Sentencing Multiple Crimes

Recent Titles in

Studies in Penal Theory and Philosophy
R.A. Duff, Michael Tonry, General Editors

Popular Punishment
On the Normative Significance of Public Opinion
Jesper Ryberg and Julian V. Roberts

Just Sentencing
Principles and Procedures for a Workable System
Richard S. Frase

Punishment, Participatory Democracy, and the Jury
Albert W. Dzur

Retributivism Has a Past
Has It a Future?
Edited by Michael Tonry

Taming the Presumption of Innocence
Richard Lippke

Sentencing Multiple Crimes
Edited by Jesper Ryberg, Julian V. Roberts and Jan W. de Keijser

Sentencing Multiple Crimes

EDITED BY
JESPER RYBERG
JULIAN V. ROBERTS
JAN W. DE KEIJSER

OXFORD
UNIVERSITY PRESS

OXFORD
UNIVERSITY PRESS

Oxford University Press is a department of the University of Oxford. It furthers the University's objective of excellence in research, scholarship, and education by publishing worldwide. Oxford is a registered trade mark of Oxford University Press in the UK and certain other countries.

Published in the United States of America by Oxford University Press
198 Madison Avenue, New York, NY 10016, United States of America.

Library of Congress Cataloging-in-Publication Data
Names: Ryberg, Jesper, editor. | Roberts, Julian V., editor. |
Keijser, Jan Willem de, 1968– editor.
Title: Sentencing Multiple Crimes / edited by
Jesper Ryberg, Julian V. Roberts and Jan W. de Keijser.
Description: New York, NY, United States of America :
Oxford University Press, [2017] | Includes bibliographical references.
Identifiers: LCCN 2017010037 | ISBN 9780190607609 (hardcover) |
ISBN 9780190607616 (updf) | ISBN 9780190607623 (epub)
Subjects: LCSH: Sentences (Criminal procedure) | Compound offenses.
Classification: LCC K5121 .M67 2017 | DDC 345/.0772—dc23
LC record available at https://lccn.loc.gov/2017010037

1 3 5 7 9 8 6 4 2

Printed by Sheridan Books, Inc., United States of America

CONTENTS

ACKNOWLEDGMENTS

The chapters in this volume are the result of an international seminar held at the Social Sciences Building, University of Oxford, December 10–12, 2015. Financial support for the seminar was generously provided by the Centre for Penal Ethics at the University of Cambridge; Roskilde University; the Institute for Criminal Law and Criminology at Leiden University; the Faculty of Law, University of Oxford; and the Centre of Criminology, University of Oxford. Our thanks to all the participants at the Oxford seminar for their valuable contributions to the discussions. We are very grateful to Dr. Gabrielle Watson for editorial and research assistance, and to James Cook from Oxford University Press for his support of the project.

Oxford, October 15, 2016
Jesper Ryberg
Julian V. Roberts
Jan W. de Keijser

CONTRIBUTORS

Andrew Ashworth is Vinerian Professor of English Law Emeritus in the University of Oxford, and Adjunct Professor of Law at the University of Tasmania.

Christopher Bennett is Reader in the Department of Philosophy, University of Sheffield.

Anthony Bottoms is Emeritus Wolfson Professor of Criminology at the University of Cambridge; Life Fellow of Fitzwilliam College, Cambridge; Honorary Professor of Criminology at the University of Sheffield; and Codirector of the Centre for Penal Theory and Penal Ethics, Institute of Criminology, University of Cambridge.

Jan W. de Keijser is Professor of Criminology at the Institute for Criminal Law and Criminology, Leiden University.

Richard S. Frase is Benjamin N. Berger Professor of Criminal Law at the University of Minnesota Law School and Codirector of the Robina Institute of Criminal Law and Criminal Justice, University of Minnesota.

Zachary Hoskins is Assistant Professor in the Faculty of Philosophy at the University of Nottingham.

Youngjae Lee is Professor of Law at Fordham University.

Richard L. Lippke is Professor of Criminal Justice and Department Chair in Criminal Justice at Indiana University Bloomington.

Allan Manson is Professor of Law in the Faculty of Law, Queen's University.

Julian V. Roberts is Professor of Criminology at the University of Oxford; Fellow of Worcester College, Oxford; and member of the Sentencing Council of England and Wales.

Jesper Ryberg is Professor of Ethics and Philosophy of Law at Roskilde University.

Michael Tonry is McKnight Presidential Professor in Criminal Law and Policy and Director of the Institute on Crime and Public Policy at the University of Minnesota and a Scientific Member of the Max Planck Society.

Natalia Vibla is a Lecturer in Criminology, Liverpool Hope University.

Andreas von Hirsch is Emeritus Honorary Professor of Penal Theory and Penal Law at the University of Cambridge; Director of the Centre for Penal Theory and Penal Ethics, Institute of Criminology, University of Cambridge; Honorary Fellow of Wolfson College, Cambridge; Honorary Professor of Penal Law, Faculty of Law at Goethe University Frankfurt; and Director, Forschungsstelle für Strafrechtstheorie und Strafrechtsethik, Law Faculty, Goethe University Frankfurt.

Martin Wasik is Emeritus Professor of Criminal Justice in the School of Law, Keele University.

1

Sentencing the Multiple Offender

Setting the Stage

JULIAN V. ROBERTS, JESPER RYBERG, AND JAN W. DE KEIJSER

Most people's image of a sentencing hearing involves an offender being sentenced for a single crime. Questions about legal punishment are framed from this perspective: What is an appropriate sentence for a crime of this seriousness, committed by an offender with this level of culpability? If custody is appropriate, how much time in prison does the offender deserve for this offense?

These questions are far from easy to answer, yet the sentencing exercise is even more complicated when the offender stands convicted of multiple crimes. These may be multiple counts of the same offense (a series of burglaries or thefts) or they may be a constellation of diverse crimes (two burglaries, an assault, possession of stolen property and possession of a weapon). It is hard to know the exact volume of such cases, as the question has attracted little empirical research. However, in England and Wales, the Sentencing Council has estimated that approximately 40% of sentencing decisions involved multiple crimes. Michael Tonry (this volume) provides data showing comparable trends in the United States. Can the approach to sentencing single crimes be directly applied to multiple count cases? Not easily. Transposing the logic of single-offense sentencing—assigning a specific sentence for each crime independent of the other, and cumulating the total sentences—creates a number of problems.

Although sentencing systems around the world pursue multiple objectives, the retributive principle of proportionality is common to almost all. A court sentencing under a retributive rationale imposes a sanction commensurate with the seriousness of the crime and the offender's culpability. Offenses of differing seriousness will attract different sentences: more serious crimes will be punished more severely, thus respecting the subprinciple of "ordinal proportionality" (von Hirsch, 1993).[1] Sentencing represents a complex challenge for courts which have to weigh crimes of different seriousness and compare offenders of very variable culpability.

Sentencing multiple offenses has been described by Jareborg (1998) as "the most complicated topic in criminal law—in those countries that care about it at all" (p. 57). An intuitive approach to sentencing fails to appreciate the complexities of multiple-offense sentencing.[2] After all, in many contexts people are held to account for multiple transgressions in a straightforward and cumulative way. For example, the motorist who receives tickets for five separate episodes of illegal parking pays five fines. The builder whose criminally shoddy workmanship results in three houses generating roof leaks will be punished for the harm inflicted on three householders. Each transgression generates a corresponding quantum of punishment. Why does this approach not read across to legal punishment for multiple crimes?

The logic of single-offense sentencing breaks down in the context of contemporary sentencing. First, the severity of prison sentences relative to the human lifespan is onerous (discussed in more detail later). Second, at sentencing, courts around the world attempt to reflect multiple, sometimes competing sentencing philosophies. These are reflected in statutory sentencing objectives. For example, in England and Wales (and most other jurisdictions) sentencers consider both utilitarian and retributive sentencing philosophies.[3] Deciding whether deterrence or desert should guide the sentence in any particular case is not easy; when the offender stands convicted of multiple crimes, now and in the past, the task becomes more problematic. The volume of individual crimes may suggest that a deterrent sentence is appropriate, while the nature of the crimes, or the resulting sentencing, may require stricter desert-based limits on the sanction imposed. As Ashworth notes, "the wide variety of combinations of offences . . . and the equally wide variations in the timespan of the offending . . . are sufficient to test any general philosophy of sentencing" (2015, p. 276).

Multiple offenses may well vary greatly in their relative seriousness, and the offender's culpability may differ across all of her crimes. For example, consider an offender convicted of domestic burglary and assaulting a police officer upon arrest. The offender may be maximally culpable for the burglary, but if he had been mistreated and provoked by the victim he may be less culpable than otherwise would be the case for assaulting the arresting officer. To further complicate matters, in addition to a complex constellation of *current* crimes, the offender may well have many *prior* convictions: He may be a multiple *and* serial offender.[4] Criminal courts in most jurisdictions will take these prior crimes into account and aggravate the sentences to reflect his current crimes.[5]

This volume addresses what may be described as a "sleeper" problem in sentencing. Determining the total sentence (or sentences) when an offender has multiple convictions has attracted little attention from legal scholars and even less from other disciplines. The only monograph on the subject is now 20 years old (Lovegrove, 1997) and since the publication of that seminal volume multiple-offense sentencing has been the subject of only a limited number of scholarly publications (e.g., Bennett, 2012; Lippke, 2011, 2017; Jareborg, 1998; Wasik, 2012; Bagaric and Alexander, 2013; Manson, 2013; Lovegrove, 2004; Ryberg, 2001).

Penal Arithmetic: Why Not Simply Add Up the Sentences for Each Individual Offense?

How then does a court weigh multiple current and previous crimes to arrive at a total sentence or sentences? A simplistic approach would see a court assign a specific sentence for each crime and then cumulate the sentences. An offender convicted of five burglaries, each worth one year in prison, would receive a total of five years' imprisonment. No jurisdiction follows this approach to multiple-crime sentencing, and for two principal reasons. First, it would result in many offenders facing very long periods of imprisonment. By committing multiple crimes an offender can easily rack up decades in prison. The consequence would be a crushing prison sentence for what may be a couple of days of criminal activity. A humanitarian perspective—touched on by several contributors to this volume—would oppose such a literal sentencing policy.

The second possible objection to simply adding up the individual sentences to arrive at a total is that the cumulative approach may blur the distinction between categories of offending that seem distinct when sentenced individually. An offender convicted of a spree of burglaries (say 12 in one night) might receive something like seven years in prison if burglary attracted a six-month sentence. He would remain in prison long after offenders admitted at the same time for much more serious offenses—rape or manslaughter—had been released. This outcome may strike many people as being inappropriate, since two offenses that seem very different are now attracting similar sentences.[6]

The Totality Principle

Courts have long been aware of these problems, and have devised pragmatic solutions, the most common of which invokes the "totality principle" (Thomas, 1979). This requires a court to impose a sentence that is not disproportionate to the volume of offending, or crushingly onerous upon the offender. If a large number of trivial crimes (say shoplifting) resulted in a lengthy prison term because each one attracted a few weeks in prison, the result would be disproportionate to the harm caused, which remains just a series of minor thefts. Shoplifting, it might be argued, should never result in such a lengthy term of custody. At the other end of the seriousness spectrum, consider a case of insider trading, including an attempt to pervert the course of justice. Imposing three or four years per conviction for eight crimes of fraud, embezzlement, and intimidating witnesses would result in a very lengthy sentence which would effectively ruin the offender's life. Some other approach to sentencing multiple crimes is clearly needed.

The totality principle can be implemented in several different ways. One way of achieving a more moderate penal response is by imposing a specific, deserved sentence for each offense—five one-year terms for five burglaries—but then allowing the offender to serve the terms *concurrently*. As stated, this simple approach fails to differentiate between the offender convicted of one such crime and the offender convicted of five burglaries. If the sentences are served concurrently the two offenders will leave the prison at the same time, one having served all his terms concurrently. For this reason courts often increase the sentence for the most serious offense and then order the remaining ones to be served concurrently. In this example the court may impose an 18-month term for the first burglary and then add 12-month terms for the remaining four crimes, with all sentences to be served concurrently rather than consecutively. In this case the multiple burglar spends appreciably longer in prison than the single conviction burglar—but nowhere near as long as he would if he had received the single-crime sentence for each of his crimes. There is no denying the importance of concurrent sentencing as a means of mitigating dauntingly long prison sentences, particularly in the United States. If all sentences of imprisonment currently imposed in western jurisdictions were served consecutively rather than concurrently, the consequence would be a massive increase in prison populations.

There is a powerful intuitive appeal to some form of totality—which then results in the "discounting" of sentences in multiple-offense cases. Research suggests that the public reject the strictly cumulative approach whereby all crimes carry a separate and independent sentence and these are then simply totaled. Respondents in research by Robinson and Darley (1995) were asked to assign liability to offenders described in scenarios. People sentenced offenders convicted of assaulting one, two, four, or seven victims during the same day. If respondents were applying a cumulative liability model, the offender convicted of seven assaults would have received a sentence seven times the length imposed for the single victim assault. However, this was not the case. For example, the average assigned liability in the case with two victims was only marginally higher than the sentence for the single victim case. The sentence for the seven victim case was higher still, but nowhere near the level expected if a cumulative model had been applied. In short, the public were applying an intuitive version of the totality principle. Their sentencing preferences were consistent with judicial practice around the world.

Multiple and Serial Offenders

The first challenge then is to ensure that an offender convicted of multiple crimes does not end up with a crushingly onerous sentence. A second challenge confronting courts arises when comparisons are made with serial offenders—those sentenced for multiple crimes over time, in separate sentencing hearings.[7] The problem is caused by a controversial sentencing policy known as the recidivist sentencing premium or the criminal history enhancement (for discussion, see Lippke, 2016; Frase et al., 2015; Roberts, 1997). This is the near-universal practice of imposing progressively harsher penalties as the offender accumulates more convictions. In some US jurisdictions, a recidivist may receive a sentence 10 or more times harsher than that which is imposed on a first offender convicted of the same crime (see Frase and Hester, 2015). Recidivist sentencing premiums have attracted a great deal of scholarship in recent years (e.g., Tamburrini and Ryberg, 2012; Frase, 2012; Roberts and von Hirsch, 2010). We understand the practice and its problems much better today as result of this work, although the policy remains controversial. Indeed, most retributivists reject the use of robust criminal history enhancements (see Roberts, 2008).

Comparing multiple-crime cases to serial offenders yields the result that when an offender commits five crimes over time, he receives a sentence which is much harsher than the sum of the individual sentences—as a result of the recidivist premium. Despite its prevalence, many scholars contest this policy (e.g., Tonry, 2010; von Hirsch, 2010). In contrast to this pattern, the offender sentenced for the same five offenses will receive a discounted sentence relative to the five-crime total. This penological paradox, if it is indeed one,[8] has been noted by scholars over the years, but most trenchantly by Kevin Reitz (2010):

> When plural offending comes to the courts in the case of prior criminal convictions, the quantum of punishment dispensed over successive prosecutions tends to explode in severity. When plural offending manifests as multiple counts of conviction, the quantum of punishment for successive crimes tends to collapse in severity. (p. 138)

Several contributing authors in this volume question whether the two patterns of offending (simultaneous or concurrent; serial or consecutive) are actually comparable. Yet the simple arithmetical comparison certainly implies a paradox. Multiple crimes sentenced separately and over time create a multiple-crime (repeat offender) sentencing enhancement; multiple crimes committed and ultimately sentenced simultaneously attract a bulk "discount."

If moderating sentence severity in multiple-crime cases is a near-universal practice, the central question then is the following: Why should the sentence for an offense be less severe when it is one of several for which he is being sentenced? Why is the offender's total penal liability less than the sum of liability for the individual crimes?

Justifying the Multiple-Offense Sentencing 'Discount'

Few theorists have addressed the justification for multiple-offense discounts. From a consequentialist perspective—such as traditional utilitarian penal theory—a bulk discount may be justified by reference to the fact that there is no extra crime preventive effect related to the longer prison terms that would follow from a purely cumulative scheme (Jareborg, 1998; Ashworth, 2015). Whether there are such desirable consequences is obviously an empirical question. However, given the dominance of retributivism in the modern era of penal theory, it is not surprising that the justification question has been addressed mainly from a desert-theoretical perspective. Two approaches have been defended.

One approach invokes the concept of *overall* proportionality. While ordinal proportionality considerations usually concern the relative punishments of individual crimes, the idea is that overall proportionality concerns the comparison of *types* of crime. More precisely, the idea is that no number of less serious crimes can be as morally wrong—and therefore deserve a more severe punitive response—as a single instance of a crime of a more serious type. For instance, it might be held that no number of offenses of stealing cars can be regarded as the moral equivalent of a single rape (Ashworth, 2015). Moreover, it has been suggested that this idea of overall proportionality reflects the idea that each new crime should contribute less to the overall punishment. That is, each crime is punished, but with the punishment reduced each time (until the curve flattens out when the ceiling is reached; see Jareborg, 1998; Ashworth, 2015; Lovegrove, 1997, 2004).

Others have advanced different proposals to justify the 'bulk discount' for multiple offending. Bottoms, for example, argues that the discount is justified by reference to mercy (Bottoms, 1998). As an illustration, suppose that an offender, aged 25, has committed 30 separate residential burglaries and that each of these offenses would, if committed as a single offense, be deemed to merit a custodial sentence of six month's duration. Thirty times six months results in 15 years in prison, during the prime of the offender's life. Therefore, the court should reduce the punishment out of mercy. Related to this concept, Jareborg (1998) articulated the "principle of humanity," which precludes cumulation of sentences. These ideas—overall proportionality, the exercise of mercy or the principle of humanity—have been criticized (Ryberg, 2005; Lippke, 2011).

The degree to which sentences are discounted is often determined by the temporal relationship between the crimes. Many jurisdictions apply a "single transaction" rule. If the crimes all form part of a single criminal event, then discounting should be significant. The offender who steals five books on a single visit to the bookstore is essentially committing a single offense with multiple counts. The burglar breaking into three adjoining houses within a few minutes will be treated as having committed a single criminal transaction. The likelihood of receiving three concurrent sentences is very high, and the offender will not spend much more time in prison than one who commits a single burglary. On the other hand, consider an offender who is sentenced for three burglaries, possession of burglary instruments, and assault of a police officer. The assault occurred three months after the burglary when officers came to search the offender's residence. This last offense seems unrelated to burglary and the sentence imposed would likely be consecutive to the concurrent crimes of burglary. The single transaction rule seems clear and universal, but the justification for this practice remains elusive, and is one of the issues addressed in this book.

The justifications for a multiple-offense reduction therefore fall into two categories. One group is external to retributive theories. For example, it may be argued that a cumulative sentencing approach simply results in too much punishment for an individual to bear. This reasoning suggests that reduced sentences in multiple-crime cases are justified out a sense of mercy, or recognition that the sentencing process should not result in penalties which have the effect of eradicating the offender's prospects for a normal life. The exercise of mercy needs to be justified, however, and courts need guidance as to how much mercy to grant. For example, should the exercise of mercy simply cap all sentences in multiple-crime cases, and if so would this not differentially benefit offenders convicted of the most serious multiple crimes?

The second group seeks to justify sentence reductions for multiple crimes by appealing to desert theory. On these accounts, the multiple-crime offender deserves less punishment than would be suggested by a strict summation of the individual "deserved" sentences. But why? The twin components of a proportionate sentence are harm and culpability (von Hirsch and Ashworth, 2005). The aggregate harm of the constellation of offenses seems no less than the sum of the individual harms. There is no scope to discount sentences in multiple-offense cases on the grounds that five burglaries committed in one night somehow results in less harm than five spread over a year. When an offender steals five cars, the loss is never less than five vehicles. That leaves the issue of culpability. Can it be argued that the aggregate culpability of the multiple-crime offender is less than the accumulation of his individual culpabilities (for each offense)? If the multiple offender is somehow less culpable, on what basis is this reduced culpability justified? These questions are addressed by several contributors.

Overview of Volume

Contributors to the present volume explore the potential justifications for adopting a different approach when sentencing multiple offenders, one that results in more lenient sentences than would be the case if the crimes had been committed (and punished) as single offenses. Justifying an alternate methodology is only one of the objectives pursued by contributors. Any justification (or set of justifications) needs to give rise to a regime which courts can apply in order to ensure consistency across cases. At present, only minimal guidance is offered trial courts—usually in the form of general statements from appellate courts.[9] More (and better) guidance is clearly needed; if courts are left relatively free to determine the extent to which multiple crimes should be discounted relative to the sentences which would be appropriate in single convictions, inconsistency will be inevitable. A number of authors propose and discuss specific ways in which general guiding principles may be put into practice. Finally, although the volume addresses the relationship between sentencing a single crime as opposed to multiple convictions, many authors also grapple with the tension which exists between multiple concurrent crimes, and multiple crimes committed and punished sequentially. The comparison is inescapable, since any sentencing system needs to have a coherent set of guiding principles for single, multiple, and serial offending.

A principled approach to sentencing multiple crimes is necessary to achieve consistency and fairness. If courts are left free to discount sentences to the extent they believe is appropriate in multiple-crime cases, inconsistency will inevitably arise. The need for principled guidance is more pressing in multiple rather than single-crime cases; the more complex the decision, the more diverse the judicial response. This is why appellate courts have developed guidance for trial judges (the totality principle) which and suggests when sentences should be served concurrently or consecutively. In jurisdictions with guidelines, sentencing commissions and councils have issued formal guidance in this regard. Scholarly reaction appears to be that these efforts have failed to deliver an adequate degree of guidance or to provide a principled justification for the practice of multiple-offense discounts.[10]

Two elements are needed. First, a clear justification for the practice of imposing a different penalty or penalties when the crimes are sentenced together rather than as individual offenses. Second, a set of procedures to ensure that this practice is consistently applied. Contributors to this volume approach the problem of multiple-offense sentencing in different ways and reflecting diverse perspectives. The chapters shed further light on the practice of multiple-offense sentencing. Some authors propose a principled approach to discounting sentences for multiple-crime offenders. Others examine the practice of the courts, with a view to offering some guidance as to the most appropriate way of taking multiple crimes into account at sentencing. No single volume can hope to resolve the complex philosophical and procedural problems surrounding sentencing in multiple-count cases. At best, we aspire to provide insight which may lead to a more humane, principled, and consistent approach to sentencing the multiple offender.

Notes

1. Ordinal proportionality of the requirements of a proportional sentencing regime. This requires offenses to be spaced appropriately at different levels of a punishment hierarchy (see discussion in von Hirsch, 1993).
2. Here we refer to an intuitive, top-of-the-head response to sentencing the multiple offender. Drawing upon daily life in a more sophisticated way may suggest some support for the practice described later as a bulk discount for multiple offending. Bennett (2012), for example, argues that in interpersonal interactions we do not adopt a unitized approach to transgressions, but rather take a series of transgressions in the round. Our response to multiple wrongs, he argues, "will not just be a matter of doing the arithmetic" (p. 148).
3. According to section 142 of the Criminal Justice Act 2003:

    (1) Any court dealing with an offender in respect of his offence must have regard to the following purposes of sentencing—
    (a) the punishment of offenders,
    (b) the reduction of crime (including its reduction by deterrence),
    (c) the reform and rehabilitation of offenders,
    (d) the protection of the public, and
    (e) the making of reparation by offenders to persons affected by their offences.

4. To further complicate matters, in England and Wales, offenders may ask the court to take additional crimes into account when imposing sentence. These are offenses that have not even been charged; the offender accepts responsibility for these crimes in return for a more lenient sentence than would otherwise be imposed if he were to be prosecuted and sentenced for the additional offenses (see Sentencing Council, 2012).
5. Prior convictions trigger additional punishment for reasons related to both crime prevention and retribution, and this makes the sentencing exercise even more complex.
6. Throughout this volume the contributors discuss multiple-offense sentencing by reference to sentences of imprisonment. Time in prison provides a convenient metric for comparing different profiles of offender. However, the principles and issues arising from multiple-offense sentencing must also consider the range of sanctions used at sentencing, thus further complicating the challenge to courts.
7. There are other challenges. When an offender commits multiple crimes against a number of individual victims the sentencing court will attempt to ensure that each victim's individual harm is reflected in the sentence. This will be difficult, whether a single sentence is imposed to reflect the total number of victimizations or multiple sentences are ordered to be served concurrently.
8. This qualification reflects the fact that several contributors to this volume regard the paradox as more apparent than real. They argue that there are significant retributively relevant grounds for distinguishing multiple and serial offenders in ways that justify the differential sentencing arrangements.

9. England and Wales is the only jurisdiction where there is a stand-alone sentencing guideline addressing the issue of multiple-offense sentencing (Sentencing Council, 2012). Yet this guideline is relatively light touch, offering a modest degree of guidance regarding the key decision to make a sentence run concurrently or consecutively, and it has been criticized for this lack of ambition (see Wasik and Ashworth, this volume; Wasik, 2012).
10. As Jareborg and others note, no "genuine guidance to the courts" is offered by statutory law either (1998, p. 63).

References

Ashworth, A. 2015. *Sentencing and Criminal Justice*. 6th ed. Cambridge: Cambridge University Press.

Bagaric, M., and T. Alexander. 2013. "Rehabilitating Totality in Sentencing: From Obscurity to Principle." *University of New South Wales Law Journal* 36(1): 139–167.

Bennett, C. 2012. "Do Multiple and Repeat Offenders Pose a Problem for Retributive Sentencing Theory?" In C. Tamburrini and J. Ryberg (eds.), *Recidivist Punishments*, pp. 137–156. Lanham, MD: Lexington Books.

Bottoms, A. 1998. "Five Puzzles in von Hirsch's Theory of Punishment." In A. Ashworth and M. Wasik (eds.), *Fundamentals of Sentencing Theory: Essays in Honour of Andrew von Hirsch*, pp. 53–102. Oxford: Oxford University Press.

Frase, R. 2012. *Just Sentencing*. New York: Oxford University Press.

Frase, R., J. V. Roberts, K. Mitchell, and R. Hester, 2015. *Sourcebook of Criminal History Enhancements*. Minneapolis: Robina Institute.

Frase, R., and R. Hester, 2015. "Magnitude of Criminal History Enhancements." In R. Frase, J. V. Roberts, K. Mitchell, and R. Hester. *Sourcebook of Criminal History Enhancements*, pp. 19–28. Minneapolis: Robina Institute.

Jareborg, N. 1998. "Why Bulk Discounts in Sentencing?" In A. Ashworth and M. Wasik (eds.), *Fundamentals of Sentencing Theory: Essays in Honour of Andrew von Hirsch*, pp. 129–140. Oxford: Clarendon Press.

Lippke, R. 2011. "Retributive Sentencing, Multiple Offenders, and Bulk Discounts." In M. D. White (ed.), *Retributivism: Essays on Theory and Policy*, pp. 212–231. New York: Oxford University Press.

Lippke, R. 2017. "The Ethics of Recidivist Sentencing Premiums." In J. Jacobs and J. Jackson (eds.), *The Routledge Handbook of Criminal Justice Ethics*, pp. 17–27. London: Routledge.

Lovegrove, A. 1997. *The Framework of Judicial Sentencing*. Cambridge: Cambridge University Press.

Lovegrove, A. 2004. *Sentencing the Multiple Offender: Judicial Practice and Legal Principle*. Canberra: Australian Institute of Criminology.

Manson, A. 2013. "Some Thoughts on Multiple Sentences and the Totality Principle: Can We Get It Right?" *Canadian Journal of Criminology and Criminal Justice* 55(4): 481–495.

Reitz, K. 2010. "The Illusion of Proportionality: Desert and Repeat Offenders." In J. V. Roberts and A. von Hirsch (eds.), *Previous Convictions at Sentencing: Theoretical and Applied Perspectives*, pp. 137–160. Oxford: Hart Publishing.

Roberts, J. V. 1997. "Paying for the Past: The Role of Criminal Record in the Sentencing Process." In M. Tonry (ed.), *Crime and Justice. A Review of Research*, Volume 22, pp. 303–362. Chicago: University of Chicago Press.

Roberts, J. V. 2008. *Punishing Persistent Offenders. Community and Offender Perspectives on the Recidivist Sentencing Premium*. Oxford: Oxford University Press.

Roberts, J. V., and A. von Hirsch (eds.) 2010. *Previous Convictions at Sentencing: Theoretical and Applied Perspectives*. Oxford: Hart Publishing.

Robinson, P. H., and J. M. Darley. 1995. *Justice, Liability, and Blame: Community Views and the Criminal Law*. Boulder, CO: Westview Press.

Ryberg, J. 2001. "Recidivism, Multiple Offending and Legal Justice." *Danish Yearbook of Philosophy* 36: 69–94.

Ryberg, J. 2005. "Retributivism and Multiple Offending." *Res Publica* 11(3): 213–233.

Sentencing Council of England and Wales. 2012. *Offences Taken into Account and Totality. Definitive Guideline*. London: Sentencing Council of England and Wales.

Tamburrini, C., and J. Ryberg (eds.) 2012. *Recidivist Punishments: The Philosopher's View*. Lanham, MD: Lexington Books.

Thomas, D. A. 1979. *Principles of Sentencing: The Sentencing Policy of the Court of Appeal Criminal Division*. 2nd ed. London: Heinemann.

Tonry, M. 2010. "The Questionable Relevance of Previous Convictions for Later CrimesTitle." In J. V. Roberts and A. von Hirsch (eds.), *Previous Convictions at Sentencing: Theoretical and Applied Perspectives*, pp. 91–116. Oxford: Hart Publishing.

Von Hirsch, A. 1993. *Censure and Sanctions*. Oxford: Clarendon Press.

Von Hirsch, A. 2010. "Proportionality and the Progressive Loss of Mitigation: Some Further Reflections." In J. V. Roberts and A. von Hirsch (eds.), *Previous Convictions at Sentencing: Theoretical and Applied Perspectives*. Studies in Penal Theory and Ethics, pp. 1–16. Oxford: Hart Publishing.

Von Hirsch, A., and A. Ashworth. 2005. *Proportionate Sentencing: Exploring the Principles*. Oxford: Oxford University Press.

Wasik, M. 2012. "Concurrent and Consecutive Sentences Revisited." In L. Zedner and J. V. Roberts (eds.), *Principles and Values in Criminal Law and Criminal Justice: Essays in Honour of Andrew Ashworth*, pp. 285–306. Oxford: Oxford University Press.

2

Retributivism, Multiple Offending, and Overall Proportionality

JESPER RYBERG

Despite the fact that penal theorists disagree on what constitutes the most plausible approach to the justification of state punishment, among theorists it is a generally shared belief that there is wide divergence between current penal practice and what penal theory prescribes. Penal theory is not regarded as merely offering a justification for the way in which the existing penal system is operating. On the contrary, it is generally held that there exists a significant discrepancy between penal practice and what is ideally desirable. However, when it comes to the question concerning the punishment of multiple offenders—that is, offenders who are, on one occasion, being sentenced for a series of crimes—the picture is different.

In many countries, sentencing judges do not deal with multiple-offense cases by simply adding up the respective sentences which each crime in a series of offenses separately merits (for example, Reitz, 2010). Rather, the standard practice is to award a discount (in fact, often of a significant extent) to multiple offenders. And this, several penal theorists contend, is precisely how it should be. Though the literature is still sparse, theorists who have taken up the issue almost unanimously reject a purely cumulative approach by recommending some sort of discount to multiple offenders. The obvious interesting question then is what constitutes the theoretical background for the (exceptional) contention that penal practice is on the right track.

Following a traditional consequentialist approach to the justification and distribution of punishment, a rejection of the cumulative approach to multiple offending is precisely what one should expect. As is often emphasized in the literature on crime prevention, there is little evidence linking longer sentences and increased marginal deterrence or offender rehabilitation (see, for instance, Doob and Webster, 2003; Pratt et al., 2006; Nagin, 2013).[1] However, it is noteworthy that this is not the type of justification that has been advanced by penal theorists. All theorists who have defended a discount for multiple offenders have done so on the ground of retributivist considerations. Given the dominance of retributivism in modern penal theory, this is not surprising. But it is also clear, that when the issue is addressed from a desert theoretical perspective, the answer as to why multiple offenders should receive a discount becomes much less straightforward. If each crime in a series, considered separately, should be responded to with a punishment of a certain degree of severity then prima facie it would seem that the deserved sentence for the whole series should be reached simply by doing the arithmetic, that is, by following the cumulative approach. Thus, if mere cumulation is rejected, then it is clear that some sort of justification is required. At this point, and from an overall perspective, two routes are open to the retributivist (see also Bennett, 2011).

The first possibility is to hold that, even though retributive justice implies that one should follow a cumulative approach, there are particular reasons that trump the requirement of justice in multiple-offense cases. Thus, although retributivism constitutes the plausible approach to punishment, with regard to this particular group of offenders, there are reasons for tempering (or tampering) with what justice strictly requires. Though this approach faces several more detailed challenges, the main problem is how it can possibly be justified. If retributivism is held to provide a justification of state punishment and to guide the distribution of penalties, then it clearly requires a strong argument to explain why the prescriptions of retributivism should be overruled in multiple-offense cases. To my knowledge, no convincing argument to this effect has been presented in the debate and it is hard to imagine the contours of this sort of reasoning.[2]

The other possibility, then, is to suggest that the rejection of the cumulative approach can be justified *within* the framework of the retributive view of justice. On this approach the multiple-offense discount is not a justified deviation from justice but rather what justice itself requires. Theoretically speaking, such an approach may seem more elegant. However, even though it does not require one to explain why it is suddenly acceptable to overrule justice, it still needs to be explained why multiple offenders deserve to be dealt with noncumulatively. The purpose of this chapter is to consider whether such an argument can be provided. More precisely, what I shall be concerned with is the view that retributive justice implies overall proportionality constraints, that is, proportionality prescriptions with regard to *classes* of offenses. Several theorists have defended the idea of overall proportionality as a way of sustaining multiple-offense sentencing discounts. In fact, some have even proposed more detailed accounts of how this notion of proportionality should manifest itself in numerical sentencing guidelines (see, for instance, Lovegrove, 2000). However, I will argue that there are strong reasons to be skeptical with regard to the justification of overall proportionality.

Overview

In order to reach this conclusion the chapter proceeds as follows. In section (1), a few initial conceptual considerations are presented concerning the notion of overall proportionality and its implications in multiple-offense cases. Moreover, I consider how overall proportionality coheres with the standard retributivist idea of proportionality and what kind of justificatory challenges this type of proportionality gives rise to. Sections (2) to (4) examine possible ways of justifying overall proportionality. Firstly, it is considered whether proportionality between categories of crimes can be justified in terms of criminal harm. It is argued that despite certain theoretical attractions, a justification along these lines rests on an implausible value-theoretical assumption. Secondly, in section (3), it is shown that it is very hard to believe that a satisfactory justification of overall proportionality can be developed on the ground of culpability considerations. Thirdly, in section (4), an attempt to justify this type of proportionality on the ground of an analysis of how we assess serial wrongdoings in interpersonal nonlegal contexts is briefly assessed. This leads to section (5), in which the alleged underlying intuition in favor of overall proportionality will be questioned. Drawing on recent moral psychological research, it is suggested that the intuitive appeal of overall proportionality and, more generally, of the view that multiple offenders should be treated with some degree of leniency may be the result of "scope-insensitivity," which means that there is reason to regard this intuition as morally highly dubious. Finally, section (6) summarizes and concludes that the idea of overall proportionality as an ingredient in the retributivist approach to multiple offending cannot be held to rest on firm ground.

Preparatory Conceptual Considerations

Overall proportionality concerns the relative seriousness of classes and subclasses of offense, implying that no number of a certain type of crime should ever attract a sentence above that imposed for a single instance of an offense belonging to the class of more serious offenses (see e.g., Lovegrove, 2000, p. 455). As an influential proponent of this idea of proportionality, Ashworth provides the following simple example. Suppose that the punishment for a middle-range rape is four years in prison, for a burglary nine months, and for the crime of stealing a car four months. Suppose that an offender has committed four burglaries or that another offender has committed nine car thefts; then, by "doing the arithmetic," the four burglaries amount to three years and the nine car thefts amount to three years. However, as Ashworth notes, "there is a feeling that any calculation which results in such a close approximation of sentence between a rape (4 years) and a moderate number of burglaries or of 'auto-thefts' goes against common sense" (Ashworth, 2005, p. 210). This, in other words, seems to violate the idea of overall proportionality.

From a purely theoretical point of view, it is possible to think of different variations of this idea (e.g., one possibility would be to connect overall proportionality levels to the number of offenses so that, for instance, the sentence for up to 10 instances of a certain offense should never reach the lower level of a more serious class of offense, while up to 30 instances should never reach beyond the level of a mid-range instance of an offense in the class of more serious offenses, and so on.) However, it is obvious that when a scheme becomes more complex the task of sustaining it theoretically becomes conspicuously more challenging. Thus, in the following I shall stick to the concept of overall proportionality as setting strict barriers between the sentences for offenses in different classes.

That overall proportionality has implications for the sentencing of multiple offenders has already been indicated. Suppose, drawing on the above example, that the ceiling for burglaries is 27 months in prison. The offender who has committed a single burglary will then get nine months, the multiple offender who has committed two burglaries will get 18 months, and the multiple offender who has committed three burglaries will get 27 months. However, since the ceiling has then been reached for this class of offense, no further instances of burglary committed by a multiple offender will add to the sentence. Now, some theorists believe that this is not fully satisfactory. For instance, Ashworth and Jareborg have suggested that, once we move forward in the series of offenses, each new offense should contribute less to the overall sentence (see Jareborg, 1998). However, whether one should follow a scheme prescribing strict cumulation or gradually reduced sentences below the ceiling for a certain class of crime is not a question that is answered merely by subscribing to the idea of overall proportionality constraints. Thus either one can hold that overall proportionality in itself provides a complete guide to how multiple offenders should be sentenced, or one can hold that such constraints should be regarded as one ingredient in a scheme also involving other components (such as, for instance, a theory concerning gradual sentence reductions).[3] In the following, the focus will be restricted to considerations of overall proportionality.

The obvious question that confronts the idea of overall proportionality is how does this type of constraint for classes of offenses relate to the standard retributivist account of proportionality? As has been comprehensively described in the modern retributivist literature, standard ordinal proportionality concerns the relative sentences for offenses of different (or the same) severity, while cardinal proportionality concerns what nonrelatively constitutes the appropriate sentence for a certain offense (see, for instance von Hirsch, 1993; Ryberg, 2004). Since overall proportionality does not say anything about how severely offenses in different classes should be punished—that is, it is not concerned with cardinality issues, but only with the relative sentences of offenses in different classes—the following question arises: What is the connection between ordinal proportionality for single offenses and overall proportionality? Are the two types of constraints justifiable on the ground of the same desert theoretical reasons or is it rather the case that there exists some sort of internal conflict?

As previously indicated, the prima facie answer is that there seems to be some sort of conflict between the two types of proportionality. Following the standard account, the gravity of offenses is determined on the ground of harm and culpability, where harm is usually attributed a significant weight in the equation. However, given this view there seems to be a problem with regard to overall proportionality. It is indisputable that each new crime in a multiple-offense series adds to the total amount of harm caused by the offender. But when a series of offenses has reached the sentence ceiling for offenses in a certain class then further instances of the offense in the series no longer add to the severity of the sentence (e.g., the fifth or sixth burglary will not be reflected in the severity of the sentence in the example above). Does this establish that standard ordinal proportionality and overall proportionality are basically inconsistent devices? No, it does not. However, what this does show is that the retributivist who subscribes to the idea of overall proportionality faces a serious challenge in terms of justification. Let us now see how the immediate tension between standard ordinal proportionality and overall proportionality can possibly be dealt with by the retributivist.

Harm and Overall Proportionality

Any attempt to justify overall proportionality on the ground of an analysis of criminal harm must from the outset be regarded as an uphill battle. It is, as mentioned, beyond dispute that each new crime in a multiple-offense series will add to the total harm of the collective misdeeds for which the multiple offender should be sentenced.[4] As we have just seen, it is precisely this fact that causes the tension between standard ordinal proportionality and overall proportionality. However, there is one possibility that should be considered.

Several philosophers working within value theory subscribe to the view that we can have a value which, no matter how often a certain unit of it is added to itself, cannot become greater than a single unit of another value. Put in less abstract terms, we can think of some (lower) pleasures (e.g., the pleasure in eating a nice apple) which can never, no matter how often this pleasure is experienced, outweigh a single experience of another (higher) pleasure (e.g., the pleasure given by a magnificent piece of art). John Stuart Mill is the traditional exponent of the view that qualitative distinctions exist between pleasures, differences which cannot be reduced to mere quantitative differences. How Mill and other later adherents have defended this idea of some pleasures being qualitatively superior to others is by referring to a simple preference test. Which would you prefer: the pleasure of an infinite number of apples or of a single excellent performance of Mozart's Requiem?[5] Now, the discussion of the comparison of types of pleasure is obviously not relevant in relation to considerations of crime gravity. However, a similar qualitative distinction exists between certain types of harm (in fact, this was also Mill's view) and that, if this is the case, then we might have reached a way of sustaining the idea of overall proportionality. Following the idea of the preference test, would it not be plausible to hold that, even though a minor theft may be experienced as inconvenient by the victim, it is still the case that no number of this kind of experience can ever become as harmful as a single instance of a serious violent crime (say aggravated rape or assault)? If the answer to this question is in the affirmative, then it seems that the retributivist would have a simple answer as to why multiple instances of theft should never be sentenced as harshly as a single instance of rape; the latter offense simply causes greater harm.

This way of underpinning overall proportionality is theoretically attractive for the obvious reason that by maintaining the focus on the cardinal concept of criminal harm, it allows the retributivist to stay within the justificatory framework of standard theorizing on proportionality. And it might be said that the feeling to which Ashworth refers, that a close approximation of the sentences for rape and multiple instances of car theft "goes against common sense," simply reflects the view that there is a qualitative difference between the harms involved in these two types of crime. Furthermore, it is clear that the task confronting the adherent of overall proportionality does not consist merely in delivering some sort of justification of the idea of this kind of constraint, but also in establishing in a nonarbitrary way how many classes of crimes there should be and where the line should be drawn between one class and another. But at this point it could be held that the answer will be provided by an analysis of the harm involved in the respective types of criminal harm: There is a step from one class to another when offenses can be distinguished in terms of qualitative superiority of the involved harm. However, despite these theoretical attractions, I believe there is reason to be skeptical about this proposal.

The crucial question obviously is whether it is plausible to believe that there is a type of qualitative distinction between different types of harm. The more general question as to whether there are any values at all which are qualitatively different from others is indeed a controversial axiological one that needs not to be considered here. In the present context, it is sufficient to ask if there is reason to believe that such a distinction exists between the types of harm that are relevant for the assessment of crime gravity. There is, I believe, a strong reason to question this. Suppose we adopt a step-by-step approach to the comparison of criminal harms. A minor theft may cause less harm than a more aggravated theft. The more aggravated instance of theft may cause the same type of deprivation as a minor burglary which, in addition, may cause psychological harm. The burglary may be only slightly less harmful than a minor violent crime, which again is less harmful than a more serious assault, and so on. In other words, it is clearly possible—irrespective of the standard legal categorizations of crimes—to imagine a sliding scale (in fact, one that is much more finely graduated than just indicated) ranging from the least to the most serious crimes where there is only a minor difference between the harmfulness of two subsequent crimes in the ordering. However, given this ranking, it becomes much less plausible to believe that there are genuine qualitative differences. If one compares one crime and another slightly more harmful one, then it is hard to believe that one would prefer any number of the less harmful crime to a single instance of the one slightly more harmful. In fact, given the close approximation between the harms of the two crimes, one would probably prefer a single instance of the more harmful crime to two instances of the crime just below it in the ordering. But if this observation is correct, what does it establish?

As noted, the idea that there are genuine qualitative distinctions—that is, distinctions that cannot be reduced to mere quantitative comparison—between different harms is usually supported by a preferences test, such as if one holds that no number of minor thefts can ever be as harmful as a single instance of a serious rape. However, if one uses a preference test in the comparison of each pair of crimes in the gradual ordering then it seems that there are no places involving a genuine qualitative step. On the contrary, all the involved harms are comparable in purely quantitative terms. But if in this way we have preferences pointing in different directions—that is, respectively the preference when we compare the poles of the ordering on the one hand, and the preferences involved in the step-by-step ordering on the other—then there is no longer a ground for affirming that there are qualitative differences.[6] The preference test simply does not validate this conclusion. Of course, it might at this point be worth considering how we should react if our preferences are inconsistent; that is, whether there is reason to have more confidence in some of the preferences than in others. As I shall shortly note, there are powerful reasons to regard the preferences in the step-by-step comparison as more reliable than the preference comparing the harms at each end of the crime scale. However, for the present it is sufficient to conclude that the idea of basing overall proportionality constraints on the existence of a qualitative distinction between criminal harms seems unconvincing. In fact, it is hard to imagine any other harm-based arguments that can possibly support overall proportionality.

Culpability and Overall Proportionality

The standard retributivist view on crime gravity, as mentioned, is that the seriousness of an offense should be determined on the grounds of harm and culpability. Thus, if as we have just seen, it is correct that overall proportionality constraints cannot plausibly be justified with reference to criminal harm, are there reasons then to believe that considerations of *culpability* can supply an adequate justification? Is it not precisely a reference to an offender's culpability that seems to constitute the obvious starting point for a way of sustaining overall proportionality? Whatever the prima facie attractions of this view might be, it is, as we shall now see, very hard to believe that this suggestion constitutes a viable option.

The culpability of an offender is usually held to comprise different types of considerations. First and foremost it is generally agreed among retributivists that one aspect of culpability concerns the mental state or attitude of the person who commits a misdeed, that is, more precisely the mens rea of the offender. Even though different fault terms have sometimes been used, the traditional mens rea distinctions are between intention, knowledge, recklessness, and perhaps negligence (see, for instance, Ashworth, 1995; Ryberg, 2004). Another aspect of culpability concerns the offender's degree of responsibility for the act that was committed. However, it is easy to see that these two aspects of culpability—mens rea and responsibility—cannot provide a justification of overall proportionality. Even though it might well be the case that a multiple offender was not fully responsible for all the misdeeds committed in a series of offenses, or did not commit all offenses intentionally, this does not mean that each offense does not deserve a punishment. And, more importantly, it clearly does not imply that extra instances of offenses at some point reach a ceiling where they no longer add to the overall gravity of the collective criminal conduct of the offender. Furthermore, it is clear that one can have cases where all offenses in a series were committed with the highest degree of mens rea and by a fully responsible offender. What this demonstrates, is that insofar as one believes that overall proportionality can be justified on the ground of culpability, one will have to draw on another interpretation of culpability that goes beyond the standard idea of mens rea and responsibility (for a discussion of an alternative interpretation, see the chapter by de Keijser and Roberts in the volume). However, even without trying to consider what such interpretations of culpability could possibly amount to, there are more formal reasons to hold that culpability considerations cannot justify overall proportionality.

Let us for reasons of simplicity assume that the offenses committed by a multiple offender are all identical (say, numerous instances of burglary) in terms of the harm. If this is the case, then there will, as we have seen, be a point at which the total aggregated harm of the offenses exceeds that harm caused by a single instance of an offense belonging in a class of more serious crimes. Thus, in order to reach the result that the overall gravity of the series of offenses cannot for reasons of culpability exceed this upper limit, it will have to be the case that the degree of culpability of the multiple offender decreases in a way inversely proportional to the increase in the total harm; that is, roughly, the increase in the aggregated harm resulting from each extra offense in the series must be precisely counterbalanced by a decrease in culpability. Unless this is the case, it will not be possible to keep the overall seriousness of the series of offenses below the upper ceiling. However, it is extremely hard to believe that it is plausible to devise a new account of culpability, and explain why the ascription of culpability to the multiple offender follows precisely the kind of mathematical function required to preserve overall proportionality.[7] Not only has such a justification of such an account not even tentatively been provided, but it is also very difficult to imagine what it would possibly look like. What this means is obviously not that there cannot be certain culpability considerations that are of relevance particularly with regard to multiple offenders, but simply that it appears as an unpromising task to try to justify *overall proportionality* on considerations related to culpability.

Bennett's Theory of Interpersonal Assessment of Wrongdoing

Given the role that harm and culpability play in the determination of the seriousness of a crime it would, as noted, from a theoretical point of view be attractive if it were possible to arrive at overall proportionality constraints directly from an analysis of culpability or harm involved in separate classes of crimes. However, if this, as argued, does not constitute a viable option are there any other routes open to the retributivist who believes that the appropriate sentence of any number of less serious offenses should not reach the level of the sentence of a single instance of a more serious offense? Does it still make sense to insist that a single rape is a more serious crime than any number of thefts? The only theorist, to my knowledge, who has attempted to propose a justification for an affirmative answer is Chris Bennett. Let us consider the structure of his argument.

The point of departure for Bennett's proposal is a version of an expressionist retributive theory of sentencing and, more precisely, the view that sentencing practice should, at least to some extent, reflect our sense of justice in interpersonal moral relations between people. Thus, the main part of Bennett's argument consists in an analysis of what would constitute an appropriate reaction to wrongdoing in nonlegal moral life. More precisely, Bennett asks his readers to imagine the case of Ben and Jenny. Jenny goes into business with her friend Ben. They have a mutual understanding of how much profit the enterprise will allow each partner by way of earnings, and how much should be ploughed back into the business (Bennett, 2011, p. 145). However, the partnership is troubled by the fact that Jenny starts to fiddle the accounts, siphoning off money into her private bank account. After some years, Ben eventually discovers Jenny's series of wrongdoing. The question now is: how seriously should one regard Jenny's wrongdoing? Or as Bennett puts it, how much would Jenny have to do to make up for it in her relation to Ben? The answer, he suggests, is that an analysis of what it takes to make up for a wrongdoing shows that there are two elements at stake: a purely restitutive element which implies that one returns what one owes, but also a retributive element in which one engages in acts of contrition and "expresses one's sense of the gravity of what one did" (Bennett, 2011, p. 147). Bennett suggests that it is the latter element that provides an answer to how one should react to multiple offending and which sustains the view that mere cumulation should be rejected.

Considering how much it takes for Jenny to make up for her wrongdoing against Ben, Bennett contends that she might take over some of his duties, donate money to good causes, or undertake other acts showing that she is genuinely contrite and "seeking to nullify deserved blame" (Bennett, 2011, p. 148). However, asking how much more Jenny would have to do in terms of retributive amends to make up for her string of wrongdoings rather than if she had committed only a single wrongdoing, Bennett's feeling is "not very much" (Bennett, 2011, p. 148). When Jenny starts thinking about making retributive amends, she will not do the arithmetic. Rather what happens is some sort of organic assimilation of the range of wrongs as a whole where the number of wrongdoing does not matter much. More precisely, the idea is that no matter how many wrongdoings Jenny has committed in a series, they will not be regarded as bad as if she had inflicted some really serious harm upon Ben. When this judgment concerning interpersonal relations is added to the premise that the legal practice should reflect our nonlegal intuitive judgments, one ends up with the conclusion that cumulative sentencing of multiple offenders should be rejected in favor of the view that does not allow any number of less serious crimes to be punitively dealt with as seriously as a single instance of an offense belonging in a more serious class of crime. Have we here reached a plausible justification for the idea of overall proportionality?

Bennett's proposal provokes several questions. A crucial question—of which Bennett is obviously well aware—is whether one should accept the normative premise that sentencing should conform to our intuitive sense of desert and retributive amends in a nonlegal personal relationship. I shall not here pursue this question. However, even if this premise is accepted, the analysis of our intuition in relation to wrongdoing also prompts several questions. First, in considering how much Jenny would have to do to make up for her misdeed, is it only her intuition that matters? If the answer is in the affirmative, then this sounds somewhat odd if we imagine a case where Jenny's view diverges from that of Ben's. If, on the other hand, it is ultimately Ben's judgment that counts with regard to what it takes for Jenny to make up for her wrongdoings, then the answer that follows cannot readily be extrapolated to questions concerning the sentencing of multiple offenders. The reason simply is that the Jenny and Ben case is not analogous to standard cases of multiple offending, in the simple sense that in such cases the victim is usually not the same person in the series of offenses (in some cases, such as serial murder, this would even be impossible). Thus in order to have a case that can be extrapolated to cases of multiple offending, one would have to consider what it would take for Jenny to make up for her wrongdoings if she has betrayed Ben, Jim, John, and so on.

Second, even if it can be argued that it is only the intuition of the individual who has committed a series of wrongdoing that counts in the assessment of what it takes to make up for these misdeeds, one is also confronted with the challenges that intuition may vary between different wrongdoers. Even though Bennett holds that people have a fairly fine-tuned sense of what is enough in terms of the amount of amends it takes to show proper recognition of wrongdoings, it could well be the case that people's intuitions vary at this point. Jenny's intuitions may not be the same as another serial wrongdoer. But does this imply that we should accept cases where, when we move to the legal setting, multiple offenders should not necessarily be sentenced equally severely even if they have committed exactly the same series of offenses? Or put a little differently, how is the idea of extrapolating intuitions in individual relations between people compatible with the standard retributivist view that equally serious crimes merit equally severe sentences?

What these questions indicate, in my view, is that there are still some open ends in Bennett's proposal that call for discussion. However, though much more could be said, I shall not engage in further discussion of these issues here. The principal reason for outlining Bennett's theory is to direct attention to the fact that it is based on a basic intuition about how one would assess serial wrongdoings. It is "our intuitive sense of desert and retributive amends" in cases of serial wrongdoing that constitutes the crucial premise in Bennett's proposal. But this naturally prompts the question as to whether we should accept this type of intuition or whether there could be reasons for rejecting it. As we shall see in the following section, I believe the latter to be the case.

Moral Intuitions and Scope Insensitivity

There is no doubt that if one takes a closer look at what has as yet been written in favor of the view that any number of minor offenses cannot amount to something that equals an instance of a more serious crime, and that cases of multiple offenders should, therefore, not be punished in a purely cumulative manner, the reference to the basic *intuitive appeal* of these views plays a prominent role in the considerations.

As we have initially seen, Ashworth explicitly referred to the feeling that the cumulative approach goes against common sense. Richard Lippke has, along the same lines, underlined that the impetus for rejecting a cumulative approach is that it produces sentences of multiple offenders that *strike* us as excessive (Lippke, 2011, p. 216). And, as we have just seen, Bennett's theory—to my knowledge constituting the most elaborate attempt at justifying overall proportionality—specifically draws on the intuition we have in the assessment of serial wrongdoings. Speaking in general terms, it seems to me that the retributivist approach to the sentencing of multiple offenders is characterized, on the one hand, by the acknowledgment that standard proportionality seems to imply that one should do the arithmetic and, on the other, the view that it is highly counterintuitive to accept that a number of less serious offenses should be regarded as more serious misbehavior than a single instance of a more serious offense. However, given the tension between these views it is remarkable that retributivists have not started out by critically considering whether there could be reasons to disregard this intuitive reaction.

That there is a temptation to take moral intuitions seriously and to make room within a theoretical framework for what they prescribe is perhaps not surprising. It is widely accepted within ethics that ethical theory cannot do without drawing on moral intuitions and that, everything else being equal, one ethical theory would be preferable to another if it to a larger extent succeeds in accounting for some of our basic moral intuitions. However, it is also generally acknowledged that there may often be strong reasons to reject our spontaneous moral intuitions. In fact, the whole point of engaging in moral philosophical considerations is that we cannot always trust our more immediate answers and that we are often well advised to reject intuitions when we provide answers to how we should act. Thus, what should we do in the present case? Should the retributivist try—as has yet constituted the preferred approach—to embrace the intuition that no number of minor offenses can be as serious a single instance of a more serious offense and that multiple offenders, therefore, should be treated with a corresponding degree of leniency—or is the more reasonable reaction to reject this intuition and stick to whatever follows from standard proportionality considerations? As I shall now argue there are strong reasons to believe that the retributivist should follow the latter route.

The reason for adopting a skeptical attitude lies in the fact that our intuitive moral reactions are, in rough terms, not very good at figures. This aspect of our intuitions has been revealed in numerous moral psychological studies. For instance, when asked how much participants in a study would pay to save 2,000, 20,000, or 200,000 migrating birds from drowning in uncovered oil ponds, they stated their willingness to pay respectively $80, $78, and $80 (Desvousges et al., 1993). The large difference in the number of birds saved was not at all reflected in the participants' willingness to pay. In another study conducted by Kahneman, it turned out that the participants were willing to spend the same amount of money to clean up several hundreds of polluted lakes compared to the clean-up of one polluted lake (Kahneman, 1986). Similar findings have been reached in many other studies revealing people's attitudes to "large numbers." The phenomenon that our more intuitive reactions are not designed to reflect differences in numbers is usually referred to as "scope-insensitivity" or "scope neglect" (see Nordgren and McDonnell, 2011, p. 97). But if we know that our inability to intuitively grasp large numbers is a general feature of our moral psychological setup, is it not reasonable to believe that it is precisely the same type of scope-insensitivity that lies behind the intuitive reaction that numbers do not make a significant difference when we are assessing instances of multiple offending? In other cases involving scope-insensitivity, this feature of our intuitive reactions is usually regarded as a violation of rational choice. When asked, the participants in the studies would all subscribe to the view that it is more important to save more rather than fewer birds or to clean up more rather than fewer polluted lakes. However, when it comes to our intuitive reactions, our sense of proportion is lost. Would it therefore, not be equally reasonable to hold that if retributivists believe there are strong reasons to assess crime gravity in terms of harm and culpability and to maintain standard proportionality, then they should not be worried by the fact that we are unable to intuitively grasp the extent of the gravity of 20 burglaries or 50 cases of car theft and, consequently, simply skip the attempt to incorporate the latter intuition within a theoretical framework into which it does not fit? In my view, this is the conclusion which the retributivist ought to draw. There is no reason why retributivism should not be informed by the results of modern moral psychology, especially when this makes it possible for the retributivist to explain away and reject intuitions that throw a spanner in the theoretical works.

It might perhaps at this point be objected that it is premature to assess our intuitions in multiple-offense cases in the light of moral psychological reactions in relation to subjects that are very different (such as drowning birds and polluted lakes). However, there is reason to believe that our tendency to display scope-insensitivity is equally at stake in relation to offense gravity assessment. In fact, this is precisely what Nordgren and McDonnell have forcefully demonstrated in a recent study. Drawing on the lessons from earlier studies on scope-insensitivity, the two researchers hypothesized that the number of people victimized by a crime would not be reflected in the perceived severity of a crime. Participants in the study were all asked to read the following vignette: "Frank Aaker was found guilty of fraud. He ran a Ponzi scheme that defrauded (three or 30) people out of their life savings" (Nordgren and McDonnell, 2011, p. 98). However, they were randomly assigned either to the small scope condition (three people being defrauded) or the large scope condition (30 people being defrauded). After reading the vignette, participants were asked to assess the severity of the offense on a 10-point scale from 1 (not at all serious) to 10 (extremely serious) and to recommend a sentence. What the researchers found was not only that the evaluations of the gravity of the crimes were not positively correlated with the number of victims, but in fact that "participants in the small scope condition judged the fraud case to be *more severe* compared to participants in the large scope condition" (Nordgren and McDonnell, 2011, p. 99). Correspondingly, participants in the small scope condition recommended *more severe* punishments (i.e., longer terms of imprisonment) for the perpetrator than participants in the large scope condition.

The result of this study may strike some as highly surprising. How can it possibly be the case that people tend to regard an offense as less serious if they are considering an instance involving fewer victims rather than an instance involving more victims, everything else being equal? However, given the knowledge we possess today within moral psychology this result is actually not surprising at all. Consider the reactions in another field where our judgments have been demonstrated to be vulnerable to scope-insensitivity, namely cases in which people are suffering from poverty or are in other ways in need of assistance. What has been demonstrated is that people's willingness to give donations decreases rapidly when we move from cases involving a single victim of poverty to cases involving several victims (see Small, 2003; Slovic, 2007). And the obvious explanation is that it is much easier to identify with a single victim than with many victims.

Even if the amount of information one receives about the single victim and the multiple victims is the same, the mere fact that we are considering a single victim is psychologically perceived in a different light than if we are asked to consider larger numbers of victims. Interestingly, this phenomenon seems also to be what is at stake in the case involving crime victims. In addition to the evaluations of the seriousness of the offense in the vignette, Nordgren and McDonnell also asked the participants to describe one of the victims in this case. What they subsequently found was that participants in the small scope condition described the hypothetical victim in much greater detail compared to the description of a victim in the large scope condition, thereby confirming the hypothesis that the evaluations of offenses in the two cases is driven to a large extent by the degree to which participants identify with a victim and it is this degree of identifiability that is weakened when the number of victims increase; as the two researchers underline: "people form more vivid mental representations of a small number of victims" (Nordgren and McDonnell, 2011, p. 99).

In light of these results it is not at all surprising that there is a strong intuition in favor of overall proportionality. Our mental system is not designed to comprehend larger numbers of victims. Thus when we compare a single instance of a more serious crime, say rape, with a large number of less serious crimes, say theft, it is not surprising that we tend to regard the former misdeed as more serious. As we have seen earlier, Bennett was absolutely right when he observed that we tend not to assess serial wrongdoings cumulatively. However, while he—as other retributivists—believes that one should try to embrace this intuition, the more plausible conclusion, as suggested, is to acknowledge that this intuition leads us astray, that it is simply a result of our limited mental capacity when it comes to identifications with statistical victims, that is, our vulnerability to scope-insensitivity. When people regard it as worse if one person suffers from poverty or other problems, compared to how they assess a corresponding situation involving several people suffering, then this is not an evaluation which we should reflect in our final ethical judgments. Rather, we should trust our reasoned evaluations that it is worse if more people are suffering (and perhaps regret that this is not always captured in our cognitively limited intuitive response system). Neither should we try to incorporate the evaluation in Nordgren and McDonnell's study that a crime is seen as less serious if it involves more victims. Having realized this deficiency in our moral intuitions, the proper conclusion for the retributivist is to let her theory be informed by the lessons from moral psychology (that scope neglect is a standard defect of our psychology set-up), to trust the essential elements in her theory (i.e., that crime gravity should be determined on the ground of harm and culpability) and abandon the idea of overall proportionality.

As a minor digression, let me conclude this section by noting that Nordgren and McDonnell conducted a follow-up study, designed to examine whether the results found in the experiment could also be observed in real-life jury verdicts. Using Westlaw's database of US jury verdicts, they examined toxic tort cases (civil suits against defendants who allegedly harmed plaintiffs by negligently exposing them to toxic substance). Such cases vary greatly in the number of victims. What the researchers found, in a 10-year period (between 2000 and 2009), was a significant *negative* association between the number of plaintiffs and the punitive awards, that is, that "juries have historically punished defendants less harshly when their offence harmed more people" (Nordgren and McDonnell, 2011, p. 101). Apparently the inverse relation between the amount of damage awarded and the number of victims was also observed outside the experimental setting.

Conclusion

What this chapter has been concerned with and has critically discussed is the retributivist approach to the sentencing of multiple offenders. As noted, there are compelling reasons for giving discounts to multiple offenders if one favors a consequentialist approach to sentencing. But it is much less obvious that an argument to this effect can be provided on the ground of desert theoretical considerations. More precisely, what I have considered is the possibility of advancing a retributivist rationale for the view that no number of offenses of one class should ever lead to a sentence as severe as the one that should be given for a single instance of an offense belonging in a class of more serious offenses.

What I have suggested, firstly, is that overall proportionality cannot be justified on the grounds of harm and culpability. Secondly, I have considered whether such proportionality constraints can plausibly be justified on the grounds of moral intuitions. As we have seen, the appeal to intuitions played an important role in Bennett's approach to multiple-offense sentencing. And, more generally, several retributivists have strongly emphasized that the intuitive attraction of the view that no number of minor offenses should be punished as severely as an instance of a more serious offense in itself constitutes a reason for adopting overall proportionality constraints within the retributivist theoretical framework.

However, I have argued that there are strong reasons to question the widespread appeal of this kind of intuition. Retributivism ought to be informed by the lessons from moral psychology revealing that scope-insensitivity constitutes a general feature of our psychological set-up, that is, that we are simply not designed to intuitively grasp large numbers. As the study by Nordgren and McDonnell has demonstrated, this is also the case with regard to our assessment of offenses involving multiple victims. Rather than trying to accommodate such intuitions within a theoretical framework with which they are incompatible, the retributivists should disregard the intuitions. The retributivist should simply react in the same way as philosophers often do when they reject intuitions (sometimes also powerful ones) in favor of theoretical reasons. Moreover, it should be noted that even though I have focused on the question as to whether a certain approach to multiple offending can be justified *within* the framework of desert theory, it is also clear that those theorists who favor the approach that multiple-offense sentencing should be dealt with by introducing considerations that overrule just deserts, should also seriously consider whether they are basically motivated by the type of intuition which they would be well-advised to debunk.

Finally, in order to avoid premature conclusions, it should be emphasized that even if the arguments of this chapter are plausible, it does obviously not follow that some sort of noncumulative approach to multiple offending cannot be justified on retributivist grounds. An argument to this effect would require much more comprehensive analysis. More modestly, all I have argued in the previous sections is that penal reductions for multiple offenders cannot be justified on the ground of overall proportionality constraints.

Notes

1. For a comment on the lack of an incapacitative effect, see Lippke 2011, p. 214.
2. For a criticism of the view that a multiple-offense discount can be justified in terms of mercy, see Ryberg, 2005.
3. For a critical discussion of the latter view, see Ryberg, 2005.
4. It could of course be held that it is impossible or morally undesirable to aggregated harms. In this paper, I cannot discuss this more general view except by noting that it would have rather radical implications (e.g., that it is not worse to kill many people rather than a single person). In the following it will be assumed that harms can and should be aggregated. For a classical discussion of the moral significance of numbers, see J. M. Taurek, 1977; for a critique of Taurek, see D. Parfit, 1978.
5. See J. S. Mill's discussion in, "Utilitarianism," J. Gray 1991, p. 138.
6. For a more elaborated discussion of this type of criticism against qualitative hedonism, see Ryberg, 2002.
7. That this view is very difficult to sustain theoretically can be illustrated in various ways. For instance, suppose that A has committed eight burglaries which are each slightly more harmful than eight burglaries committed by B. Suppose, furthermore, that if the two offenders were punished cumulatively the overall punishment would exceed the punishment ceiling for this type of crime. What this implies is that they should both receive that same sentence, namely, the one constituting the ceiling. However, in order to sustain this view of overall proportionality on the ground of culpability considerations one will have to establish: 1) that A is less culpable than B and 2) that the lower degree of culpability ascribed to A precisely counterweighs for the fact that A's crimes were more harmful (if this is not the case, then A and B will not end up with the same punishment, namely, the one constituting the punishment ceiling). While it is not easy to see how the first condition can be established it is even harder to imagine a convincing argument in favor of the second condition. Thus, the idea of sustaining overall proportionately on the ground of culpability considerations faces serious challenges.

References

Ashworth. A. 1995. *Principles of Criminal Law*. 2nd ed. Oxford: Clarendon Press.

Ashworth. A. 2005. *Sentencing and Criminal Justice*. 4th ed. Cambridge: Cambridge University Press.

Bennett. C. 2011. "Do Multiple and Repeat Offenders Pose a Problem for Retributive Sentencing Theory?" In C. Tamburrini and J. Ryberg (eds.), *Recidivist Punishments: The Philosopher's View*, pp. 137–156. Lanham, MD: Lexington Books.

Desvousges, W. H., F. R. Johnson, R. W. Dunford, S. P. Hudson, and K. N. Wilson. 1993. "Measuring Natural Resource Damages with Contingent Valuation: Tests of Validity and Reliability." In J. A. Hausman (ed.), *Contingent Valuation: A Critical Assessment*, pp. 91–164. Amsterdam, London: North-Holland.

Doob, A., and C. N. Webster. 2003. "Sentence Severity and Crime: Accepting the Null Hypothesis." In M. Tonry (ed.), *Crime and Justice: A Review of Research* 30: 143–195. Chicago: University of Chicago Press.

Gray, J. (ed.) 1991. *John Stuart Mill. On Liberty and Other Essays*. Oxford: Oxford University Press.

Jareborg, N. 1998. "Why Bulk Discounts in Multiple Offence Sentencing?" In A. Ashworth and M. Wasik (eds.), *Fundamentals of Sentencing Theory: Essays in Honour of Andrew von Hirsch*, pp. 129–140. Oxford: Clarendon Press.

Kahneman, D. 1986. "Comments on the Contingent Valuation Method." In R. G. Cummings, D. Brookshire, and W. D. Schulze (eds.), *Valuing Environmental Goods: An Assessment of the Contingent Valuation Method*, pp. 185–193. Totowa: Rowan and Allanheld.

Lippke, R. 2011. "Retributive Sentencing, Multiple Offenders, and Bulk Discounts." In M. D. White (ed.), *Retributivism: Essays on Theory and Policy*, pp. 212–231. New York: Oxford University Press.

Lovegrove, A. 2000. "Proportionality, Sentencing and the Multiple Offender." *Punishment & Society* 2(4): 453–469.

Nagin, D. S. 2013. "Deterrence in the Twenty-First Century." In M. Tonry (ed.), *Crime and Justice: A Review of Research* 42(1): 199–263. Chicago: University of Chicago Press.

Nordgren, J. F., and M. M. McDonnell. 2011. "The Scope-Severity Paradox: Why Doing More Harm Is Judged to Be Less Harmful." *Social Psychology and Personality Science* 2(1): 97–102.

Parfit, D. 1978. "Innumerate Ethics." *Philosophy and Public Affairs* 7(4): 285–301.

Pratt, T. C., F. T. Cullen, K. R. Blevins, L. E. Daigle, and T. D. Madensen. 2006. "The Empirical Status of Deterrence Theory: A Meta-Analysis." In F. T. Cullen, J. P. Wright, and K. R. Blevins (eds.), *Taking Stock: The Status of Criminological Theory* vol. 15, pp. 367–395. New Brunswick, NJ: Transaction.

Reitz, K. R. 2010. "The Illusion of Proportionality: Desert and Repeat Offenders." In J. V. Roberts and A. von Hirsch (eds.), *Previous Convictions at Sentencing: Theoretical and Applied Perspectives*, pp. 137–160. Oxford: Hart Publishing.

Ryberg, J. 2002. "Higher and Lower Pleasures—Doubts on Justification." *Ethical Theory and Moral Practice* 5(4) 415–429.

Ryberg, J. 2004. *The Ethics of Proportionate Punishment: A Critical Investigation*. Dordrecht, Boston: Kluwer Academic Publishers.

Ryberg, J. 2005. "Retributivism and Multiple Offending." *Res Publica* 11(3): 213–233.

Small, D. A., and G. Loewenstein. 2003. "Helping a Victim or Helping the Victim: Altruism and Identifiability." *Journal of Risk and Uncertainty* 26(1) 5–16.

Slovic, P. 2007. "If I Look at the Mass I Will Never Act." *Judgment and Decision Making* 2(2): 79–95.

Taurek, J. M. 1977. "Should the Numbers Count?" *Philosophy and Public Affairs* 6(4) 293–316.

Von Hirsch, A. 1993. *Censure and Sanctions*. Oxford: Clarendon Press.

3

Exploring an Institutionalist and Post-Desert Theoretical Approach to Multiple-Offense Sentencing

ANTHONY BOTTOMS

The topic of multiple-offense sentencing (MOS) presents scholars with a troubling disjunction between everyday sentencing practice and a central feature of recent punishment theory. Legal systems across the world vary widely, both in their procedural approaches and in their substantive content, yet there has so far been not a single report of a jurisdiction that does not include, in MOS cases, some version of a totality principle, sometimes informally described as a "discount for bulk offending." When we turn to punishment theory, however, we observe that in the last half-century there has been a significant turning away from previously dominant consequentialist approaches; and, while the main (broadly retributivist) theories on offer espouse some significantly different principles relating to various matters, many of them endorse, to a greater or lesser extent, the principle of "equal punishment for equal crimes"—a principle that is clearly in tension with the totality principle (Reitz, 2010). This disjunction between practice and theory appears to leave scholars who endorse the principle of equal punishment for equal crimes with three principal options. These might be described as follows:

First, they could press upon Sentencing Commissions and appellate courts the need for a significant revision of existing practices relating to MOS, so as to better conform with the theoretical requirement of "equal punishment for equal crimes."

Secondly, such scholars might decide that, given the tension between their theories and (at least some aspects of) settled sentencing practice, it would be beneficial to examine existing sentencing practice as carefully and closely as possible, in order to consider whether there is a need to revise one or more features of their chosen theoretical approach.

Thirdly, rather than choosing either of the preceding options, scholars might explore the possibility of altering the terms within which this debate is standardly conducted, and thus perhaps lessening the apparent conflict between practice and theory.

In this chapter, I will focus initially on the second of these possibilities. This choice has been made because, in my judgment, there are good reasons, based in what is sometimes described as an "institutionalist theory of law," for believing that theorists can sometimes gain valuable normative insights from the careful study of institutionalized legal practices. Accordingly, when analyzing a puzzling legal phenomenon, until we have made a thorough and "appreciative" analysis of existing practices,[1] and then subjected the results of that study to careful normative assessment,[2] it will be premature to conclude that existing practices are normatively deficient.

In pursuit of this approach, the first three sections of this chapter will explore an institutionalist approach to MOS. The final two sections will then consider normative issues relevant to MOS, with appropriate reference to the findings of the institutionalist analysis. It is hoped that together the analyses in the chapter will be helpful to those wishing to develop a version or versions of the third option described above.

An Institutionalist Approach to Legal Theory

What is "institutionalism"? There are various versions of it, but for simplicity I shall discuss only that developed by Neil MacCormick. He begins from the position that human beings are daily *norm-users*, as evidenced for example in their use of language. He points out that "languages have a structure . . . that depends on highly complex norms that were never consciously made by anybody, . . . [yet] experts . . . struggle to express (or rationally reconstruct) . . . the norms implicit" in any given language (MacCormick, 2007, p. 1). Hence in everyday oral exchanges, complex and subtle normative structures are deployed in a socially useful way, without those structures necessarily being consciously understood by their users. The same is also often true of behavioral norms. Such norms signify usual practice within a given social group; they are sometimes the product of human design and planning, but frequently, just like a language, they have evolved through regular usage (Bicchieri, 2006). Usually we simply work within and with such norms as part of our daily patterns of living, although sometimes we are able to explicate such practices when we think carefully about them.

From this starting point, MacCormick (2007, p. 11) develops the idea, central to his jurisprudence, that law and legal systems are a form (although not the only form) of *institutional normative order.* Within such an order,

> discourses about law use a network of interrelated concepts like "persons," "duties," "rights," "obligations," "powers" [or] "immunities" . . . *An analytical approach to elucidating the meaning of such terms* is one that seeks to see how they all *interconnect in linkages of mutual implication or opposition* . . . . [This] requires a reflexive inquiry into the norms of the discourse we engage in when we are discussing the legal rights and duties of persons, or [other legal topics] . . . . This can be a relatively abstract discourse, or, in a lawyer's chambers trying to solve a client's legal problem, an intensely practical one. The complexity of life under highly developed systems of law guarantees also that the network one analyses is *a dense and thickly concatenated one.* (MacCormick, 2009, p. 190, emphasis added)

The italicized phrases in this passage are, in my judgment, of great importance in understanding legal practices. This is because they stress, first, that considerable analytical effort is sometimes necessary in order to understand legal practices; and secondly, that in a given empirical context there can be significant *interconnection* and *concatenation* of legal-institutional norms and practices.[3]

The potential relevance of this approach to legal phenomena can be illustrated In the present context by reference to a historically dominant account of MOS in common-law jurisdictions. According to this account, the sentencer first decides the appropriate sentences for the several offenses considered separately and singly; then he or she relates these sentences to one another in a preliminary fashion (for example, by deciding whether terms of imprisonment should in principle be ordered to be served consecutively or concurrently); then, finally, consideration is given as to whether any downward adjustment of the total punishment is necessary in the light of the full set of circumstances in the case.[4] In the helpful formulation of an appellate court in Canada, in the concluding stage of this process the court takes "*one last look* at the combined sentence to determine whether it is unduly long or harsh";[5] or, otherwise stated, it assesses whether the unadjusted combined sentence would be *unfair*. Within an institutionalist analysis, to understand why such adjustments are made it is appropriate to assess them in the context of the preceding norms and practices, and to consider in particular why, and on what basis, courts so often judge that a final "fairness adjustment" is necessary to reflect the totality of the situation.

An implication of an institutionalist approach is that careful empirical analyses of MOS in various jurisdictions would help to enhance understanding of this topic. Unfortunately, however, that presents us with a significant difficulty, because empirical research on this topic is very sparse indeed. In the next section, I shall therefore focus on the most extensive (although still fairly small-scale) published English-language empirical research on MOS, which was conducted by Austin Lovegrove in Victoria, Australia. Perhaps surprisingly, relatively few academic papers on MOS have cited this important study.

An Empirical Study of Multiple-Offense Sentencing

Lovegrove's research is principally reported in two book-length publications. The first of these contains an analysis of the decisions and reasoning of eight experienced judges in 60 hypothetical cases, from which a "decision framework" of sentencing in MOS cases was inferred (Lovegrove, 1997). In the second study, aspects of this decision framework were tested, using a sample of archival MOS cases in which one of three crimes (armed robbery, burglary, or rape) constituted the principal offense (Lovegrove, 2004). Within the context of an institutionalist analysis, the second of these studies is of special significance, because its focus is on actual decided cases.

As Lovegrove (2004, p. 9) notes, Fox and Freiberg's (1999, p. 725) well-respected legal textbook on sentencing in Victoria states that "the principle of totality is the product of two others, namely proportionality and mercy." In Lovegrove's (1997) initial work using hypothetical cases, the main "justification for constraint" articulated by judges in MOS cases was found to be mercy, alternatively described by Lovegrove (2004, p. 55) as "the need to minimise the potentially crushing effects of imprisonment on offenders." In the later archival study, this assessment was broadly confirmed by a qualitative examination of the transcripts of judges' sentencing remarks, in which matters relating to "rehabilitation prospects" were found to be "commonly canvassed in judgments, and . . . the stated allowance for [them] is sometimes substantial" (Lovegrove, 2004, p. 56); moreover, this seemed to apply "not just at the upper levels of imprisonment, but . . . [potentially] as a moderating influence on . . . all sentences of imprisonment" in MOS cases (Lovegrove, 2004, 67–68). However, as we shall see, the statistical evidence from Lovegrove's 2004 study also supported Fox and Freiberg's legal analysis in showing that "evidence of proportionality in one way or another [acts] as a powerful limiting factor" on the severity of sentences in MOS cases (p. 55). The focus of these two principles is, of course, different: proportionality focuses on the series of acts (*offenses*) that are before the court, whereas mercy considers particularly the likely effect of the sentence on the *offender*. Yet as Lovegrove (2004, p. 55) rightly commented, in principle these "two justifications are not incompatible."

Lovegrove's archival study contained 118 MOS cases, in each of which the defendant received a custodial sentence. The sample was limited to cases in which the set of offenses to be sentenced was adjudged to consist of two or more separate "transactions"—a restriction that was applied because of the rule of law (in Victoria as in England and Wales) that where "two or more offences are committed in the course of a single transaction, all sentences in respect of these offences should be concurrent" (Thomas, 1979, p. 53; see also Fox and Freiburg, 1999, p. 714).[6] Despite this restriction, however—and to Lovegrove's surprise—fully concurrent custodial sentences were "very common" in his Victoria sample, comprising nearly half (54) of the cases (Lovegrove, 2004, p. 52). That left only 64 cases for the principal analysis, which was focused upon cases that included some element of sentence cumulation (the term used in Victoria for consecutive sentences); and among these 64 cases, the principal offense was armed robbery in 27 cases, rape in 24, and burglary in thirteen. The term "some element of sentence cumulation" has been used advisedly, because in Victoria, unlike England and Wales, a sentence of imprisonment can be ordered to be served partly concurrently and partly consecutively.

Qualitative data in Lovegrove's (1997) first study had suggested that judges often had only a "superficial understanding" of the issues involved in MOS cases; hence, "their expressions of what they thought to be correct by way of a general approach lack[ed] detail and [were] incomplete" (Lovegrove, 2004, p. 58). A consequence of this imprecision was that the quantitative data in the later archival study were statistically "noisy." However, as we shall see, certain statistical patterns were discernible in the data; the judges "could be said to be applying a more-or-less common and general policy badly" (Lovegrove, 2004, p. 59).

To make progress with an institutionalist analysis of MOS using Lovegrove's data, it is necessary to identify the main features of this "common and general" policy, while bearing in mind that the policy has not been applied with full consistency. There are, I believe, four particularly significant features of judicial sentencing practice in MOS cases in Victoria that are revealed by Lovegrove's statistical analysis; each will be considered in turn.

Linkages Between Offenses

The first feature concerns the nature of the linkages between the offenses falling to be sentenced. In his research study, Lovegrove distinguished four principal categories for such linkages. The first two of these were: (i) a single offense of the principal type (armed robbery, etc.), together with other offenses connected with it ("single-connected"); and (ii) an "escapade" of two or more offenses on the same day or night (and therefore connected in time).[7] These two categories therefore have in common an obvious degree of *connectedness*; by contrast, Lovegrove's other two categories were less connected and more disparate in character.[8] For present purposes, it is useful to work with two groups rather than four, so I shall consider only the broad differentiation between cases with "connected" (N = 76) and "less connected" (N = 42) groups of offenses.

Using this distinction, and comparing the 54 cases in which judges had ordered full concurrency with the remainder of the sentenced cases, offenders in the connected group were significantly more likely to receive fully concurrent sentences. The difference was large: 59.2% of offenders with connected groups of offenses received fully concurrent sentences, as against only 21.4% of those whose offenses were less connected (data calculated from Table 6 in Lovegrove, 2004, p. 51). More detailed analysis showed that the same pattern held when separate analyses were conducted for cases with different principal offenses (i.e., armed robbery, burglary, and rape). Thus, the data clearly showed that offenders whose offenses were less connected were more likely to receive consecutive sentences.

Aggregate Sentence Length

The next finding to be highlighted is restricted to the 64 cases in which there was some cumulation of sentence. The variable of particular interest in this analysis is the proportion of the (unadjusted) secondary sentences in each case that were made cumulative (consecutive); this proportion was then plotted against what was termed the total sentence in each case (where "total sentence" means the length of sentence for the principal offense, plus the aggregate unadjusted length of those sentences for secondary offenses that were made wholly or partially consecutive).[9] In these analyses, a similar data pattern emerged for each of the three offenses studied (see Lovegrove, 2004, Figures 2, 4, and 5, pp. 38, 44 and 47[10]); this pattern is illustrated here in a simplified form from a prototypical analysis in Lovegrove's (1997) earlier study (Figure 3.1).

As may be seen, the general relationship found is that the proportion of the secondary sentences made cumulative (consecutive) is highest when the total sentence (as defined above) is low, then diminishes as the total sentence increases. Indeed, there is a point at which the curve flattens out almost completely, which suggests that beyond a certain (unadjusted) total sentence length, judges in Victoria are reluctant to add further consecutive sentences for secondary offenses. In principle, this pattern is explicable by reference to the "mercy"

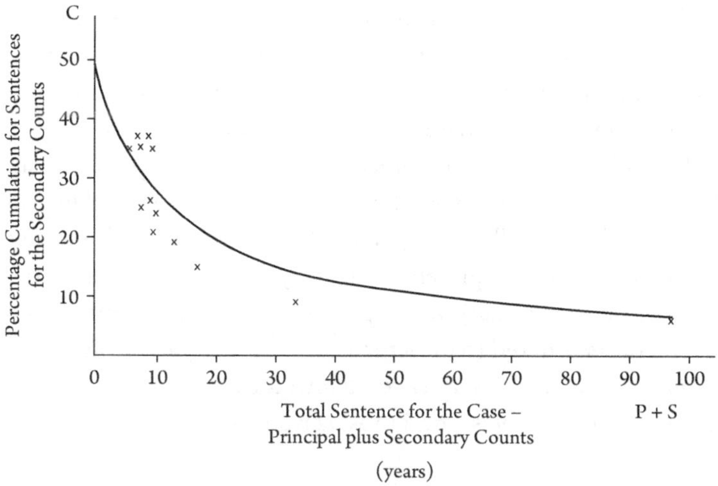

Figure 3.1 A Prototypical Analysis of the Relation between the Percentage Cumulation of Sentences for Secondary Offenses and the Total Sentence
Source: Lovegrove 1997, Figure 9.2, p. 242.

dimension of Victorian sentencing philosophy identified by Lovegrove, though as we shall see later it is also consistent with a more consequentialist approach to sentencing.

It is of great interest that the general shape of the curve shown in Figure 3.1 is remarkably similar to that found in an earlier German study by Albrecht (1994) (not cited by Lovegrove), notwithstanding that one of these studies was conducted in an Australasian common-law context, and the other in a European civil law jurisdiction. Like Lovegrove, Albrecht studied MOS for the three offenses of rape, robbery and burglary, and he found a lesser degree of cumulation as total sentence length increased (Albrecht, 1994, Figure 35, p. 391). For burglary, he expressed the results in percentage terms (in his Figure 36), and Jareborg (1998, p. 135) has provided a useful English-language summary of the results:

> discounts were hardly noticeable where the sum of the punishments was imprisonment for less than one year: the average total punishment was 78 per cent of the sum of the individual punishments. For almost each additional one-year interval the percentages fell: (2) 73 per cent, (3) 69 per cent, (4) 58 per cent, (5) 56 per cent, (6) 47 per cent, (7) 38 per cent, (8) 45 per cent, (9) 31 per cent.

In addition to this analysis, Albrecht (1994, pp. 392–393) also analyzed the data from his study in a different way. For the horizontal axis, instead of the aggregate sentence for all offenses in the case (as in Figure 3.1), Albrecht plotted the: "penal value" (that is, the unadjusted deserved sentence) for each separate offense, considered sequentially, with the highest penal value at the left-hand end of the graph. The vertical axis then measured the proportion of each sentence that the court ordered to be served. On this basis, a curve of a very similar shape to that in Figure 3.1 was obtained—perhaps not surprisingly, since there is clearly some conceptual overlap between the two analyses. Subsequently, a replication in Finland of Albrecht's penal value analysis again found very similar results: Hinkkanen and Lappi-Seppala (2011, pp. 363–366) showed that over a five-year period (1999–2003), the percentage of the identified penal value that Finnish courts ordered to be actually served was (obviously) 100% for the most serious offense in the sequence, followed by a clear decline as the penal value lessened (29% for the second most serious offense, then 18%, 13%, 10%, and 7%).

From these analyses, we can conclude that empirical research analyses in Australia, Germany and Finland have produced very similar results. The increasingly followed "Borgeke scale" used by judges for MOS in Sweden (see Borgeke, 2008, also the chapter by Natalia Vibla in this volume) also follows the same broad pattern.

Variations By Offense

Returning to Lovegrove's study, we noted that the shape of the curve shown in Figure 3.1 was found to be consistent across the separate analyses conducted for cases with different principal offenses (armed robbery, rape, and burglary). However, there was an interesting further finding, which was that the substantive proportion of cumulation of the secondary offenses in these three analyses differed, and was greatest where rape was the principal offense. For example, where the total sentence (as measured in the horizontal axis in Figure 3.1) was four years, the percentage cumulation for secondary offenses (the vertical axis of Figure 3.1) was 53% in rape cases, but only 41% in armed robbery cases. The corresponding data for a total sentence length of 15 years was 25% as against 16%; and so on (Lovegrove, 2004, Table 7, p. 55).[11] In other words, for any given length of total sentence, the proportion of the secondary sentences that were cumulated (made consecutive) was consistently greater in the rape subsample.

It is worth spelling out the subtlety of this finding. The findings in the previous subsection show that when the total offending pattern is very serious, leading to very high unadjusted total sentences, there is a *lower* degree of cumulation. But the present subsection also shows that *for any given value of total sentence length* (as shown in Figure 3.1) the degree of cumulation will be *higher* when the offense is more serious. Nor does this seem to be a chance finding, because there was again a similar finding in Albrecht's (1994, Figure 35) study—he showed that for any given aggregate sentence length, German courts ordered a greater degree of cumulation of sentence when rape, rather than burglary, was the principal offense.

Accordingly, it seems that when they apply the totality principle, courts often take into account not only the degree of connectedness of the offense group and the length of the total sentence, but also the seriousness of the type of principal offense.

Staying Within the Standard Sentence Range?

In his archival study, Lovegrove (2004, pp. 83f) paid some special attention to a conceptual approach to MOS that had been articulated in legal analyses in England, but not explicitly in Victoria. Following Wasik (2012, p. 292) I shall describe this as "Thomas's principle," because it was first articulated in David Thomas's (1979) pioneering work on the sentencing practice of the Court of Appeal in England and Wales. Thomas stated that precise formulation of the principle was difficult, because of some inconsistencies in the cases decided by the Court. However, he defined "the essence of the principle" as follows: "the aggregate sentence should not be longer than the upper limit of the normal bracket of sentences for the category of cases in which the most serious offense committed by the offender would be placed" (Thomas, 1979, p. 59).

For Thomas (p. 58) this principle is "an extension" of a central principle of sentencing in single-offense cases, namely that of "proportionality between offense and sentence" (including ordinal proportionality). In MOS cases, he saw the focus of the principle—as developed by the Court of Appeal—as that of proportionality between the sentence and the seriousness of the *principal* crime in the cluster of offenses. As an example, he cited an unreported case (*Holderness*, 1974) in which the judge at first instance had imposed consecutive sentences totaling four years' imprisonment for a group of mainly motoring offenses. In this case, the Court of Appeal held that in making the sentences consecutive, the trial judge had failed to "take the step . . . of standing back and looking at the overall effect of the sentences"; had he done so, he "would at once have appreciated" that he had imposed an aggregate sentence of a length that should be reserved for cases of "really serious crime" (Thomas, 1979, p. 58). Thus, the Court seemed to be saying that it was important for sentencers to think about sending the right message to the public about the "headline" seriousness of the crimes involved, and therefore to keep the sentence within the normal range for the principal offense. (The public might, for example, have said in response to the original sentence in *Holderness*: "You mean he got four years for some *motoring offenses*?").

Lovegrove attempted to test empirically whether the courts in Victoria were abiding by Thomas's principle, and for this purpose he used archival sentencing data to establish a "normal range" of sentences for the three principal offenses represented in his study. He found that Thomas's principle was followed in the majority of the 64 cases where some cumulation of sentence was ordered, as well as, obviously, in the 54 "fully concurrent" cases. He developed two different criteria to establish whether sentences for the specified offenses were "disproportionate," and found that, on the more stringent criterion, 21 cases (just under a fifth of the 118 cases) had been sentenced disproportionately (Lovegrove, 2004, pp. 108–109).[12] But such sentences were carefully targeted: 16 of the 21 disproportionate sentences (76%) were imposed on offenders who had committed a group of less-connected crimes (see previous discussion). This again suggests that courts often see less-connected MOS offenders as deserving of more severe punishment than those who have committed a group of connected offenses.

Overview and Implications

Lovegrove's statistical analysis, together with his qualitative examination of judicial transcripts, provides strong empirical support for Fox and Freiberg's claim that proportionality and mercy are the two key principles underpinning MOS in Victoria. In some of the academic literature on MOS, there has been a tendency to treat the proportionality and mercy explanations of the totality principle as separate and alternative theoretical principles, but Lovegrove's study suggests that in court practice they can be, and are, applied together, in what MacCormick (2009, p. 190) described as an "interconnected" and "concatenated" way.

Overall, we can summarize Lovegrove's empirical research as having found that:

(i) in the usual case, courts did not sentence above the highest level of the normal range of the principal offense; but
(ii) they were willing to break that guideline in a minority of cases, especially less-connected offenses (see (iii));
(iii) their practice varied according to the connectedness of the set of offenses (less-connected offenses were more likely to be sentenced consecutively);
(iv) they were much less likely to make secondary sentences consecutive (cumulative) where the aggregate of the unadjusted individual sentences was long;
(v) the practice described in (iv) above varied by the type of principal offense; and
(vi) courts were willing to endorse the principle of a reduction of sentence in MOS cases on grounds of mercy, understood as avoiding "crushing" sentences and facilitating rehabilitation.

Thus, despite its relatively small scale, Lovegrove's study can be seen to have made a valuable contribution to an institutionalist analysis of MOS; as such, it provides significant data for normative theorists to engage with.

Dealing with a "Trouble Case"

Empirical analyses of MOS, such as that of Lovegrove, are clearly valuable, but from an institutionalist perspective it is also valuable to examine MOS in action, in a specific case or cases. This could be done in many ways, but I have chosen to remain in the state of Victoria, and to examine what is now the leading appellate case on the totality principle within that jurisdiction. This case, *Azzopardi v. R.* [2011] VSCA 372, was decided in the Victoria Court of Appeal seven years after the publication of Lovegrove's archival analysis.[13] It can, I believe, contribute to the argument of this chapter in two ways. First, it illustrates some of the stark realities of trying to determine an appropriate and just sentence in cases where a defendant is convicted simultaneously of many offenses; secondly, it contributes a fresh thought on the justification of MOS.

Azzopardi and his main codefendant, Baltatzis, both aged 19, were jointly convicted of 46 separate offenses committed over a period of seven weeks; and both the sentencing judge and the appeal court ruled that in principle each of these offenses constituted a separate transaction that merited a custodial sentence, to be served cumulatively (consecutively). The principal conviction (the one with the longest sentence) was one of intentionally causing serious injury; there were also three further convictions for this offense, plus 32 convictions for robbery or attempted robbery (all but two of which were armed robbery). The appeal court reduced the originally imposed sentences for both defendants, but even so it ruled that before any application of the totality principle, the unadjusted aggregate of the deserved sentences for Azzopardi was 128 years, and for Baltatzis 105 years, 4 months. This case therefore dramatically illustrates the practical difficulties faced by judges in MOS cases. If we apply the language and logic of the Canadian case previously cited (see note 5), *Azzopardi* raises the question: exactly how should a court apply an appropriate "last look" or "final fairness check" in a set of circumstances such as these?

The appeal court in *Azzopardi* was acutely aware of the difficulties raised by this question, and it openly expressed a degree of frustration with some prior judicial formulations, such as one which spoke of the application of the totality principle in terms of arriving at an "instinctive synthesis" as "a matter of impression." As the court rather politely put the matter, in this type of formulation "the content of the principle remains unstated"; accordingly, "some further explication must be undertaken" (para. 58).

The key theoretical passage in the court's judgment (para. 61) reads as follows:

> The rationale underlying the [totality] principle is that a "just measure" of an offender's total criminality is *a sentence which satisfies all sentencing objectives applicable to the entirety of the criminal conduct.* Only implicitly in all of the statements of the principle of totality in its application is the proposition that a sentencing judge undertaking the adjustment of the sentence does so in order to ensure that *the final sentence is no more than necessary to satisfy the various objectives of sentencing. Considerations of mercy may further influence the sentencing judge to increase any downward adjustment.* As Wickham J was to recognise in [the Western Australian case of] *Magee v. The Queen* [(1980) WAR 117] . . . once the aggregate sentence satisfies both the mitigatory sentencing objectives as well as the punitive principles of just punishment, retribution, denunciation and protection of the community, "that is enough." Wickham J. also opined that *"more than enough is wrong because the excess is not only purposeless but might be harmful".* (at 119, emphases added)

The suggestion in this passage that the totality principle should be applied having regard to the stated sentencing objectives in a given jurisdiction seems obviously right, but such a principle has rarely been articulated in the past, either by courts or in the academic literature.[14] Notably, also, the sentencing objectives mentioned by the court include both retributive and consequentialist aims, raising the possibility that a mixed-theory justification of the exercise of the totality principle might be considered.

The final sentences ordered by the appeal court in *Azzopardi* are of interest. For Azzopardi himself (unadjusted total sentence= 128 years), these were: principal offense = seven years; cumulation of the secondary sentences = nine years; therefore total effective sentence = 16 years. For Baltatzis (unadjusted total sentence = 105 years 4 months), the corresponding figures were five years, seven years, and 12 years. The percentage cumulation of the secondary sentences (as shown in the vertical axis of Figure 3.1) was therefore low; less than 10% for both defendants. This is consistent with Lovegrove's (2004, p. 38, Figure 2) data for those with very long unadjusted total sentences in armed robbery cases. It is also noteworthy that, for both defendants, the aggregate cumulation of the secondary sentences exceeded the sentence for the principal offense, so in its final sentences for these offenders the court did not adhere to Thomas's principle.

Readers who are familiar with the work of the American jurist Karl Llewellyn will know that the title of the present section ("dealing with a trouble case") is derived from his famous article on "law jobs theory" (Llewellyn,

1940). Briefly, Llewellyn postulated that every legal system, and indeed every social group however small or informal (sports clubs, families, etc.) needs to have in place mechanisms to deal with some core issues of group functioning (= "law-jobs"); and one of these (expressed in Llewellyn's typically folksy language), concerns how the community should deal with the trouble case. In the present context, the concept of the trouble case seems to have particular resonance. Of course, in Llewellyn's terms, any sentencing process is a way of dealing with a trouble case; but in MOS cases, the trouble that the sentencing judge has to try to resolve can be very complex indeed, as the case of *Azzopardi* well illustrates. In dealing with such a case, the judge has to be aware that his or her decision may be being closely watched by the victims of relevant offenses and their families, possibly by the press and politicians, and certainly by the offender and his family. In developing the "last look" that the application of the totality principle standardly requires, the judge therefore needs to balance the (potentially conflicting) legitimate expectations of these various interested citizens, and also to apply any settled legal provisions operative in that particular jurisdiction. MOS, in short, is a very practical matter, yet one with significant moral and political dimensions. In this and the previous section, I have tried, through an institutionalist analysis in one jurisdiction, to elucidate descriptively some aspects of this complex piece of decision-making, in order to try to reach a more realistic stance from which to consider appropriate normative principles for the practice of MOS. But it is now time to address those normative issues more directly.

Post-Desert Theory

We saw in the introduction to this chapter that the point of particular tension between contemporary punishment theory and sentencing practice in MOS cases lies in the principle of equal punishments for equal crimes. That principle is espoused to a greater or lesser degree by most contemporary punishment theorists, yet it seems to be clearly placed in jeopardy when sentencers decide (as they did, for example, on several of the counts in *Azzopardi*) that an offender will receive a partially consecutive sentence of three months for a secondary offense of armed robbery that would, if it were a principal offense, merit a three-year sentence. The purpose of this section is to explore this tension more fully, which I shall do with special reference to the work of the leading advocate of ordinal proportionality in sentencing, Andreas von Hirsch (von Hirsch, 1993; von Hirsch and Ashworth, 2005) and a more recent critical commentary by Matt Matravers (2011). I shall focus the discussion around two propositions that can be derived from Matravers's essay.

> Proposition 1: The retributive revival of the 1970s "was not about desert"; it was rather about fairness [or "sweeping away many practices that resulted in actual injustices"]. (Matravers, 2011, p. 43)

For Matravers (2011, p. 32), a true desert theory of punishment holds that "a person who has committed a (legitimate) criminal wrong deserves to suffer some loss, and it is the function of the system of punishment to impose that loss for the wrong done." On this basis, he argues, we cannot describe as true "desert theories" either of the two most influential retributive theories of the 1970s—namely, von Hirsch's proportionality theory and Norval Morris's (1982, ch. 5) "limiting retributivism." What motivated both these theorists was a deep concern about some of the injustices being perpetrated under the largely unrestrained consequentialist practices then dominant in criminal justice systems in the United States, such as the widespread use of indeterminate sentences. Hence fairness, or justice, was a central motif of both theories. Although retributivism was at that time deeply intellectually unfashionable both in philosophical and in criminological circles, both scholars rightly saw (albeit in different ways) that some aspects of a retributive approach had the potential to improve criminal justice practice by creating credible blocks on unrestrained consequentialism. But neither of them rejected consequentialism completely; hence neither was, in Matravers's terms, a true desert theorist. Moreover, Matravers (2011, p. 35) explicitly states that ordinal proportionality (the central concept in von Hirsch's theory) "has nothing to do with the desert thesis" as traditionally understood.

Matravers acknowledges that this approach might seem to be driving us to a "dead end," since the "traditional understanding of deserved punishment" that he has definitionally prescribed is one that few contemporary punishment theorists would wish to share (p. 37). So he reasonably asks what gains there might be in taking this kind of approach. He reveals that he is particularly interested in the potential challenges to punishment theory posed by "recent therapeutic or restorative practices," and rightly says that if we are to respond adequately to these challenges then "we need to know what the issue is." His answer is expansive; he contends that if his previous arguments about desert are correct, "then the issue is not one of reconciling those practices to desert . . . but rather it is one of thinking about the requirements of liberal justice as a whole." Although he does not quite put it this way, the implication seems to be that, as punishment theorists, we should be willing to be as open-minded and creative as were our predecessors in the 1970s, and like them—with their primary emphasis on fairness—we should give priority to thinking about the nature of liberal justice as a whole.

This leads to the question: what are the implications of this line of argument for the issue of ordinal proportionality?

> Proposition 2: "Proportionality has an important role in our thinking about punishment. . . . However, it is not an independent principle. Rather, it is one of many considerations that must be taken into account when we devise a system of criminal justice and punishment . . . It is not a liberal trump card that can be played without further need for justification in proposing or criticizing a penal system." (Matravers, 2011, p. 40)

If this second proposition can be adequately defended, it obviously has potentially significant consequences for analyses of MOS.

Andreas von Hirsch would certainly concede Matravers's (2011, p. 37) claim that "proportionality does not provide the ultimate rationale for having a system of punishment (as opposed to not having one)." With Andrew Ashworth, he has developed a sophisticated account of the "general justifying aim" of a penal system, arguing that this must include considerations of both censure and prevention (von Hirsch and Ashworth, 2005, ch. 2). In an interesting footnote (p. 32), they also comment on the balance between these two factors:

> The question of primacy [as between censure and prevention] depends on the issue being addressed. When speaking of the justification of punishment's impositions on those punished, emphasis should be given to treating persons as moral agents—which suggests . . . a primacy for the censuring element. When speaking, however, of the reasons for the *state's* involvement in punishment, consequences may matter more—because the state's primary concerns relate to the consequences of its measures for its citizenry (emphasis in original).

Despite this comment, and despite the "mixed" (deontological and consequentialist) character of the general justifying aim in his theory, von Hirsch has always been clear that when discussing the amount of punishment to be ordered by a court (in cases involving a single offense), issues of ordinal proportionality must trump consequential considerations. The reason given is that, if it were otherwise, the crucial fairness requirement that ordinal proportionality represents will be lost. This is a central point that Matravers (2011, p. 39) challenges. Assume, he argues, that there are good reasons of public policy for the state to crack down on gang-related crime, and that this has led to sentencing guidelines that make gang-related crime subject to an additional tariff.[15] In this situation, if two offenders—one (A) a gang member and the other (B) not—commit equivalent crimes, A will receive a greater punishment than B. On von Hirsch's approach to punishment, this would not be permitted; but Matravers's (2011, p. 39) view is that such an outcome would not necessarily violate the requirement of a liberal state that citizens should be treated equally. "Of course," he argues, "their treatment *is* unequal, but the respect we are owed as citizens is, as Dworkin (1978) has usefully phrased it, not a matter of equal treatment, but of 'treatment as an equal'" (emphasis in original).

It is this analysis that underpins Matravers's proposition that ordinal proportionality should not be treated as an "independent principle" or a "liberal trump card." Matravers does not consider MOS, but if he has successfully argued that proportionality is not a trump card, then perhaps there is room to fashion a somewhat different theoretical approach to MOS, in which the clash between punishment theory and the practice of the courts becomes less stark. Following Matravers's nomenclature, although with a somewhat different meaning, this might be described as a "post-desert" approach to MOS;[16] that is, an approach which seeks to retain some of the best insights of proportionality theory, but also to provide some fresh ways of thinking about how one might develop just sentences in MOS cases.

Charting a Way Forward

To take matters forward from the analysis so far developed, it seems appropriate to begin with the principles identified in the institutionalist analysis, but to work also with the insights afforded by Matravers's post-desert approach. Within this framework, the obvious place to start is with Fox and Freiberg's (1999, p. 725) statement, validated in Victoria by Lovegrove's subsequent study, that "the principle of totality is the product of two others, namely proportionality and mercy." These matters will be considered separately.

Mercy

As noted earlier, in the Victorian case law the concept of mercy seems to have been used with two main connotations, namely: first, the "need to minimise the potentially crushing effects of imprisonment on offenders" (Lovegrove, 2004, p. 55; see also earlier English cases to a similar effect, discussed in Thomas, 1979, pp. 57ff); and secondly, the need to maximize the offender's rehabilitation prospects.[17] These two approaches, although closely related, are in principle distinguishable because rehabilitative considerations might be relevant even where the sentence is not likely to be considered crushing.

In considering the justification of these two approaches, an apparently promising theoretical resource is the concept of *responsive censure*, which has been recently developed by Hannah Maslen (2015). In the MOS context, the potential use of this theory is of special interest because—as we have seen—there is an obvious tension between MOS practice and proportionality theory, yet Maslen describes the concept of responsive censure as arising in part from the insights of proportionality theory.[18] Indeed, in developing her argument Maslen (2015, p. 98) gives prominence to the following passage from von Hirsch and Ashworth (2005, p. 92):

> Punishment, we believe, should be conceptualized as an expression of censure. Penal censure has important moral functions that are not reducible to crime prevention. A response to criminal wrongdoing that conveys disapprobation gives the individual the opportunity to respond in ways that are typically those of an agent capable of moral deliberation: to recognise the wrongfulness of the action; to feel remorse; to express regret; to make efforts to desist in future—or else to try to give reasons why the conduct was not actually wrong.

The central concept underpinning this paragraph is that of *dialogue*; the offender is censured, but it is hoped that he or she will respond in various ways, including expressions of regret and making efforts to desist.[19] (And we need to remember that as recent research has shown, most offenders, even persistent offenders, not only wish to desist, but usually do successfully desist: see Bottoms, 2014). But if one is serious about developing responsive dialogues in relation to sentencing, it follows that (i) the punishment arising out of the state censure must not be so harsh or overwhelming (crushing) as to make a positive response by the offender impossible or very unlikely; and (ii) even in cases where this crushing rationale does not apply, the state will wish to encourage a desisting/rehabilitative response by the offender, and in some cases might modify the sentence in order to maximize this possibility, while still adequately censuring the offender. These conclusions are, of course, entirely congruent with the two main meanings of mercy developed in MOS cases in Victoria.

But there is a further issue. Extensive empirical evidence suggests that censures are more likely to be positively responded to if they are seen to be both procedurally and distributively fair (Bottoms and Tankebe, 2017), and fairness requires that when punishing someone, careful account needs to be taken of their situation. That is why, when courts impose fines, they routinely take into account the resources of the defendant, imposing lower fines on those who are less well-off.[20] In Dworkin's (1978) language, this is not "equal treatment," but it is actually *fairer* than technically equal treatment, because—by taking account of differential resources—it treats everyone "as an equal." Developing this line of thought, one can argue that just as fines bite into an offender's economic resources, so custodial sentences can be seen to bite into an offender's most basic and precious resource—his or her lifespan. (A seven-year real-time prison sentence takes away a person's freedom for as much as 10% of the proverbial lifespan of 70 years.) These considerations help to explain how a court could reach the conclusion—as it did in Azzopardi's case—that the 46 offenses committed by the principal defendant had, in aggregate, what the Swedish Penal Code calls a penal value of 128 years, yet the same court could also, and entirely rationally, take the view that to impose such a sentence on a 19-year-old man for seven weeks of very bad behavior would be unjust, because it would deprive him of his liberty for his whole natural lifespan, and leave him with no opportunity to respond to the censure by altering his ways. Arguments of this kind obviously become more compelling when—as in Azzopardi's case—the aggregate of the unadjusted sentence is very long. Clearly, an account of this kind would support a sentencing pattern such as the one shown in Figure 3.1, which, as we have seen, has been independently observed in empirical studies in Australia, Germany, and Finland.

That same curve can, however, also be explained by another principle, described by Marianne Wells (1992, pp. 45–48), in a study of MOS in Western Australia, as the "enough is enough" principle. That principle is best exemplified in the statement by Wickham J in *Magee v. The Queen* [1980] WAR 117 that a custodial term which is "longer than is necessary to meet the various purposes of criminal punishment—retribution, deterrence and reformation . . . is too long" (*Magee* at 118, quoted in Wells, 1992, p. 45).[21] It was this version of the enough is enough principle that was later adopted and developed by the Victoria Court of Appeal in *Azzopardi*, and it can be regarded as a principle of some importance. The court in *Azzopardi* was in effect saying that when making the final fairness check that the totality principle requires (see earlier discussion), courts should *"ensure that the final sentence is no more than necessary to satisfy the various objectives of sentencing"* in the given jurisdiction (para. 61, emphasis added). In the present context, the point of particular interest in this formulation lies in the fact that, in virtually all jurisdictions, "the various objectives of sentencing" will include some consequentialist aims.

In a previous essay, I argued that consequentialism has much less of a problem with MOS than does proportionality theory; indeed, I suggested that for consequentialists it does not greatly matter

> whether a given offender is before the court for one offence, or twenty, or two hundred; what is important is whether the sentence to be passed on this offender will have the appropriate effect of deterring him and others from future offending, reforming him, or producing appropriate incapacitation from likely future depredations. (Bottoms, 1998, p. 64)

While this statement was perhaps slightly hyperbolic, the basic point is sound: consequentialists are more interested in forward-looking outcomes than in backward-looking matters relating to the number of offenses before the court. Accordingly, when consequential considerations are part of the court's objectives, we could expect them to use cumulative (consecutive) sentences less often where the aggregate of the unadjusted sentences in the case is very large, because the deterrent or incapacitative purpose will already have been met by the aggregate of the sentences already awarded for other offenses. This is, of course, exactly the pattern of sentencing shown in Figure 3.1.

But how would a committed proportionalist respond to this version of the enough is enough principle? It would seem that the response would not necessarily be unfavorable. It was noted earlier that for von Hirsch and Ashworth (2005, n32), whether censure or consequence is primary among the justifying aims of a punishment system "depends on the issue being addressed"; and that when speaking of the state's involvement, "consequences may matter more." Of course, these authors also say that when looked at from the perspective of the person punished, there should be "a primacy for the censuring element" because "emphasis should be given to treating persons as moral agents." However, in MOS cases one can safely predict that few defendants will wish to insist on receiving consecutive censures for each of their offenses; and in any case—as we have seen—that kind of cumulation will very likely lead to significant difficulties for the important "responsive" dimension of censure-based punishments.[22] Thus there seems to be no bar, in von Hirsch and Ashworth's theorization, to acceptance of the enough is enough principle, as it was articulated in *Azzopardi*.[23]

We can conclude, therefore, that the discussion in this subsection provides at least a prima facie case for the justification of the pattern of MOS shown in Figure 3.1. That case is based upon the dual principles of (i) responsive censure, and (ii) the enough is enough principle. Both of these principles seem consistent with Matravers's (2011, p. 37) suggestion that in developing sound theories of punishment for a liberal-democratic state, a primary requirement is to "[think] about the requirements of liberal justice as a whole"

Proportionality

From Lovegrove's statistical analysis in Victoria, three issues relevant to issues of proportionality were identified: these concerned Thomas's principle and differences in cumulation by offense type and by the connectedness or otherwise of the group of offenses. The last two of these issues require little discussion here. There is an obvious logic, within the principles of proportionality, in saying that other things being equal, (i) a group of very serious offenses (such as rape) merits greater cumulation than a group of less serious offenses; and (ii) a group of unconnected offenses merits greater cumulation than a group of connected offenses. This last point is further considered in the chapter by Roberts and de Keijser, in this volume.

Substantially greater attention must be paid to Thomas's principle. In an important paper, Martin Wasik (2012) insightfully argued that there is a significant tension between this principle and the standard account of the totality principle (as discussed at the beginning of this chapter), whereby totality is the last matter that the sentencer considers. In Wasik's (2012, p. 290) view, if we take Thomas's principle seriously, then the sentencer's approach cannot be that of

> determining all the individual sentences first, and then scaling back for totality . . . Instead, an early task .. should be to identify the appropriate range for the "lead" sentence (to be imposed for the most serious of the offences), and then to fit the other sentences in and around it, using concurrent or consecutive sentences as appropriate, while ensuring that the total sentence remains within that range [for the lead offense]. Totality then becomes not a limiting principle but a determining principle for sentencing the multiple offender.

Wasik is clearly right about the potential tension between the two approaches, but his final suggestion (totality becomes a determining not a limiting principle) is correct only if Thomas's principle is universally applied in all MOS cases. In my view, however, there are some good reasons why that principle should not be universally applied, and to tease these out it is necessary to go back to first principles.

Marianne Wells (1992, p. 38), in her Australian study, rightly argued that in an MOS case, it is one thing to say that the accumulated (unadjusted) sentences for all the offenses would be "excessive by reference to [the standard punishment for] a more serious offence" (Thomas's principle); but it is "quite another" thing to say that "the total is excessive in relation to the total conduct involved." (This contrast is the nub of the tension identified by Wasik.) Andrew Ashworth (2015, p. 290), agreeing with Wells on this point, poses an important consequential dilemma:

> One might wish to say that the sentence for 14 indecent assaults on children should remain below the normal sentence for [a single] rape, but what if there were 24 or 34 indecent assaults on children? In that eventuality it could be argued that the overall sentence should remain below the level for rape, . . . but it might be thought that the sentence was disproportionately low in terms of the serial sex offending involved. Which kind of proportionality should prevail ?

Ashworth's own answer to this key question is, ultimately, similar to that of Wasik: "there seems to be a powerful public and judicial intuition that inter-offence proportionality [that is, Thomas's principle] should be the principal driver" (Ashworth, 2015, p. 290). But on what is this intuition based?

In an earlier essay, I noted that Thomas's principle "invests the 'appropriate sentencing range' for a single offense with a very considerable symbolic importance, within the communicative scheme that any overall sentencing system represents" (Bottoms, 1998, p. 65). Symbolism and communication are, unquestionably, important and insufficiently studied topics within criminal justice systems, as the work of Martin Innes (2014) on "signal crimes" and "control signals" has powerfully demonstrated.[24] In the present instance, the symbolic communication is about the "headline seriousness" of a particular offense, and it is easy to see that messages of this kind have an importance in setting and maintaining societal understandings about the ordinal seriousness of the various wrongs that the criminal law proscribes. But should Thomas's principle override all other considerations relating to MOS, and therefore be, as Wasik proposes, a *determining* principle?

As previously noted, David Thomas himself regarded the principle of interoffense proportionality in MOS cases as an "extension" of the general principle of proportionality in sentencing (p. 58). That being the case, Matravers's suggestion that proportionality is neither a liberal trump card nor an independent principle in punishment theory must, if correct, apply to MOS sentencing as much as to the sentencing of single offenses. In which case, Thomas's principle should not be a determining principle in MOS cases, but rather "one of many considerations that we take into account when we devise a system of criminal justice and punishment" (Matravers, 2011, p. 40).

But where does this leave us? To tackle this question, a return to the institutionalist analysis derived from Lovegrave's data might be helpful. To Lovegrave's evident surprise, the judges in Victoria imposed fully concurrent sentences in nearly half the cases in his sample, notwithstanding that all the cases consisted of more than one transaction; the judges also applied Thomas's principle in the majority of cases where there was a degree of cumulation. Judicial intuitions were therefore clearly sympathetic to this principle, even though there was no rule of law to this effect in Victoria. But in a minority of cases, the statistical analysis showed that sentencers were willing to breach the principle, especially in less-connected cases. It was therefore not a determining principle (see also note 12). Further aspects of the institutionalist analysis in Victoria revealed that Thomas's principle was applied by judges alongside other principles, each of which seemed to carry a degree of normative plausibility. There seems to be no compelling reason why all of these principles should be subordinated to the principle of interoffense proportionality. It is also worth noting that, if they were so subordinated, in a case like *Azzopardi* where many offenses have been committed, the defendants would receive a significantly greater discount than they actually received, and the justice of such a result is at least open to question.

There is also a further point. As Marianne Wells (1992, p. 44) has pointed out, when courts treat Thomas's principle as a determining principle, this can sometimes lead to a neglect of the details of the individual crimes that form part of the set of multiple offenses before the court. (She cites a Western Australian case in which the court simply imposed concurrent sentences for six offenses without even discussing whether a cumulative sentence might have been considered.) While Wells does not make this point, this kind of behavior by a sentencing judge is surely disrespectful to victims, who are entitled to a careful consideration by the court of the appropriate sentence for "their" crime, even if, ultimately, the court takes a decision that on other grounds there are good reasons for not imposing that sentence in full. As was argued at the end of the discussion of *Azzopardi*, there are good grounds for holding that the judge in an MOS case needs to balance the potentially conflicting legitimate expectations of the state and of various interested citizens (including the defendant and the victim, and their supporters). That, it is suggested, requires a full consideration of all the issues for each offense before the court, and then, if appropriate, the traditional last look for a final fairness check. In that final check, Thomas's principle will be an important, but not necessarily decisive, matter to be considered.

Conclusion

This essay is built upon an institutionalist approach to law, according to which legal theorists can sometimes benefit from making a careful study of legal norms and practices in action. Victor Tadros (2009, p. 84) is skeptical about this enterprise: he is primarily interested in justice, and he considers that there is "little reason to be confident" that the values revealed by an institutionalist analysis will be "motivated by justice"; instead, he thinks that "they are likely to favour those who have had most influence in shaping the law, or who would have the power to advocate change when they are disadvantaged by it." Perhaps this skepticism would be justified in some circumstances, but it has not proved accurate in relation to MOS. Instead, the institutionalist analysis developed in this chapter, drawing principally on Lovegrove's (2004) data, has provided a fuller, more complex and more nuanced account of MOS than will be found in most academic papers on the subject. This suggests that judges in MOS cases do make serious attempts to develop just solutions to what can be very complex sets of issues. Moreover, in the normative discussion in this chapter, none of the principles discovered in the institutionalist analysis has been found to be without normative merit. Each of these principles does, therefore, at least potentially make a contribution to the ultimate normative question in this field, namely: what principles should optimally guide sentencers in cases involving multiple offenses?

An exploratory essay such as this one cannot tackle that question. However, it is hoped that both the instititutionalist and the normative analyses in this chapter may have helped to clear the ground in a way that may lead scholars and judges together to develop, in the future, a better answer to the question than we can currently provide. Serious efforts in that direction will require further empirical research, both quantitative and qualitative, to strengthen the currently slender base of our institutionalist understanding (see also Ashworth, 2015, p. 292). It will also require careful normative work, preferably of the kind recommended by Amartya Sen (2009), in which various possible principles of MOS sentencing, as identified in institutionalist analyses, would be directly compared with one another, and evaluated, within a framework of rigorous normative reasoning.

Notes

1. On the importance within social science of appreciative description, or understanding social phenomena from the perspective of the actors, see, for example, Runciman (1983).
2. In undertaking such an analysis, it is important to maintain a clear awareness of the distinction between "positive morality" (morality as understood and practised in the empirical context under discussion) and "critical morality" (an external normative assessment of the practices observed). On the distinction between positive and critical morality, see Hart (1963, p. 20).
3. Victor Tadros (2009, p. 84) has argued that an institutionalist approach of the kind advocated by MacCormick "will tend to suffer from conservatism" and "tend to defend the values that the law in fact adopts." While these might be dangers for the institutionalist to guard against, they do not constitute an argument against undertaking an institutionalist analysis, since there is no necessary connection between "understanding the normative structure of the law in action" and "defending the normative structure of the law in action."
4. This approach to MOS cases has recently been the subject of challenge, notably by Wasik (2012). This issue will be considered in the final section of this chapter.
5. *R v Hutchings* [2012] NLCA 41 at para 84 (Court of Appeal of Newfoundland and Labrador; emphasis added).
6. Thomas added a comment that the difficulty in applying this rule "lies in establishing a sufficiently precise definition of the concept of a single transaction" (p. 53). Fox and Freiburg concurred, saying that "the so-called . . . 'one transaction' rule provides no simple guide" (p. 715). This difficulty has been noted by many subsequent commentators: see for example Ashworth (2015, pp. 281–282).
7. The definitions given are those used by Lovegrove where either robbery or burglary was the principal offense; the definitions used for the rape subsample were slightly different (Lovegrove, 2004, p. 46).
8. These categories were described by Lovegrove (2004, p. 31) as "multiple" and "single multiple," but to avoid confusion I have avoided this terminology since all the cases in his sample by definition contained multiple offenses.
9. In Victoria, courts routinely state the full (deserved) sentence for each secondary offense, and also the portion of it that is made cumulative to the principal offense: for example, "3 years (6 months cumulation)." When calculating the "total sentence" it is the *unadjusted* sentence

for each secondary sentence that is counted, not the number of years/months that are finally made cumulative.

10. The proportion of the statistical variance explained in these analyses (R-squared) was considerable: for armed robbery 49%, for burglary 56%, and for rape 27%.
11. There were only 13 burglary cases with full or partial cumulation of sentence, so this comparison is restricted to the two larger principal offense groups.
12. Note also Lovegrove's (2004, p. 56) observation that in a few rare cases (too few to analyze statistically), the degree of "cumulation might . . . be greater, and demonstrably so." These cases tended to be those where "the comprising offences were uncommonly serious or the period of offending particularly protracted or there was striking variation in the constituent criminality."
13. This case was drawn to my attention by Michael Keks, a Victorian lawyer who was a postgraduate student at Fitzwilliam College, Cambridge, in the academic year 2015–2016. I am most grateful to him.
14. As noted in the extract from the judgment in *Azzopardi,* the principle was enunciated in an earlier case in Western Australia (*Magee*). However, it appears from the discussion in Wells (1992, pp. 45–48) that the quoted formulation in *Magee* was not particularly influential in the subsequent case law in Western Australia: see further at note 21.
15. To improve the example, we might add the stipulation that there are good reasons to believe that greater punishment will enhance the deterrent effect. Given the right circumstances, this is now not a fanciful stipulation: see Braga and Weisburd (2012).
16. Given his definition of "desert," what Matravers (2011, p. 43) means by "post-desert" is basically post-Hegelian: "our best theories of punishment are post-desert, and have been since long before the retributive revival at the end of the twentieth century." I am using the term to mean a theoretical approach that takes seriously the insights of proportionality theory (often called "desert theory"), but, following Matravers, does not treat it as an independent principle.
17. In an earlier essay (Bottoms, 1998, pp. 63–70) I defended the concept of mercy as a possible general principle in MOS cases. That analysis has received some reasoned criticism (e.g., Ashworth, 2015, pp. 288–289). More could be said about mercy in this general sense, particularly in light of more recent writings on mercy (e.g., Tasioulas, 2003), but in the present context I have chosen to remain within the concept of mercy as articulated by judges in the institutionalist analysis in Victoria.
18. Maslen (2015, p. 108) describes responsive censure theory as a way of thinking about punishment that uses a "dialogical model" which is "an appealing modification of von Hirsch and Ashworth's [proportionality] theory."
19. Brownlee (2011) has raised objections to a dialogical conception of punishment, but these are fully responded to by Maslen (2015, pp. 108–116).
20. In many countries, this takes the form of a "day fine" system (that is, the penalty is set as the defendant's income for a stated number of days). In other countries, including England and Wales, the amount of the fine is adjusted downward for those with limited ability to pay.
21. Wells (1992, pp. 45–48) notes, however, that the history of the enough is enough concept in relation to MOS in Western Australia was confusing, since at least three different meanings of the phrase can be identified in the case law after *Magee.*
22. Victims, of course, might take a different view. But, for reasons that one can develop from legitimacy theory (see Bottoms and Tankebe, 2017), while victims' views should be fully respected in MOS cases (see further discussion in next subsection), those views should not necessarily be decisive.
23. Proportionality theorists might respond that for them these matters are not very important, and the decisive principle is that of "inter-offence proportionality" (Ashworth, 2015, p. 290), or Thomas's principle. This matter is discussed in the next section.
24. Innes (2014, p. 129) defines a "control signal" as "an act of social control sending a message to an audience. The message can be intentional but also an unintended product of social control interventions." He also rightly emphasizes that actions intended to promote social control "are irrevocably dependent upon processes of tacit and explicit communication." It seems that judges in

many jurisdictions are aware of communicative mechanisms of this kind, and believe that there are good control signal reasons for maintaining—at least in most cases—the principle that the overall sentence in an MOS case should not exceed the upper limit of the sentence range for the principal offense, in order to maintain an easily understood "ladder" of ordinal proportionality.

References

Albrecht, H-J. 1994. *Strafzumessung bei Schwerer Kriminalität*. Berlin: Duncker and Humblot.

Ashworth, A. 2015. *Sentencing and Criminal Justice* 6th ed. Cambridge: Cambridge University Press.

Bicchieri, C. 2006. *The Grammar of Society: The Nature and Dynamics of Social Norms*. Cambridge: Cambridge University Press.

Borgeke, M. 2008. *Att bestämma påföljid för brott*. Stockholm: Norstedts Juridik.

Bottoms, A. E. 1998. "Five Puzzles in von Hirsch's Theory of Punishment." In A. Ashworth and M. Wasik (eds.), *Fundamentals of Sentencing Theory: Essays in Honour of Andrew von Hirsch*, pp. 53–100. Oxford: Clarendon Press.

Bottoms, A. E. 2014. "Desistance from Crime." In Z. Ashmore and R Shuker (eds.), *Forensic Practice in the Community*, pp. 251–273. Abingdon: Routledge.

Bottoms, A. E., and J. Tankebe. 2017. "Police Legitimacy and the Authority of the State." In A. Du Bois-Pedain, M. Ulväng, and P. App (eds.), *Criminal Law and the Authority of the State*, pp. 47–88. Oxford: Hart Publishing.

Brownlee, K. L. 2011. "The Offender's Part in the Dialogue." In R. Cruft, M. H. Kramer, and M. R. Reiff (eds.), *Crime, Punishment and Responsibility: The Jurisprudence of Antony Duff*, pp. 54–67. Oxford: Oxford University Press

Braga, A. A., and D. L. Weisburd. 2012. *The Effects of "Pulling Levers" Focussed Deterrence Strategies on Crime*. Campbell Systematic Reviews 2012, No. 6: 1–90.

Dworkin, R. 1978. *Taking Rights Seriously*. London: Duckworth.

Fox, R., and A. Freiberg. 1999. *Sentencing: State and Federal Law in Victoria*. 2nd ed. Melbourne: Oxford University Press.

Hart, H. L. A. 1963. *Law, Liberty and Morality*. London: Oxford University Press.

Hinkkanen, V., and T. Lappi-Seppala. 2011. "Sentencing Theory, Policy and Research in the Nordic Countries." In M. Tonry (ed.), *Crime and Justice in Scandinavia* (*Crime and Justice: A Review of Research* 40(1): 349–404). Chicago: University of Chicago Press.

Innes, M. 2014. *Signal Crimes: Social Reactions to Crime, Disorder and Control*. Oxford: Oxford University Press.

Jareborg, N. 1998. "Why Bulk Discounts in Multiple Offence Sentencing?" In A. Ashworth and M. Wasik (eds.), *Fundamentals of Sentencing Theory: Essays in Honour of Andrew von Hirsch*, pp. 129–140. Oxford: Clarendon Press.

Llewellyn, K. 1940. "The Normative, the Legal, and the Law-Jobs: The Problem of Juristic Method." *Yale Law Journal* 49(8): 1355–1400.

Lovegrove, A. 1997. *The Framework of Judicial Sentencing*. Cambridge: Cambridge University Press.

Lovegrove, A. 2004. *Sentencing the Multiple Offender: Judicial Practice and Legal Principle*. Canberra: Australian Institute of Criminology.

MacCormick, N. 2007. *Institutions of Law: An Essay in Legal Theory*. Oxford: Oxford University Press.

MacCormick, N. 2009. "Concluding for Institutionalism." In M. Del Mar and Z. Bankowski (eds.), *Law as Institutional Normative Order*, pp. 187–200. Farnham, Surrey: Ashgate.

Maslen, H. 2015. *Remorse, Penal Theory and Sentencing*. Oxford: Hart Publishing.

Matravers, M. 2011. "Is Twenty-First Century Punishment Post-Desert?" In M. Tonry (ed.), *Retributivism Has a Past: Has it a Future?*, pp. 30–45 New York: Oxford University Press.

Morris, N. 1982. *Madness and the Criminal Law*. Chicago: Chicago University Press.

Reitz, K. R. 2010. "The Illusion of Proportionality: Desert and Repeat Offenders." In J. V. Roberts and A. von Hirsch (eds.), *Previous Convictions at Sentencing: Theoretical and Applied Perspectives*, pp. 137–159. Oxford: Hart Publishing.

Runciman, W. G. 1983. *A Treatise on Social Theory: Vol. 1, The Methodology of Social Theory*. Cambridge: Cambridge University Press.

Sen, A. 2009. *The Idea of Justice*. London: Allen Lane.

Tadros, V. 2009. "Institutions and Aims." In M. Del Mar and Z. Bankowski (eds.), *Law as Institutional Normative Order*, pp. 83–101. Farnham, Surrey: Ashgate.

Tasioulas, J. 2003. "VI—Mercy," *Proceedings of the Aristotelian Society*. 103(1): 101–132.

Thomas, D. A. 1979. *Principles of Sentencing: The Sentencing Policy of the Court of Appeal Criminal Division*. 2nd ed. London: Heinemann.

Von Hirsch, A. 1993. *Censure and Sanctions*. Oxford: Oxford University Press.

Von Hirsch, A., and A. Ashworth. 2005. *Proportionate Sentencing: Exploring the Principles*. Oxford: Oxford University Press.

Wasik, M. 2012. "Concurrent and Consecutive Sentences Revisited." In L. Zedner and J. V. Roberts (eds.), *Principles and Values in Criminal Law and Criminal Justice*, pp. 287–305. Oxford: Oxford University Press.

Wells, M. 1992. *Sentencing for Multiple Offences in Western Australia* (University of Western Australia Crime Research Centre Research Report No 6). Nedlands: University of Western Australia.

4

Retributivism and Totality

Can Bulk Discounts for Multiple Offending Fit the Crime?

CHRISTOPHER BENNETT

The charging and sentencing of multiple offenders is an important point at which discretion enters the criminal justice system. Discretion need not be a bad thing in a legal system, but there should be principles by which its exercise is guided, and to which it is accountable, and these principles should have a transparent public justification. At present the principle that seems to operate widely with respect to multiple offenders is what has been called the "bulk discount" (Jareborg, 1998). In this chapter, I identify two ways in which multiple offenders seem to pose a problem for broadly retributive principles of sentencing. I will argue that these problems are only apparent; looking at the proper place and exercise of discretion will help us to see why.

In the first part of the chapter, I introduce the issue of multiple offending, pointing to the discretion it apparently gives sentencers, and the bulk-discount principle that appears to guide decisions. In the second part, I point out two ways in which bulk discounts may appear to conflict with retributive sentencing theory, which I call the "fittingness problem" and the "selection problem." In the third section, I introduce what I take to be the key guiding thought within retributive approaches to criminal justice, and I distinguish between two types of retributivism, moralistic and legalistic. In the fourth section I argue that moralistic retributivism should, if certain conditions are met, be happy to allow discretion at sentencing in order to allow the criminal justice system better to comply with the relevant moral ends. This addresses the selection problem, and leaves the question whether retributive sentencing goals are compatible with bulk discounts. In the fifth section I argue that the view that they are incompatible rests on a key assumption ("perspective invariantism about desert"); however, I argue against this assumption. This addresses the fittingness problem, and concludes my case for arguing that retributivism is compatible with common sentencing practice regarding multiple offenders. Finally, I draw the argument together in the last part of the chapter.

Before I begin, let me say something briefly about the philosophical methodology adopted in this chapter. Broadly speaking, my aim is a "rational reconstruction" of the practice of sentencing multiple offenders. I will take it that the persistence of the bulk discount as a part of common sentencing practice shows that practitioners find it intuitively compelling. (I also believe that a similar discount principle operates when we think about blame and blameworthiness in interpersonal relations: for some argument on this point, see Bennett, 2010, though this claim is disputed by Hoskins, this volume.) Men and women making difficult and weighty sentencing decisions, and whom we have no special reason to judge lacking in competence or commitment, are unwilling to sacrifice the bulk-discount principle. Furthermore, this unwillingness persists in the face of the lack of an articulated and satisfactory justification for the principle; even in the face of apparently good reasons to abandon the principle, as we will see. This shows a high degree of commitment to the principle, or abhorrence of its alternatives.

The persistence of the bulk-discount principle does not in itself show it to be well-grounded, of course. Other possible explanations for its persistence might be better: that practitioners are in the grip of a false ideology, or that they are not good at reckoning with cases involving many victims (Ryberg, this volume), or that bureaucratic inertia prevents sensible changes. The question, in the end, is what is the best explanation of the fact that sentencers act as they do: whether it is practitioners' grasp of some normative consideration favoring bulk discounts, or rather a disabling factor that interferes with their taking a clear view of the normative situation. My view is that taking seriously the practical wisdom of practitioners requires us to reach for "disabling factor" explanations only as a last resort. I take it that sentencing is not a matter of simple rule-following, but is in some ways a craft in which practitioners bring moral intelligence, imagination, and insight to bear on individual cases. Our initial job as theorists, then, is to attempt to articulate those considerations that practitioners, when asked to commit themselves at the moment of decision, take to be compelling—considerations about which they themselves may be inarticulate. Of course, it is a further question whether those articulations constitute satisfying justifications. But respect for practitioners as skilled and thoughtful decision-makers should make us reluctant to disregard strongly held elements of practice, or to do so only once the search for sympathetic justifications of that practice has been exhausted.

Multiple Offenders and Discretion

We can distinguish two types of multiple offender. First of all, there are those who commit a number of distinct—or at any rate distinguishable—offenses in a single episode of criminal activity. Secondly, there is the multiple offender who commits a number of offenses across a string of episodes of criminal activity. If we can usefully divide multiple offenders into these two broad categories, we can also identify two points in the criminal justice process at which the multiplicity of their offenses becomes an issue. First of all, there is the question of how many offenses police and prosecutors should decide to charge the offender with—and on what basis, if the answer is not all, they should select offenses. Andrew Ashworth sets out four options that are open to prosecutors when dealing with multiple offenders: charging all offenses, charging specimen offenses, using a general charge, or taking offenses "into consideration" (Ashworth, 2010, pp. 261–263). It seems from this as though the prosecution does have the option of taking what Ashworth calls the "straightforward route" of charging "all the offenses of which the prosecution have sufficient evidence," although it is not required to. But in practice this seems unlikely to happen in many cases. Prosecutors have legal discretion, and they exercise it by taking one of the other options.

Secondly, there is the question of how the multiplicity of offenses should be dealt with at sentencing. Again, we could say that the straightforward route is to sentence for each criminalisable offense, to give a sentence for that offense which is within the normal range for the offense, and to set the sentences consecutively, so that the offender would only start serving one sentence upon the completion of the last. Again, however, we can say that it seems unlikely that the offender will be sentenced according to this straightforward route. Certainly sentencers do not seem to be obliged to take this route. The law appears to be that sentencers are restricted to sentencing only for those offenses that have been charged, even where the offender has admitted to committing other, possibly serious, offenses (following Lord Bingham in *Canavan and Kidd* [1998]).[1] However, even if sentencers' discretion is limited in that they cannot sentence for more offenses than are on the charge sheet, it seems as though they can decide not to pass sentence for each offense that *is* on the charge sheet. Furthermore, for all the sentences that are passed, they have the option to set the same activity as the sentence for a number of offenses—for instance, serving a term in prison—and allowing the sentences to run concurrently, thus allowing the offender to discharge a number of sentences without doing anything more than he would have had he been serving one sentence. Finally, if the decision is made to set the sentences to be served consecutively, sentencers will tend to abide by what Thomas has called the totality principle (Thomas, 1979, pp. 56–57). This principle says that the sentence should reflect the totality of the criminal activity, and should not allow the sentence for a string of minor offenses to mount up to something that is more like the sentence for a really serious crime. All of which means that sentencers are highly unlikely to take the straightforward route, and that the amount of time served by an offender who is sentenced for multiple offenses after a string of episodes of criminal activity is much less than that which would be served by someone who was apprehended after each bout of such activity and sentenced separately on each occasion (Reitz, 2010).

Multiple Offenders and Retributive Sentencing Theory

There are two ways in which the bulk-discount principle might appear arbitrary, at least from the point of view of retributive sentencing theory. The first is that it seems to go against the principle that the punishment should fit the crime, since it is not the case, under the bulk discount, that each offense is punished separately and given the sentence that, considered in isolation as that particular offense, would be appropriate to it. Not all offenses are put on the charge sheet; some offenses are not sentenced for even if they are on the charge sheet; sentences are effectively "collapsed" and served concurrently. Retributive principles might seem to favor the straightforward approach; it seems that insofar as the straightforward approach is universally abandoned in sentencing practice, sentencers must be responding to principles other than retributive principles. This is therefore grist to the mill of anti-retributivists, who claim that retributivism put into practice leads to unacceptable results, and that its principles cannot explain the decisions of experienced sentencers (Reitz, 2010). I will call this the fittingness problem: common practice in the punishment of multiple offenders seems to abandon the principle that punishment should fit the crime.

The second problem arises even if we accept that there might be a justification in retributive sentencing principles for giving a bulk discount for multiple offenses; it concerns rather the principle by which it is decided which offenses should be put on the charge sheet in the first place. The case of multiple offending demonstrates that it is often the case that not all offenses are put on the charge sheet—rather some selection is made. Retributivism, it might be thought, claims that criminal justice systems should respond to the need to do justice to instances of wrongdoing by treating them *as* wrongdoing, to vindicate victims, and to pass punishments appropriate for such wrongdoing. This would appear to favor taking each instance of criminal action seriously and reflecting the moral nature of that criminality in sentencing. It is unlike a deterrent theory where playing fast and loose with individual offenses might be quite appropriate as long as it gets results: it seems that retributivism on principle favors a kind of rigorism, since its justification for punishment looks to do justice to past offenses rather than bring about some future good. So retributivism again seems to stand against the common sentencing practice of selecting among offenses at charging and sentencing. I will call this the "selection problem": common practice in the sentencing of multiple offenders appears to abandon the retributive principle of taking each instance of wrongdoing seriously.

My approach in this essay is to suggest that the conception of retributive principles outlined here, and which is claimed to be incompatible with common sentencing practice for multiple offenders, is overly simple, and that a more sophisticated version of retributivism can avoid these concerns. In this next section I will start by outlining some assumptions about retributive sentencing theory on which the bulk-discount principle would be problematic: specifically on a conception I will call "legalistic retributivism." This will include a certain understanding of "fitting the crime." However, I will argue that this understanding of retributivism is not the most common, or likely to be the most adequate; in its place I will suggest some form of what I will call moralistic retributivism.

Retributivism: Legalistic and Moralistic

First of all, let me say something about what I take retributive sentencing theory to be. I intend this to be a broad category encompassing all those views that take a noninstrumental view of the purposes of sentencing, and therefore take some kind of response to wrongful or criminal activity as deserved or inherently fitting. One thing to make clear at the outset, therefore, is that retributivism is not simply to be understood as the view that wrongdoers, or criminal offenders, deserve to *suffer* in proportion to the seriousness of their transgression. The fundamental point that distinguishes retributivism from instrumental justifications of punishment such as deterrence or preventive detention is rather this: that retributivists hold that *some* response of a *specific character* is called for intrinsically because of the wrongful character of the criminal action (Bennett, 2016). Retributivists hold, in other words, that some specific response is morally necessary, independently of the contingent fact that making such a response is likely to lead to some independently desirable end, but rather because the offender's action *merits* such a response (or he *deserves* that response).

Why is such a response necessary? I think that what is characteristic of retributivism is that it involves the claim that something must be done in the wake of wrongdoing to *dissociate* oneself from the wrongdoing—and that in the absence of such dissociating response, one will be in the position of acquiescing in, becoming complicit in, or condoning the wrong. This is the essential claim behind retributivism, which explains the position that some response is morally necessary independently of other extraneous effects (beneficial or detrimental) that that response may have. Retributivists think that the transgression alters the way it is morally acceptable to treat or relate to the wrongdoer; if our behavior toward the transgressor does not change to reflect the transgression then it will be as though nothing morally impermissible had happened, as if no basic limit was violated. This is the claim that those who take a purely instrumental view of responses to crime have to reject.

However, if one accepts retributivism thus far, it is a further question what that specific response needs to be—and those I am calling retributivists disagree widely on *this* question. Retributivists believe that what I am calling the "specific" response to the transgression needs to be the right one, because only if it is the right type of action can it successfully dissociate those who make it from the transgression; therefore retributivists need to claim that the nature of the appropriate response is nonarbitrary. But there is substantive moral disagreement over what the form of the response needs to be in order to bring this about. The caricature of retributivism is that what is required is to make the wrongdoer suffer. My own view is rather that what is necessary is a partial and temporary *withdrawal of recognition* such as we find in the canonical expression of interpersonal blame (Bennett, 2013). The essential thing is that the response should mark and do justice to the wrongdoing as a wrongdoing.

We can make a further distinction among varieties of retributivism between legalistic retributivism and moralistic retributivism. Is punishment a response to lawbreaking, and specifically the wrong of lawbreaking, in which case it should be proportionate to the legal categorization of the crime, and the desert that arises from breaking that law? That would be the position I have called legalistic retributivism. One version of this view might derive the importance of retributivism from the specifically political need to vindicate the authority of the law itself. If punishment is not a consequence of lawbreaking, this legal retributivism might hold, the law is not really valid. Given that the law needs to claim authority, and its authority hence needs to be vindicated in the face of defiance, this explains why punishment is morally important independently of its results.

By contrast, according to moralistic retributivism, legal punishment should be seen as at best an attempt to approximate a prelegal moral desert arising from wrongdoing. My intention here is not to debate the merits of these two approaches to retributivism, but simply to note that influential retributivists like Moore and Duff (as well as the present author) defend the moralistic version (Moore, 1992; Duff, 2001; Bennett, 2008). It is enough to note this because it will be enough to show that there is some sensible "live" version of retributivism that holds that a) the point of the criminal justice system is to treat people as they deserve to be treated, whether that is in terms of some quantum of suffering, or in terms of deserved condemnation; and b) the legal framework for classifying criminal offenses and providing procedures for settling on a sentence should be seen as at best approximations of that prelegal desert.

If we adopt moralistic retributivism, this does not yet show that we should allow sentencers a breadth of discretion to decide on cases of multiple offending which might lead to results that appear paradoxical in the context of the existing legal framework for classifying crimes (as the treatment of multiple offending might appear). There might be further reasons to restrict such discretion—we will see that there are. But it opens up space at least for a position that holds that, when it comes to sentencing, sentencers should aim to decide on the merits of the case, and in particular to ask what the appropriate prelegal desert of the offender is, and that they should not be decisively constrained by the prior legal classification of the criminal activity. Moralistic retributivism holds that at least in principle, discretion at sentencing is necessary to allow for the aims of the criminal justice system (in adjusting the way the state punishes to prelegal desert) are realized.

The desirability or not of moralistic retributivism raises some questions about the proper role of discretion. The question I would like to turn to at this point is therefore what attitude we should adopt toward the fact that legal officials have the discretion that they do when charging and sentencing multiple offenders.

Attitudes to Discretion

We should note before we proceed that the existence of discretion in a legal system does not mean that an agent is legally free to decide in any way they want with impunity. Often a legal role is structured on the assumption (sometimes tacit) that, although the agent's decision will be binding, the agent has a responsibility to make a decision through conscientiously paying attention to a range of relevant considerations, and only those. So for instance—to give a nonlegal example—I may have discretion in marking my students' essays to give them the mark I see fit to give. Yet my possession of this discretion does not mean that it would be permissible for me to assign the marks randomly. Although I have discretion, I have a binding professional responsibility to exercise my discretion by paying attention to the quality of the essays. In part, this limited discretion is reflected in rights of appeal. Yet it seems clear that the enforcement of the proper exercise of discretion can only be partial. Appeals are time-consuming and costly, they are often resolved by appeal to the discretion of another marker, and the justifications that have to be given for decisions are rarely such as to explain decisively why that particular mark was appropriate. By and large, the university and its students rely on the assumption that its teaching staff are dedicated and of good will, and can therefore be trusted to exercise their discretion wisely. So exercising discretion wisely can be part of the responsibility of one's professional role, even if that responsibility is only partially enforceable.

The existence of discretion raises two sorts of questions. First of all, a *substantive* question: how should that discretion ideally be exercised? This is to ask the question: given that it falls to this agent to make a decision, what is the right decision for her to make? But another question is *procedural*: by what right does this agent get to have the discretion to make this decision as she sees fit? This is to ask the question: what procedures should we have for making decisions about multiple offenders? The procedural question asks how we should decide on the process by which the decision will be made (or at least guided): how to decide to decide (Sunstein and Ullman-Margalit, 1999). We will look in more detail at the dimensions on which discretion may be assessed.

We can categorize attitudes to discretion in something like the following way. First of all, one might argue that discretion is morally necessary because it allows leeway within an otherwise rigid system of rules for equity and doing justice to the demands of the individual case (Meyer, 2014). In other words, discretion is necessary, this approach says, to avoid absurdities that mechanically applying the rules would inevitably lead us into. But the reason behind the need for discretion then gives us an explanation of how discretion should be used: to allow officials scope within the legal framework to make a decision on the moral merits of the case rather than being constrained by what prior legislative or adjudicatory decisions have provided for. What the moral merits of the case consist in might be given two different interpretations: on the one hand, it might be taken to encompass all morally relevant considerations (such as, in the case of sentencing, the welfare of the offender, the welfare of his dependents, the likely effect on the economy of the local area, etc.); or on the other one might understand the merits of the case to consist in the right way for the institution of which one is part to deal with this case, given what one takes to be the best interpretation of the defining values of that institution (in our case, the basic purposes of sentencing, which, according to a moralistic retributivist, would confine the range of reasons to be taken into account to those of prelegal desert). Given the impossibility of having the right rule for any eventuality, discretion allows for the exercise of a kind of practical moral reasonableness on the part of officials. For the sake of having a label, and in order to connect it to our previous discussion of legalistic and moralistic retributivism, we can call this attitude "morality": the idea that legal structures have to leave room for the exercise of conscience by officials in order to avoid rigorism leading to morally wrong decisions.

Secondly, however, one might take against giving such discretion to officials on the grounds that it opens the way to abuse and inconsistency. Therefore one might have the attitude that, on the basis of rule of law values such as certainty, predictability, stability, the limiting of the unaccountable power of public officials, and fairness and consistency across cases, exercises of discretion should be limited as far as possible, and a rule-governed framework introduced to ensure that the decisions are made in a consistent and publicly accountable way. The implication of this view is that officials should be constrained in their decision-making by a tightly focused body of rules, and will therefore be constrained to decide cases in ways that do not always reflect their best understanding of the moral merits of the case. This is the view that we will call "legality": the idea that discretion should be minimized as far as possible for the sake of accountability, consistency, and predictability and replaced with binding rules.

These two options cover the distinction drawn between moralistic and legalistic retributivism. But there is another broad type of attitude to discretion that is worth noting. So thirdly, one might be troubled by the power such points of discretion invest in particular individuals—even if these individuals are public servants who have a professional ethos and a professional responsibility to decide the cases in circumscribed ways. After all, even if officials strive to make the decision they think a person in their role ought to be making rather than the decision that they think any person of conscience should make, it will nevertheless be their outlook and attitudes that shape the nature of the decision. Rather, one might feel that such decisions will lack democratic legitimacy since they will simply reflect the view taken by the particular individual in charge rather than the will of the people taken as a whole. Democracy is a system, one might argue, that provides a fair way of coming to what can properly be called collective decisions on matters of basic rights, where the reason that it is maximally fair is that it gives no person any more influence than any other. Discretion invested in one individual goes against this democratic promise by making it the case that public servants end up doing more than merely serving the people (Waldron, 1999). I will call this view "democracy," the view that decisions about the actions of public agencies which are properly taken in the name of the people should be made *as far as possible* in such a way that no any one individual has greater sway over the decision than any other.

This concern about democratic legitimacy might be assuaged in either of two ways, one of which aims to minimize discretion while the other seeks to preserve it (hence my claim at the start of the preceding paragraph that there were two further types of attitude to discretion worth considering). The first way seeks to minimize discretion by identifying the will of the people with the deliverances of the elected legislative assembly: if the assembly is the source of democratic legitimacy, to ensure that the will of the people is preserved in the decisions made by public agencies, the transmission of the directive from the assembly to the individual case has to be made as watertight as possible, and this means the minimization of discretion. This first way therefore comes to some of the same conclusions as legality, but it does so for different reasons: whereas legality was grounded in a concern for rule of law values, this first approach to democracy sees the importance of those rule of law as merely derivative of the need to preserve the democratic will.

The second way is more sanguine about the usefulness of rules in anticipating the vagaries of individual cases. It may also see something procedurally important about dealing with individual cases as individuals rather than just as the instances of a rule. Therefore the second way shares something with the reasons given under morality for leaving space for discretion as long as it is used to give consideration to the merits of an individual case, but it argues that fairness requires that the decision be made in a way that is compatible with each having an individual say. This may seem wholly impractical—are we going to arrange a plebiscite for each sentencing decision? But in fact a more feasible, though perhaps still revolutionary, alternative is at hand. This is to increase lay participation in criminal justice decision-making in a way modeled on the institution of the jury (Dzur, 2012). A jury is randomly selected, so in principle anyone could be chosen to make the decisions. This preserves fairness, but assembles a group of people who can then deliberate meaningfully about what ought to be done. Like the jury, these decision-makers would be operating within a legal framework, and would be advised by legal officials. They would not be expected to make their decisions out of nowhere. However, they would be allowed to make the decision. In this model of democracy, those making the decision may not see the decision made according to their best understanding of the merits of the case. In this it departs from morality. But the procedural values that constrain an individual from deciding the case on its merits are not those of legality but rather those of democracy: the need to make the decision in a way that reflects and does justice to the fact that ultimate political authority rests with the people as a whole, a body in which each citizen is an equal.

So far, this section has illustrated a range of positions a broadly retributivist approach might take on the desirability of having a legal framework that allows for discretion in sentencing. This allows us to resist the charge that retributivism per se cannot deal with the selection problem. The selection problem says that that each criminalisable action committed by the offender should find its way on to the charge sheet, and should be reflected in sentencing; that sentencers should not have discretion to pick and choose. However, moralistic retributivism opens up the possibility that such discretion is necessary to correct for distortions introduced by the form of legality. Therefore, selection as such is only a problem if one makes certain (legalistic) assumptions about the relation between sentencing and offense classification. There may still be a problem with selection: namely, if the exercise of discretion leads to a failure to respond appropriately to the moral gravity of offending behavior. But that is the fittingness problem, which we will discuss next. Therefore, if moralistic retributivism is plausible, the selection problem is not an independent problem. The question, then, is whether some variant of moralistic retributivism is plausible.

We can distinguish extreme from moderate versions of moralistic retributivism. The extreme version is not prepared to give any weight at all to the considerations underpinning legality. For the extreme moralistic retributivist, the state of the law should make no difference whatsoever to the decisions made at sentencing. Now I take that to be an implausible position. One reason for this is that the values of accountability, equity, predictability and so on underpinning the case for legality are not negligible. A publicly accessible framework of law makes it possible for citizens to know in advance of sentencing roughly how they are likely to be treated, and it makes it possible for the state to aspire to treating like cases alike, and thereby approximating a kind of unity or integrity in its dealings with citizens. Those are hugely important advantages of a system of law, yet they would be lost if sentencers did not take themselves to be constrained by general and publicly accessible rules. However, the implausibility of extreme moralistic retributivism does not mean that we should abandon morality altogether. Sentencing is the sharp end of the criminal justice system—the point at which someone has to decide what the case against the offender actually amounts to, and how he or she should be dealt with. A moderate moralistic retributivism suggests that the good sentencer does not take the legal framework—those legalistic processes and classifications that have brought the offender to the point where he requires a sentence to be given him—as the final word on what that sentence is to be. The good sentencer requires discretion, or at least she does as long as there is some evidence that by giving sentencers discretion decisions are more likely to reflect a proper balance between prelegal desert and rule of law values. Whether there is such evidence will turn on two issues: firstly, whether sentencers are in the main broadly *competent* to judge on matters of prelegal desert, or the proper balance between prelegal desert and rule of law values, and are in the main broadly motivated to do so conscientiously; and secondly, whether prelegal desert, and its balancing with rule of law values, is a complex matter determined by the particulars of individual situations, and which therefore resists adequate codification in law or sentencing guidelines.

The moral complexity of actual situations of lawbreaking suggests that the latter is highly plausible; whether the former is also plausible is beyond the scope of this chapter to determine. However, one way for the moralistic retributivist to address this question might be to make room for the concerns of democracy, in particular the second version of the view that we considered earlier, where a jury or other randomly selected body should make sentencing decisions. It may be, given that deciding upon prelegal desert is not a technical matter but is rather a matter of general moral competence, that both for reasons of fairness, but also for reasons of accurate deliberation, having decisions made by a panel (who can engage in explicit deliberation about cases) rather than by a single judge, might be desirable and compatible with the moralistic approach (Bennett, 2014).

Retributivism, Desert, and Perspective

A moderate version of moralistic retributivism can make a plausible argument for the existence of discretion at sentencing. This is because on the moderate moralistic view one cannot take the legal categorization of offenses for granted: such categorization is merely an approximation to the desert of condemnation or punishment that the criminal law aims at. Moralistic retributivism may restrict the range of discretion by arguing that the general justifying aim of criminal justice is to distribute such condemnation/punishment according to deserts, and hence that the decision on the "merits" of the case should exclude considerations not bearing on such deserts. It may also recognize the need to restrict discretion in order to accommodate rule of law values such as consistency, accountability and predictability. But discretion, on the face of it, can and should be considered as a necessary accompaniment of judicial decision-making in criminal law. This shows why the selection problem is not a deep problem for a plausible version of retributivism.

However, if we allow cases to be decided as moralistic retributivism would recommend, by some combination of legal framework supplemented by scrutiny of their moral merits, would we get to the principle of bulk discounts? No: solving the selection problem would still leave the fittingness problem. The fittingness problem points out that retributivism, for all we have said so far, is still tied to the notion that punishment should fit the crime. We have argued that moralistic retributivism doesn't have to read "crime" literally, and that punishment should in part be guided by a form of prelegal desert to which legal categories of crime are only an approximation. But the concern underlying the fittingness problem is that retributivism still has a problem with multiple offenders; for couldn't it be the case that prelegal desert is determined by each individual act of wrongdoing in a way that precludes something like a bulk discount? Even for moralistic retributivism, that is, wrongdoing requires some dissociating response, and whatever the specific nature of that response, the concern is that each transgression will require its own individual dissociation. So the concern goes, at any rate.

Let me describe the problem that multiple offending and the use of bulk discounts apparently poses for retributivism in slightly technical terms, by calling it the problem of "perspective relativity." To make bulk discounts compatible with desert it would have to be the case that what an offender deserves varies depending on when he is sentenced. If an offender has committed a string of offenses, and has been apprehended, convicted and sentenced for each in turn, he will end up serving much more time, or undergoing much more punishment, than he would have had he been convicted only after the string of offenses was completed and treated as a multiple offender. Since the discount only operates if the offender is sentenced at one time, or in one context (i.e., in the midst of sentencing for many offenses), and not in another (i.e., being apprehended and sentenced for each in turn), it seems that we can only make sense of this within a retributivist paradigm if desert also varies with the context of sentencing. In other words, desert would have to be relative to the perspective we have when we are sentencing. Yet the fittingness problem concludes that desert cannot be relative to perspective: desert is determined by the wrongdoer and his action, not by the perspective from which we are now looking back at the wrong. To use technical language again, the fittingness problem takes it as obvious that desert is property *intrinsic* to the wrongdoer and his action, and not a property of the *relation* between the wrongdoer and the person judging him at a particular time.

I would now like to explore the possibility that having made the argument for the fittingness problem explicit, we are now able to see the shape of a solution. We would have a solution, that is, if there were a good argument against the final premiss: if perspective relativity *can* affect desert. I will argue that it is not at all obvious that retributivists should accept, without further justification, the kind of perspective invariantism regarding desert that would be incompatible with bulk discounts. This is not to provide a conclusive argument against those who claim to see a conflict between retributivism and such discounts. But it is to put the ball back in their court. They would need to establish that retributivism is committed to perspective invariantism in order to establish their case.

So why think perspective invariantism is not essential to retributivism? We are perhaps prompted to think that perspective invariantism is essential to retributivism by talk of individual "desert." This phrasing suggests that it is only facts about the wrongdoer that make up his or her desert, and that facts about the person responding to the wrongdoer (in particular, facts about the person responding's temporal place in relation to the series of acts committed by the offender) must be irrelevant. However, earlier in this essay I claimed that the essential thing about retributivism is the principle that it can be morally necessary to dissociate oneself from wrongdoing independently of any other good consequences that might come from doing so or not doing so. Stated thus, this principle leaves it open whether what one needs to do to dissociate oneself from the wrongdoing is perspective invariant. The focus switches from the wrongdoer to the person relating to the wrongdoer; the question is what the latter has to do to avoid wrongfully going along with the former's conduct. Thinking about matters in this way already makes it clear that it is a further step—rather than a conceptual necessity—to the conclusion that retributivism requires perspective invariantism about desert. The theorist who claims that there is a conflict between retributivism and bulk discounts would have to show why dissociation is perspective invariant.

But it may also be the case that we can say something stronger. Perhaps looking at dissociation as the basis of retributivism favors perspective *relativity*. Looking at matters in the way I have suggested reorients things because it makes it clear that the crucial thing is a *relation* between the individual doing the dissociating and the wrongdoer. The individual dissociating herself from the wrong looks at what the wrongdoer has done, of course. But she then looks at what that means for her relationship with the wrongdoer and how that relationship must proceed differently in order that the wrongdoing should be marked as such. Many contextual factors might be relevant to this in nonlegal interpersonal contexts, factors that take account of the gravity of the wrongdoer's action, to be sure, but are not limited to it. In interpersonal contexts, moral tasks such as dissociation are carried out by expressively powerful actions—such as blame, withdrawal, apology—that are packed with meaning, and are flexible in their ability to refer to numerous aspects of the situation at once. The ideal act of dissociation in a case of multiple offending does not ignore the multiple acts in favor of responding to just one; rather it synthesizes their acknowledgment into a gesture that performs the dissociation from each of them. This process of devising a gesture by which reference to numerous acts, numerous contextual features can be brought about is an extremely important, everyday, but overlooked exercise of practical intelligence. It need not, and often cannot, be carried out additively. The process is normally one of synthesis rather than aggregation. Such synthesis is something that a developed vocabulary of expressive actions allows us to bring about, by virtue of the way in which acts like those of dissociation can refer to and acknowledge multiple features of the situation in which they are performed.

This inevitably means that proportionality between wrongdoing and response is a more complex matter than mere aggregation. A proportionate response to wrongdoing is, on this view, roughly the minimum disturbance to normal relations necessary to avoid acquiescence. Anything else is going over the top. Of course, "minimum" is not a notion that can be made entirely precise. But the idea is that one does what one needs to do to keep from going along with the wrongdoing, and that doing more than that would be vindictive, or relishing the suffering of the wrongdoer for its own sake, and so on. This already counts in favor of eschewing aggregation if possible. Furthermore, the way in which social actions bear meaning and are capable of referring to, and acknowledging, aspects of their situation, does make it possible for multiple offenses to be acknowledged nonadditively. The remaining question is the substantive one: does, and should, a nonadditive response to multiple offenses strike us as enough to do each offense justice? Here I think we can only look at individual cases and how they strike us. Say I find myself at a reception with Henry Kissinger. Say I think him culpable of numerous wrongs: colluding with Nixon, who was plainly corrupt on many levels; countless individual human rights violations relating to Vietnam; and being highly influential in making US foreign policy isolationist and disproportionately concerned with national interest. And say I also think that adopting an attitude of simple friendliness towards him—as though he were not guilty of those things—will unacceptably compromise me. Nevertheless, the situation requires that I have to choose some way in which to relate to him. I have to sum up my attitude toward him in some way of being toward him. It may be hard to say in the abstract what the appropriate response in this situation is. But it seems unlikely that practical intelligence requires that each of Kissinger's wrongs should receive individualized proportionate response.

As I have written elsewhere, state punishment can be modeled on this understanding of interpersonal dissociation from wrongdoing: ideally, state punishment should be guided by an attempt to say how things now stand between the state (or the community) and the wrongdoer as a result of the offense, given that a relationship with the offender must persist, but that the terms of the relationship have changed as a result of the wrong (Bennett, 2016). On my view, such "saying how things stand"—acknowledging the gravity of the wrongdoing—can sometimes require punishment. However, just as in the interpersonal case, it might be very unlikely that one can "say" such a thing accurately by taking an individualizing, additive response to responding to each transgression in a perspective invariant way. An additive response may well end up being disproportionate given the availability of a response that will give the offending behavior due acknowledgment at less cost to the offender. Of course, in the legal case, there is pressure to employ generalizable, transparent procedures that require regularity and uniformity in state responses. But the question is what type of uniformity is required. If moderate moralistic retributivism is correct, these procedures should be aimed at regulating accurate and proportionate moral responses to wrongdoing. If perspective relativity applies to proportionate moral response then there is no reason why legal procedures should not try to replicate that; indeed, there may be reason to think that they would be disproportionate if they did not.

In the legal case just as much as the interpersonal case, then, it is not obvious that "how things stand between us now" is composed by adding offenses up in a simple way. Focusing on dissociation rather than desert leads us instead to see that proportionate condemnation is a relational and perspective relative matter from the outset; the case of multiple offending is not an outlier. The fittingness problem arises if it is only through individualizing, additive response to each crime that one can do justice to the wrongdoing as a whole. But why should we think that? Moral commonsense seems to disagree. Although these considerations still leave the logical possibility that perspective invariantism should be correct, it puts the onus on the critics of retributivism to defend it.

Conclusion

We have now assembled the materials necessary to address the two problems this essay has posed for retributivism and for sentencing practice. I have aimed to show that we do not need to give up the bulk-discount principle by virtue of its conflict with attractive elements of retributive sentencing theory (or vice versa). I have taken it that our situation is something like this: the bulk-discount principle in the sentencing of multiple offenders appears compelling and prima facie justified, yet we find it hard to say *why* it is justified; furthermore, it seems to conflict directly with other things we find compelling, such as proportionality. My approach argues that this conflict arises because our understanding of retributive sentencing theory is too simple. By pointing to the possibility of a slightly more nuanced view of what retributivism is about, I have sought both to improve our understanding of the retributive tradition, and to remove a barrier to recognizing bulk discounts as an exercise of the practical wisdom of sentencing practitioners.

The fittingness problem said that there is no way for retributivism to explain how bulk discounts fit the crime, while the selection problem said that there is no way for retributivism to explain why it is important to charge and sentence only selectively rather than for all instances of wrongdoing. In response, I have agreed that common sentencing practice is broadly correct on this point, and I have sought to explain why it is correct by explaining how a sophisticated version of retributivism might make sense of this practice.

First of all, I distinguished moralistic from legalistic retributivism, where I argued that what is important on the former is that punishment should be guided by prelegal desert. This means that the moralistic retributivist should see legal classifications such as crimes, charges, and convictions as merely approximations to the underlying desert that the criminal justice system has the right to make its business. This response undermines the selection problem. Whether the moralistic retributivist should endorse the law stemming from *Canavan* is therefore an interesting question: the answer might be that if she should, it would only be for rule of law reasons rather than for retributivist reasons.

Secondly, I argued that on certain plausible assumptions, this first set of points should lead the moralistic retributivist to favor giving sentencers discretion to depart from the apparent requirements of the legal framework and to give out sentences that are guided directly by prelegal desert. Sentencers' ability to do so should, we argued, be tempered by rule of law values such as consistency across cases, predictability of treatment. The task facing sentencers is to find a balance between these considerations. But moderate versions of moralistic retributivism can support this incorporation of rule of law values. The thought that the state should speak with one voice and should deal alike with like situations is not, after all, entirely alien to the form of retributivism (associated, for instance, with Duff) on which the aim of punishment is condemnation in the name of the political community as a whole; if it is, consistency across cases—what Dworkin calls "integrity" (Dworkin, 1986)—is an important part of the package.

And thirdly, I completed the argument against the fittingness problem by arguing against the assumption—which I claimed underlies this alleged problem—that retributivism should take up perspective invariantism in regard to judgments of desert. Perspective invariantism would be the view that the appropriate retributive response to an offender is determined wholly by facts about the offender and her wrongdoing, and that facts about the temporal perspective of the person making the response is irrelevant. I argued that this is unsupported by what I identified as the key motivation for any form of retributivism, namely, to avoid complicity or acquiescence in the offense by dissociating oneself from it. At any rate, the critic of retributivism needs to find a compelling argument for perspective invariantism.

In conclusion, then, the plausibility of retributive sentencing theory is not threatened by the plausibility of deploying bulk discounts. And a wider lesson for retributivists is perhaps that they should be talking less about desert and more about dissociation.[2]

Notes

1. Again, I am using Ashworth as my authority here.
2. I would like to thank Jesper Ryberg, Julian V. Roberts, and Jan W. de Keijser for inviting me to the seminar on the sentencing of multiple offenders that they organized in Oxford in December 2015. I am particularly grateful to Zach Hoskins, Jae Lee, Antje DuBois-Pedain, Andreas von Hirsch, and Jesper Ryberg for helpful questions on my own presentation, and to Jesper Ryberg for written editorial comments.

References

Ashworth, A. 2010. *Sentencing and Criminal Justice*. 5th ed. Cambridge: Cambridge University Press.

Bennett, C. 2008. *The Apology Ritual: A Philosophical Theory of Punishment*. Cambridge: Cambridge University Press.

Bennett, C. 2013. "The Expressive Function of Blame." In J. Coates and N. Tognazzini (eds.), *Blame: Its Nature and Norms*, pp. 66–83. Oxford: Oxford University Press.

Bennett, C. 2014. "Public Opinion and Democratic Control of Sentencing Policy." In J. Ryberg and J. V. Roberts (eds.), *Popular Punishment: On the Normative Significance of Public Opinion*, pp. 146–162. Oxford: Oxford University Press.

Bennett, C. 2016. "Penal Disenfranchisement." *Criminal Law and Philosophy* 10(3): 411–425.

Duff, R. A. 2001. *Punishment, Communication and Community*. Oxford: Oxford University Press.

Dworkin, R. 1986. *Law's Empire*. London: Fontana.

Dzur, A. 2012. *Punishment, Participatory Democracy and the Jury*. Oxford: Oxford University Press.

Jareborg, N. 1998. "Why Bulk Discounts in Multiple Offence Sentencing?" In A. Ashworth and M. Wasik (eds.), *Fundamentals of Sentencing Theory: Essays in Honour of Andrew von Hirsch*, pp. 129–140. Oxford: Clarendon Press.

Meyer, F. 2014. "Discretion." In M. D. Dubber and T. Hörnle (eds.), *Oxford Handbook of Criminal Law*, pp. 913–940. Oxford: Oxford University Press.

Moore, M. S. 1992. "Law as a Functional Kind." In R. P. George (ed.), *Natural Law Theory*, pp. 188–242. Oxford: Oxford University Press.

Reitz, K. (2010). "The Illusion of Proportionality: Desert and Repeat Offenders." In J. V. Roberts and A. von Hirsch (eds.), *Previous Convictions at Sentencing: Theoretical and Applied Perspectives*, pp. 137–160. Oxford: Hart Publishing.

Sunstein, C., and E. Ullmann-Margalit. 1999. "Second-Order Decisions." *Ethics* 110 (1): 5–31.

Thomas, D. A. 1979. *Principles of Sentencing: The Sentencing Policy of the Court of Appeal Criminal Division*. 2nd ed. London: Heinemann.

Waldron, J. 1999. *Law and Disagreement*. Oxford: Oxford University Press.

5

Multiple-Offense Sentencing Discounts

Score One for Hybrid Accounts of Punishment

ZACHARY HOSKINS

Nearly 50 years ago, H. L. A. Hart described the state of philosophical debate about the justification of punishment as "confusing shadow-fighting between utilitarians and their opponents," namely, retributivists (1968, p. 9). Today the terrain has changed, so that pure utilitarian (or indeed, consequentialist) accounts are hard to find. Instead, theorizing about punishment is now dominated by, on one hand, various versions of retributivism and, on the other hand, hybrid accounts of one type or another. Retributivism comes in various forms, but what unites the various accounts is the claim that punishment is justified insofar as it is a *deserved* response to criminal wrongdoing. By contrast, hybrid accounts, such as the one offered by Hart himself, typically regard the question of punishment's justification as in fact a cluster of questions, which can be answered by appeal to various considerations. On most such accounts, broadly retributivist notions of desert and proportionality limit, in one way or another, consequentialist aims such as crime reduction.

Retributivists have criticized hybrid views of punishment as being ad hoc or internally inconsistent. Retributivist theories, by comparison, appear more attractive insofar as they offer integrated accounts—ones that focus on moral desert as the basis both for answering why punishment is permissible and for governing how severely the state should punish in particular cases. For their part, however, hybrid theorists might respond that retributivists often purchase theoretical tidiness at the cost of intuitive plausibility. Morality may just be messy, and as W. D. Ross put it, "it is more important that our theory fit the facts than that it be simple" (1930, p. 19). Thus it seems at least a point in favor of hybrid accounts (though obviously not a decisive argument) if they can better account for certain widely held intuitions about punishment.

This paper examines one widespread, and intuitively appealing, legal practice for which retributivist accounts struggle to find justification: multiple-offense sentencing discounts.[1] Many legal systems provide for those sentenced for multiple offenses at once to receive a total sentence that is somewhat less severe than the cumulation of prescribed sentences for each individual crime. Such discounts appear to violate retributivist commitments to desert and proportionality in sentencing. Again, retributivism holds that punishment is an intrinsically appropriate, because morally deserved, response to crime. Thus the severity of punishment should be proportionate relative to the seriousness of the crime and the offender's degree of culpability. But if this is so, and if Carter culpably commits two instances of an offense, each of which is as serious as the one offense Wilson culpably commits, then retributivism seems to imply that Carter deserves punishment twice as severe as Wilson's.

Retributivists could accept this conclusion and simply contend that bulk-sentencing discounts are unjustified—that those convicted of multiple offenses should receive a total sentence equal to the sum of what each offense considered individually would receive. But many theorists, including retributivists, regard bulk discounts as a desirable feature of sentencing. Thus the challenge for retributivists is to provide some account of why such discounts are deserved, why they do not in fact violate desert-based proportionality.

This essay examines several proposed strategies for justifying bulk discounts on retributivist grounds. I don't claim that the accounts considered exhaust the possibilities, although it is interesting how little attention retributivists have devoted to the challenge of justifying bulk discounts.[2] In particular, I consider strategies that appeal to an absolute punishment maximum, that appeal to interpersonal practices of blame and making amends, and that suggest that perpetrators of multiple offenses sometimes have reduced culpability. I contend that each of these strategies either is implausible as a ground for bulk-sentencing discounts or is plausible only insofar as it incorporates nonretributivist considerations into its account—thus is in fact a hybrid view. Then, in the paper's final section, I consider hybrid theories as an alternative, and I suggest that such views not only can provide justification for bulk-sentencing discounts but are also more plausible in general than is often thought.

Desert and an Absolute Punishment Maximum

How might retributivists justify sentencing multiple offenders less severely than would be indicated by strictly summing the sentences each of their individual offenses would receive? Nils Jareborg (1998) offers an answer grounded in two principles that he believes should guide sentencing decisions for multiple offenses: the "wet noodle punishment" principle, and the "life is short" principle (p. 138). The wet noodle punishment principle says, essentially, that punishment requires hard treatment that reflects the seriousness of the crime: beating offenders with a wet noodle would not be sufficient. The life is short principle says (not surprisingly) that life is short, and thus that basic decency requires the law to prescribe an absolute punishment maximum. Combining these principles leads Jareborg to the view that although punishment for a single serious crime should be substantial (no wet noodles), there is an upper bound on how severely the state may punish the multiple offenses in total (because life is short). Thus sentencers should punish the single crime proportionately but then "let the presence of the ceiling be felt immediately after the first (most serious) offence," and thus discount the other crimes (p. 139).

The key piece of this argument is the prescription of an upper limit on total punishment, but it is unclear how such a limit might be defended on retributivist grounds. Jareborg mentions the principle of parsimony (p. 138), which states that punishment should be no more severe than is necessary to achieve its purpose. But as Jesper Ryberg (2005, p. 222) rightly points out, whether this principle will provide the basis for an upper limit on punishment on retributivist grounds will depend on whether an upper limit is consistent with achieving punishment's retributive purpose or whether, instead, retributivism requires strict proportionality for each offense. But this is just the central question at issue. Thus rather than the parsimony principle providing a basis to support upper limits on retributivist grounds, the relevance of the parsimony principle depends on our already having an answer to whether upper limits are consistent with punishment's retributivist purpose.

Anthony Bottoms (1998) defends an upper limit on total punishment by appeal to something similar to the life is short principle: he contends that an offender's total punishment should not be so severe as to deprive him of "a high proportion of the prime years of his life" (p. 66). There is a natural affinity between the notion that life is short and the idea that individuals should not be deprived of the prime years of their lives. Bottoms, however, explicitly grounds his view in terms of mercy, not desert. What the retributivist needs is a desert-based rationale for the upper limit on total punishment.

Is there another way to flesh out Jareborg's life is short principle, then, to provide such a retributivist justification for upper sentencing limits? I think the most charitable interpretation of the view is that given the relatively short lives we live, no one *deserves* to spend all (or most) of our brief lives under the yoke of state punishment. Or conversely, no matter how serious our violations, we all *deserve* to spend some significant portion of our short lives free of punishment.

Thus desert sets an upper limit on the total punishment that may be imposed during a person's lifetime. This seems consistent with Jareborg's claim that "a minimum of moral decency requires that a ceiling is created for State intervention in human lives" (p. 138).

But there are various problems with this understanding of the life is short principle: for one thing, it may prove too much. If people deserve not to be subject to punishment for too large a portion of their lives, then it is unclear why this should only limit those who are sentenced for multiple offenses at once. In particular, it's not clear why a maximum punishment limit should apply to those who are sentenced for many crimes at once but not for those who commit the same number of equally serious crimes but do so one at a time and are sentenced and punished between each offense. In other words, if bulk discounts are deserved because life is short, then the same reasoning would seem to suggest that recidivist discounts are deserved as well, rather than the current practice of recidivist premiums. Many people find recidivist sentencing premiums intuitively appealing, but even those (like me) who do not may be reluctant to endorse recidivist *discounts*.

A more fundamental problem with the notion of a deserved upper punishment limit, at least from the retributivist perspective, is that the sense of desert at issue here is not the retributivist sense. To see why this is so, consider more closely the notion of desert. Margaret Falls (1987) provides a useful analysis of the claim "person *P* deserves *X*." The claim, she explains, is "(1) an assessment or acknowledgement of *P*'s worth (2) relative to a given role or capacity (3) based upon what already is or has been true of *P*'s characteristics, abilities, and/or acts" (p. 38). Thus *P* merits or is worthy of *X*, relative to some role or capacity, in virtue of what is or has been true of *P*. If we say Novak Djokovic deserves to be regarded as the best tennis player in the world, we seem to be making a claim that Djokovic is worthy of such regard, relative to his role as a tennis player, in virtue of his accomplishments in tournaments in recent years.

Crucial to Falls's account, however, is that we may also deserve (or be worthy of) certain treatment simply in our role as moral persons, in virtue of our status as persons. That is, we may deserve certain treatment not only in virtue of *what we have done* but also in virtue of *who we are*. Falls characterizes this latter sort of desert as *unearned* desert: for example, as a moral person, you deserve not to be lied to merely for others' convenience, or to be killed for sport. She distinguishes this from *earned* desert (p. 40): this is the sort of desert Djokovic comes to merit in virtue of his accomplishments as a tennis player. Falls's distinction between earned and unearned desert is intuitively plausible and also useful, in my view. In particular, recognizing these two distinct senses in which we can deserve certain treatment helps to highlight that the two senses of desert may come to be in tension with each other: we may deserve *as earned desert* certain treatment based on our behavior that conflicts with what we deserve *as unearned desert* simply in virtue of our status as moral persons (or perhaps as citizens, family members, etc.).

For present purposes, two points are relevant: first, retributivism is best understood as dealing in earned desert. Retributivists believe punishment is deserved as a response to (and thus should be proportionate to) an offender's prior wrongdoing. But second, if we accept the life is short principle's implication that we deserve an upper limit on the degree of punishment the state metes out, we seem to be accepting a claim about *unearned* desert. The shortness of our lives is not centrally a product of what we have done; rather, it is a feature of our human condition (this is consistent with acknowledging that some people's actions will serve to further shorten their already short lives). Thus if, as Jareborg suggests, the upper limit is justified by the requirements of minimum moral decency because we deserve not to be subject to too much state control during our short lives, then the sense of desert at issue here is unearned desert; it is not desert in the earned sense with which retributivism is concerned.

Retributivists might object, of course, to the whole notion of unearned desert, or alternatively they might accept unearned desert but suggest that insofar as it is nonetheless a form of desert, treatment according to unearned desert is also properly understood as a form of retributivism. Both claims would be unpersuasive. Consider the various types of desert claims that might be made in a commonly discussed type of dilemma in medical ethics: who among a number of candidates should receive the recently received kidney. Candidate A claims to deserve the kidney because she needs it the most: she has the lowest likelihood of survival without it. Her dire condition, however, is not a result of any reckless or ill-advised past decisions on her part. Candidate B claims to deserve the kidney because his long-term prospects if he receives it will be the best in the group: whereas A is most certain to die without the transplant, she is fairly unlikely to survive long even with the kidney; by contrast, B's life is likely to be prolonged by many years with the kidney. And again, suppose B's otherwise robust health is due more to genetic good fortune than to particular choices he has made in the past. Finally, both candidates A and B agree that candidate C does not deserve to receive the kidney because he is a serial rapist. Now, setting aside the merit of any of these claims, I suggest that each is a fairly natural use of the term "desert," but only the third claim can plausibly be construed as a claim about *earned* desert. Candidates A's and B's desert claims appeal to unearned desert. Furthermore, notice how implausible it is to suggest that the desert claims asserted by A and B represent retributivist considerations. Thus although we can recognize a sense of desert that is unearned, this sort of desert is not a basis for retributivist claims.

So even if we accept that the life is short principle will ground upper limits on total punishment, and even if we can then derive from this a case for bulk-sentencing discounts, our account will be based ultimately on a nonretributivist rather than a retributivist notion of desert. Retributivists are still in need, then, of an account of why bulk discounts are deserved in the sense of earned desert.

Richard Lippke (2011) provides a somewhat different retributivist argument for the upper limit on total punishment. On his view, "multiple offenders should not be made to endure penal losses and deprivations the total impact of which exceeds, by too significant a margin, the harms which they culpably inflicted on any one of their victims" (p. 220). Thus although a multiple offender could be punished more severely than a single offender on Lippke's account, the total punishment for the multiple offender should not be clearly disproportionate to the harm inflicted by the most serious among their multiple offenses. If we are to understand this account as a properly retributivist one—that is, one concerned with earned desert—then the point seems to be that no matter how many crimes a person commits, he can never come to deserve suffering or censure (depending on which of these is given priority in one's retributivist account) that significantly exceeds the harm he caused to his most seriously harmed victim.

But why should we think this sort of limit follows from retributivist desert? Why think, for example, that a person who batters 20 individuals (and we can stipulate, inflicts equal harm on each person) does not thereby come to deserve a sentence that is significantly more severe than is commensurate with the harm caused to any one of the victims? Lippke suggests that punishment should not impede the offender's ability to lead a decent life to a significantly greater extent than the offender's crime impedes his victim's ability to lead a decent life (pp. 220–221).[3] I think there is some intuitive appeal to this suggestion, but again, I do not see how it follows on retributivist grounds. If I impede to a moderate extent the ability of 20 victims to live decent lives, then it is difficult to see why, as a consequence of harming so many people, I don't thereby come to deserve treatment that sets my own interests back significantly more than the interests of any one of my own victims was set back. What we need is an explanation of why my earned desert does not continue to accumulate much beyond what I deserve for any one of the offenses. As far as I can tell, Lippke does not provide such an explanation.

Lessons from Interpersonal Blame and Making Amends

Christopher Bennett provides a different sort of account of why bulk discounts are deserved in the properly retributivist sense. Bennett's is an expressivist version of retributivism, in which the state expresses deserved blame, and thus dissociates itself from the offender's wrongdoing, by forcing the offender to take part in an apology ritual (see Bennett, 2008). The ritual involves suffering burdensome treatment of a degree roughly equivalent to what an offender would undertake, were she genuinely sorry, as a way to make amends. Thus his justification of state punishment in general, and of bulk-sentencing discounts in particular, is grounded in an examination of our interpersonal moral practices of blaming, apologizing, and making amends. He writes:

> When we blame, or when we apologize, when we are engaged in thinking about how much retributive amends it will take to set things right, we are giving a snapshot of how things stand between us given what you have done. We are asking how what I have done alters the relationship between us, given that we are two people who stand in a certain relation to one another, and, other things being equal, owe one another a certain standard of care and respect. (2012, p. 148)

How, then, do things stand between two people when one commits multiple offenses before being discovered and blamed by the other? Bennett considers the example of business partners Ben and Jenny. Over a number of years, Jenny repeatedly siphons money from the business before Ben eventually discovers the wrongdoing. Bennett asks, then, how much more Jenny would need to do by way of making retributive amends after the multiple instances of embezzlement than if she were only guilty of one instance of it. "My sense," he writes, "is that the answer is, not very much" (p. 148).

> In thinking about what one would have to do to make amends for such a string of wrongdoing our thinking tends to elide the string of wrongs into one—so we see it, not as a series of betrayals, but rather an ongoing betrayal represented by a series of fraudulent acquisitions. (p. 148)

Here we have a thoroughly retributivist candidate justification of bulk discounts. On this view, how much punishment a person *deserves* (in the retributivist sense of earned desert) is understood in terms of how much would be required to make amends for her wrongdoing. And what would be required to make amends for multiple instances of wrongdoing, all discovered at once, is less (perhaps much less) than would be indicated by simply adding up what would be required to make amends for each individual instance of wrongdoing considered separately. Thus it follows that what the multiple offender *deserves* is less than the sum of what each offense, considered separately, would warrant.

Bennett's view is attractive, I think, in a number of respects. In particular, by focusing on the notion of making amends, this account of punishment puts the offender front and center, as an active participant in the process of punishment rather than merely a passive object of treatment by the state. Still, I am ultimately skeptical about Bennett's defense of bulk discounts, for various reasons.

First, I'm not sure I share Bennett's intuition that, in the interpersonal context, what Jenny would owe to Ben by way of making amends for repeated wrongdoing would not be much more than what would be required to make amends for a single instance of the wrongdoing. The example of Jenny and Ben seems intended to elicit particular intuitions about blame, apology, and making amends, and this point is central to Bennett's account: if we share his intuitions about the interpersonal case, then perhaps we will be that much more sympathetic to his conclusions about bulk discounts in the legal context. But what if one's intuitions about the Jenny–Ben example don't correspond with Bennett's? My intuitions about the case are, at least, muddy.

We can distinguish three key claims in Bennett's discussion of Jenny and Ben. Each of these claims, I suggest, is suspect. First, he claims that in circumstances of blaming and making amends, we tend mentally to clump the several individual wrongs into one ongoing wrong. I acknowledge that we *may* do this in cases such as the embezzlement example he describes. Lippke terms such crimes "complex single transaction offenses": crimes that "involve a series of small criminal transactions, no one of which inflicts more than modest or moderate harms on victims but the cumulative harms of which are substantial" (Lippke, 2011, p. 226). It may be that for such series of small criminal transactions, we do tend mentally to clump the individual instances into one ongoing crime. But I doubt that this is generally so. I doubt that, for example, a woman whose partner regularly batters her will tend to elide the string of wrongs into one. Our discussion of such cases may sometimes imply such an elision, as we speak of "domestic abuse," a singular term, to describe the pattern of ongoing abusive behavior. But for many victims of such abuse, I suspect that individual beatings remain vivid and distinct—that there is no real danger of collapsing all of the individual episodes into a single instance of ongoing abuse.

The notion that we tend to clump the many offenses into one seems especially implausible when we consider cases in which the individual offenses either have different victims or are different in nature. Imagine that in addition to her collaboration with Ben, Jenny has also been working as a part-time accountant for numerous other clients around town, and she has been embezzling from each of them. If all of her wrongdoing is discovered at once, it seems counterintuitive to think of these various offenses, against distinct victims, as essentially all one offense. This is even more apparent in cases in which the multiple offenses are distinct in nature. Imagine that in addition to embezzling from Ben, Jenny also kidnaps his daughter, poisons his wife, and steals his car (Ben should have been more judicious in selecting business partners). In such cases, it is entirely counterintuitive to suggest that we will naturally tend to elide the various individual offenses into a single larger offense.

Suppose for argument's sake, however, that we accept the notion that we tend mentally to clump multiple individual offenses into one larger wrong. Bennett's second key claim is that we then tend to think that what is required to make amends for the clumped wrong is not very much more than would be required to make amends for a single instance of the wrong. Again, I am skeptical. If we asked a battered partner how much more would be required to make amends for two beatings, or three, or four, rather than one, I doubt that her answer would be "not very much." Similarly, if we consider how much more would be required to make amends for Jenny's clumped offense against Ben (the clump comprising the kidnapping, poisoning, car theft, and embezzlement) even as compared to the most serious individual offense in the clump, the murder of his wife, it is implausible to suggest that the answer is "not very much more." Indeed, it seems plausible to me that what would be required to make amends for all of Jenny's offenses considered together would be equal to the cumulation of what would be required to make amends for each one individually. My intuitions are not entirely firm on this point, in part because I have no firm intuitions about what would be sufficient to make amends in any of the individual cases. But the cumulative model of making amends strikes me as intuitively more plausible in many cases, such as the battered partner case or my modified Jenny–Ben example, than Bennett's model.

Even if we accept Bennett's first two claims—that we tend mentally to elide multiple offenses into one, and that we think what's required to make amends for the one composite offense is not very much more than would be required to make amends for one (perhaps the most serious) of the single offenses—the third key claim of which I am skeptical is that we are *justified* in each of these ways of thinking. Bennett offers a fairly brief defense of this claim, which draws on a point suggested previously by Andrew Ashworth that "no matter how many offences of a particular kind an offender is found to have committed, the sentence should remain in the range appropriate to that type of offence" (Ashworth, 1995, p. 214). Thus no matter how many instances we are considering of, say, shoplifting, the total sentence for these should be less severe than for a single instance of, say, assault. Bennett writes that in cases of blaming and making amends such as Jenny and Ben's, we should bear in mind "that however bad things are, they are not as bad as they would have been had I done something really serious against you" (Bennett, 2012, p. 148).

> Therefore whatever amount of retributive amends we settle upon as being adequate, it must be such as to leave clear blue water between that

> amount and the amount that would have been required for really serious wrongs. This is the kind of claim that justifies the elision. (pp. 148–149)

If this is the idea that justifies our eliding multiple offenses into one large one, then we must ask whether this idea is itself justified. Jesper Ryberg has offered an extensive, and in my view persuasive, critique of this idea that no number of lesser crimes can warrant as severe a punishment as a more serious crime, so I won't repeat that critique here (Ryberg, 2005, pp. 221–225; see also Lippke, 2011, p. 217). But it is important to note that Bennett himself is critical of this "clear blue water" claim earlier in his essay. He writes, "To claim that motoring offenses can never deserve the kind of punishment that a more serious crime deserves merely restates without further explaining the intuition that we are puzzling over" (Bennett, 2012, p. 141). He contends that his account of interpersonal blaming and making amends provides the needed explanation but then appears to claim that our thinking about bulk wrongdoing in the interpersonal context is justified by the clear blue water argument. This argument seems to me suspiciously close to being circular.[4]

For various reasons, then, I am skeptical about whether we find retributivist grounds for bulk-sentencing discounts by appealing to the interpersonal practices of blaming and making amends. Perhaps, however, we can justify the discounts by focusing directly on the relative culpability of differently situated perpetrators.

Multiple Offending and Reduced Culpability

As we have seen, the challenge posed to retributivism by bulk-sentencing discounts is that these discounts appear to violate the retributivist proportionality principle, which tells us that the severity of punishment should be proportionate to the seriousness of the offense and the offender's degree of culpability. Perhaps, however, such discounts can be justified on retributivist grounds because the *culpability* of perpetrators of multiple offenses is somewhat mitigated. In other words, Carter's culpability for committing two counts of an offense is somewhat less than twice Wilson's culpability for committing one count of the same offense. Julian Roberts and Jan W. de Keijser (chapter 8, this volume) endorse this sort of view. They offer two main justifications of the claim that in some cases, "multiple offenders deserve less punishment because they are less culpable than offenders convicted of the same crimes committed sequentially" (p. 1):

> First, the repeat offender has experienced penal censure and has declined the opportunity to respond to the moral message conveyed by

> the court. In contrast, the multiple offender has not had the benefit of this experience. Second, offenses committed during a single period or state of criminality reflect a lower level of culpability for each individual crime. In contrast, the serial offender has to generate an independent criminal intention for each crime. (p. 4–5)

I consider these justifications in turn. First, Roberts and de Keijser claim that an offender who commits multiple crimes in a short time span—and importantly, all before being prosecuted, convicted, or punished for any of them—should receive mitigation. Because he has not been convicted or punished, he has not "had the wrongfulness or harmfulness of his crime brought home to him by the criminal process" (p. 5) and he can also "argue that the offenses were out of character" (p. 5). Thus he is less culpable than someone who committed the same offenses one at a time, experiencing prosecution, conviction, and punishment after each offense.

There are reasons, I think, to be skeptical of this sort of view. The idea that first-time offenders are less culpable because they have not had the wrongfulness or harmfulness of their actions brought home to them through the criminal justice process implies that this process plays some sort of morally educative role for those offenders who go through it. It seems unlikely, however, that this is always, or even typically, the case. Many first-time offenders are already aware that their behavior is wrong: they do not need a process of criminal prosecution and punishment to make this clear to them. What's more, even for offenders who are not already aware that what they did was wrong, it is questionable whether the criminal justice process is typically an effective means of conveying this message.

Similarly, the idea that first-time offenders act contrary to their characters and thus deserve mitigation also is suspect. To the extent that it makes sense to draw inferences about character from behavior, surely many first-time offenders act consistently with their characters just as do many repeat offenders. We might argue that a first-timer's offense is less clearly *indicative* of bad character than is that of a recidivist, but even here this need not always be the case. If crimes are indeed indicative of character, then undoubtedly there are many first offenses that leave no real doubt about the perpetrator's character, and so there would be no less certainty about the character of the first-timer than of the recidivist.

Even if we endorse this notion of first-timer mitigation, however, it does not help in grounding a bulk-sentencing discount. Justifying the bulk discount requires explaining why a person convicted of multiple offenses deserves less severe punishment than the strict cumulation of what she would receive for each of the individual offenses. Focusing on previous convictions muddies the waters by introducing an additional variable. The first-timer mitigation claim tells us, at most, that a) someone who commits some number of crimes never having previously been prosecuted and punished deserves a lighter sentence than b) someone who commits the same number of crimes after having been previously prosecuted and punished. It does not tell us that a) a first-time multiple offender deserves less severe punishment than b) the strict cumulation of what first-time offenders would receive for each of the individual offenses. Put differently, suppose Carter's two counts of offense x are his first offenses, and Wilson's one count of offense x is his first offense. Justifying bulk discounts requires an explanation of why Carter's sentence should be less than twice as severe as Wilson's. Pointing out that Carter is a first-timer does not help.

The other justification offered by Roberts and de Keijser is that when the multiple offenses are related in certain respects, then we can often say that they "have been committed *within a continued culpable state of mind*" (p. 8). Crimes may be related in three relevant senses. First, they may be temporally related when they are committed "within a short time-span, for example a single day" (p. 9). Second, they may be causally related when, "without one particular offense, a subsequent offense would never have occurred" (p. 10). Third, they may be substantively related when they involve similar conduct (p. 10). Roberts and de Keijser describe temporal relatedness as "the most powerful dimension" of relatedness and a necessary condition (a sine qua non) for culpability reduction (p. 9). But temporal relatedness is not a sufficient condition; to justify a sentence reduction based on diminished culpability, the offenses must also be either causally or substantively related (p. 10).

Let us consider, then, a case of offenses that are both temporally and substantively related, and compare this to a case of similar offenses not temporally related (to ensure that the cases are in other respects similar, we can stipulate that both cases involve first-time offenders). Suppose Carter steals three cars in a single day. Wilson steals one car a month for three months. Each is apprehended, prosecuted, and convicted after the theft of the third car. Because Carter's offenses are temporally and substantively related, he appears on Roberts and de Keijser's account to be a candidate for a diminished-culpability sentence reduction. Wilson's offenses, by contrast, are substantively but not temporally related, so (because temporal relatedness is a necessary condition for diminished culpability) he does not deserve a reduced sentence.

Why should we think that Carter is less culpable for the three thefts than is Wilson? Roberts and de Keijser suggest that the person who offends within a small period of time "has less opportunity to reflect on the wrongfulness of his actions than the offender who has weeks or months within which to commit the same crimes" (p. 9). By committing the several offenses in a single day, Carter "deprives himself of the opportunity for rational reflection" between each offense (p. 10). And degraded decision-making diminishes culpability. Thus

Carter is less culpable for his second and third theft than Wilson, who had more time to reflect, is culpable for his second and third theft.

But there are reasons to be skeptical of this line of argument. In particular, it is unclear why we should think that a limited opportunity to reflect on a previous offense degrades one's decision-making about a subsequent offense. First, surely many offenders are already aware of the wrongfulness of their acts before they commit them. If Carter and Wilson are both already aware, even before their first car thefts, that stealing cars is wrong, then it does not seem that Carter's having a briefer opportunity for reflection between his first and second offenses compromises his decision-making relative to Wilson's about whether it is wrong to steal the second (or third) car.

Still, even if many people know their acts are wrong even before committing them, there are presumably others who do not really appreciate the wrongness of behavior they are considering. In these cases, however, we must ask why, if a person does not already realize that an act is wrong, committing and then reflecting on an act will teach her the wrongness of the act. As we saw earlier, Roberts and de Keijser suggest that one function of conviction and punishment is to bring home to an offender that her actions were wrong. But whether or not conviction and punishment are effective in this regard, here the claim under consideration is that a person who has less time to reflect on a previous offense is less culpable, because she has less opportunity for reflection, than a person would be who has more time to reflect on the previous offense. Thus this argument relies not on the controversial claim about the educative function of punishment, but rather on a claim about the educative function simply of reflecting on one's previous offense. Specifically, the claim must be that reflecting on one's prior offense can teach that acts of that type are wrong and thus that the subsequent act one is considering, of the same type, is wrong.

I doubt that committing an offense puts one in an epistemically superior position to reflect on the wrongness of acts of that type. Arguably, witnessing the effects of a crime might drive home its wrongness. But perpetrators often do not see the full effects of their crimes, and so it is not clear that reflecting on the commission of a crime will always, or even typically, foster remorse about what one has done.[5] Instead, an offender reflecting on his crime might focus on the thrill of committing it, or his cleverness in not being caught. Suppose Wilson spends the month after stealing his first car thinking in these ways, rather than reflecting on the wrongness of what he did. Or suppose he just does not think much about the previous theft at all. If so, should we say that not having engaged in the right sort of reflection, his decision-making about whether to steal another car is thereby diminished, and thus he is less culpable for the subsequent thefts? Now, one might respond that Wilson, unlike Carter, had time and therefore *should have* engaged in the proper sort of reflection. But again, we should ask why committing an offense starts the clock, so to speak, on opportunity for proper reflection on the wrongness of that sort of behavior. It is more plausible, in my view, to say that Carter, like Wilson, has ample opportunity to reflect before his first car theft about the wrongness of such behavior. But this means Carter has also had ample opportunity, as later in the day he contemplates engaging in the same type of behavior again, to reflect on its wrongness. His culpability is thus not diminished in the second (or third) theft on grounds that lack of time for reflection degraded his decision-making.

Ultimately, I am not persuaded that temporal proximity of offenses matters to culpability in the way Roberts and de Keijser claim. And as temporal proximity is the sine qua non of their relatedness account of diminished culpability, I am not persuaded that the account fares better than other retributivist attempts to justify bulk-sentencing discounts. In the final section, then, I turn to consider the hybrid alternative.

Revisiting the Hybrid View

If we admit nonretributivist considerations into our account of punishment, then there are a number of grounds on which we might argue that bulk discounts, though not justified by retributivist considerations, are all-things-considered justified.

My own view is that the reason we should want an institution of punishment is that the institution helps to reduce crime by dissuading potential wrongdoers (see Hoskins, 2011). This rationale for the institution has certain implications for how, and how severely, the state should punish. In particular, sentences should not be so light that they are ineffective in reducing crime, nor should they be more severe than crime reduction warrants. Thus considerations of crime reduction imply some, albeit vague, floors and ceilings on sentencing severity. But these do not exhaust the relevant considerations in sentencing. Retributivist considerations of earned desert are also relevant: people should not be punished more severely than they deserve given the seriousness of their crimes and their culpability, even if doing so would promote crime reductive goals. Thus retributivism constrains punishment in the pursuit of crime reduction. Furthermore, in my view offenders as moral persons deserve (in the sense of unearned desert) not to be treated in ways that tend to undermine their prospects of reform (see Hoskins, 2013).

On this account, bulk-sentencing discounts might be justified in two ways even if they are not deserved in the retributivist sense. Suppose the deserved (in the retributivist, "earned" sense) punishment for burglary is six months in prison. A person who commits 10 burglaries would thus deserve 60 months in prison. But on my account, whereas retributivist desert sets a hard upper limit on sentence severity, the lower limit it sets may be overridden by other considerations. In particular, if the sentence (or range of sentences) indicated by retributivist desert is more severe than is needed to serve punishment's crime reductive purpose, then a downward departure from retributivist desert—that is, a bulk discount—is warranted. The same is true if retributivist desert prescribes sentences so severe that they will tend to undermine offenders' prospects of reform.

I do not claim that this sort of account would justify bulk discounts in every case: *if* sentencing those convicted of 10 burglaries to 60 months in prison was not more severe than the aim of crime reduction required, and *if* such a sentence did not tend to undermine their prospects for reform, then insofar as such a sentence was deserved in the retributivist sense, a bulk discount would not be warranted on my account. But I do not claim that an adequate account of punishment must allow for reduced sentences in all instances of multiple offending. Like many scholars and practitioners, I do believe that bulk discounts are appealing in many cases. I have argued that such discounts cannot be adequately accounted for by pure retributivist views. Thus we should look elsewhere for theoretical grounding of sentencing discounts in those cases in which they are justified.

It is clear enough, I believe, that if we admit nonretributivist as well as retributivist considerations into our account, there are various plausible grounds for maintaining bulk discounts in many (though not necessarily all) cases. My account can justify discounts in many cases based on considerations of crime reduction or offender reform. One need not be persuaded by my view, however. Jareborg's is, I have suggested, essentially a hybrid view: offenders deserve (in the retributivist, earned sense of desert) punishment that is significant, but given the shortness of our lives, no one deserves (in the nonretributivist, unearned sense of desert) to spend too much of their lives under the yoke of punishment. Alternatively, we could follow Bottoms in appealing to considerations of mercy, a nonretributivist notion, as a constraint on retributivist sentencing. My goal in this chapter is not to defend my own view as preferable to alternative hybrid views. Rather, my central point is that hybrid views have a variety of resources, which retributivism does not have, to account for bulk-sentencing discounts. Insofar as such discounts strike many of us as intuitively attractive, the ability of hybrid theories to provide plausible grounds for such discounts, and the apparent inability of retributivist theories to do so, constitutes one point in favor of hybrid theories.

Of course, retributivists may respond that whatever small victory this may be for hybrid views, it is significantly outweighed by the more general implausibility of such views. Thus my aim in this concluding section is to say a bit about hybrid theories of punishment generally, and why they are more plausible than retributivist critiques often imply. What follows, of course, is not a comprehensive defense of hybrid views against the full range of objections that have been lodged against them.[6]

In his seminal statement of a hybrid account, H. L. A. Hart writes that "in relation to any social institution, after stating what general aim or value its maintenance fosters we should enquire whether there are any and if so what principles limiting the unqualified pursuit of that aim or value" (Hart, 1968, p. 10). Hart goes on to distinguish two questions, which he terms the question of punishment's "general justifying aim" and the question of its "distribution" (p. 9). He contends that once we recognize this distinction, we can avoid the "confusing shadow-fighting" between consequentialists and retributivists by offering a *consequentialist* answer to the "general justifying aim" question and a *retributivist* answer to the "distribution" question.[7]

Critics have objected that Hart's distinction of punishment's general justifying aim from its distribution is implausible: if consequentialist considerations supply the justifying aim of the practice, shouldn't these considerations also play a role in how punishment is meted out? Conversely, retributivists argue that Hart's account relegates retributivism to a merely subsidiary role, whereas giving offenders their just deserts is in fact not merely a constraining consideration but a (or the) central point of punishment (see Wood, 2002, p. 303). Thus critics have regarded Hart's two-question approach as ad hoc and internally inconsistent (see, e.g., Kaufman, 2008, pp. 45–49).

I think the criticisms are understandable given certain features of Hart's account, but I do not think they give us sufficient reason to abandon the hybrid strategy altogether. Consider a somewhat revised version of his insight about social institutions: in assessing whether a social institution is justified, we should first ask what valuable, legitimate function, if any, the institution serves. Hart endorses a consequentialist answer to this question, as I do. But there is nothing about the hybrid strategy itself that requires a consequentialist answer here. The question may be answered by appeal to retributivist or other nonconsequentialist considerations. And indeed, punishment might serve multiple functions. Admitting of different functions does create the possibility of tensions between the various functions of punishment, but such tensions might be resolved by meta-considerations about the relative priority of the various functions: that is, considerations of which function is primary, which is secondary, and so on.

Whatever valuable function an institution is to serve, its function will imply certain constraints on how the institution is administered. Hart recognized this general point—he writes that a general justifying aim of retribution would entail "retribution in Distribution" (Hart, 1968, p. 9)—although he does not elaborate on it. This is unfortunate, because doing so would have helped to highlight that the questions of punishment's function and how it is administered are, even on a hybrid view, more integrated than is sometimes recognized.

That said, I believe that an important insight underlying hybrid views is that whatever constraints on the administration of a practice are implied by the valuable, legitimate functions it serves, we should not expect that these will be the only constraints. Other sorts of considerations will be relevant as well. This insight is accepted as relatively uncontroversial in the context of other social practices. Consider taxation. We might plausibly say that the valuable, legitimate function served by levying taxes is the provision of funds for public goods such as roads, education, public safety, healthcare, and so on. As before, this consideration will imply certain constraints on how taxes are levied: namely, taxes must be substantial enough actually to provide for the various public goods, and should not be more substantial than is needed to do so. But these do not exhaust the relevant considerations regarding how taxes are levied. Questions of distributive justice are relevant, as well. The point generalizes: with virtually any social practice, we should expect there to be a valuable, legitimate function served by the practice, and that function will imply certain constraints on its administration; but we should not expect that the *only* considerations relevant to how the practice may be administered will be implied by its function.

Once we admit of various, independent constraints on a social practice, of course, we open the door to potential tensions among various constraints. Acknowledging that tensions will inevitably arise, however, need not lead to despair over the prospects for resolving them. We might attempt to resolve tensions among the constraints on that practice by prioritizing some constraints over others, or by making certain constraints absolute and others only presumptive. Or we might adopt some meta-principle such as that whichever constraint sets the ceiling lower in a particular instance should govern in that instance.

In my view, considerations of unearned desert should take priority over considerations of earned desert. That is, there are certain types of treatment that moral persons deserve simply in virtue of being moral persons, and this desert is not overridable or defeasible as a result of our behavior. (Put in rights language, we might say that there are certain moral rights that people do not forfeit even when they are guilty of especially heinous offenses.) Thus in my view unearned desert constitutes a significant constraint on how the state may punish offenders. For one thing, considerations of unearned desert ground the principle that punishment should not tend to undermine offenders' prospects for moral reform. The notion of unearned desert might also ground the principle, per Jareborg, that punishment should not deprive a person of freedom for too much of her life. Or it might ground other constraining principles on sentencing. But notice that none of these principles need be implied by the central function of punishment. We need not believe, for example, that offender reform should be one of punishment's central functions to believe that punishment at least should not tend to get in the way of reform. Thus it is entirely plausible that whatever constraints on sentencing are implied by the function of punishment, additional constraints will be grounded in considerations independent of its function. This, I suggest, is the key insight of Hart's discussion of social institutions. If we accept this point, then the prospect of a hybrid account of punishment should not strike us as particularly mysterious. Rather, given the richness and complexity of our moral lives, we should not be surprised if the moral justification of punishment is itself pluralistic.

Whether such an account will be ultimately convincing will depend, of course, on how the details are fleshed out. As I said earlier, my aim here is not to give a full articulation and defense of my own hybrid view. Rather, my central aim has been to contend that such views are plausible in their own right, and also that they offer the resources—whereas pure retributivism does not—to ground a plausible justification of bulk-sentencing discounts. Given the intuitive appeal of such discounts, it is a point in favor of hybrid views that they can provide such justification.

Notes

1. Some theorists, including some in this volume, object to the term "discounts" in this context as being misleading or question-begging. Nevertheless, I use the term in what follows, both because it is common currency in these debates and because it has the virtue of being concise. Whatever term we use, the normative question remains: Why, on retributivist grounds, should a person who has committed multiple offenses receive less than the strict sum of what each offense individually taken would receive?
2. For useful critiques of other possible strategies, see esp. Ryberg (2005) and Lippke (2011).
3. Lippke does suggest that we might allow exceptions to this rule in especially severe cases, such as serial rapists, though it is not clear on what principled (and specifically, retributivist) basis we would make such exceptions.
4. More recently, Bennett has suggested that what is essential to retributivism is not the notion of individual *desert*, but rather *dissociation* (chapter 4, this volume). Thus retributivists should focus on the question of "what one needs to do to dissociate oneself" from wrongdoing" (p. 69). As I mentioned at the outset of this chapter, retributivism comes in a range of forms, but in my view, the thread uniting these views is that punishment is an intrinsically appropriate, because *deserved*, response to crime. Thus I doubt that we can decouple retributivism from desert, as Bennett suggests. In my view, any properly retributivist account of sentencing will be grounded in the notion of desert, and thus will need to deal with the problem desert appears to pose for bulk-sentencing discounts.
5. Proponents of restorative justice often endorse bringing offenders and their victims together in part to drive home to offenders the wrongness of their actions; but again, here the reflection is spurred not just by the commission of an offense plus time, but rather by an intervention by the justice system.
6. For a fuller recent defense of hybrid views, see Frase (2013, pp. 107–119).
7. Hart's actual answer to the distribution question is not, in fact, retributivist, as various scholars have pointed out. Rather, his view is grounded in the value of protecting individual freedom. For discussion of Hart's view on this point, see, e.g., R. A. Duff (2001, p. 12).

References

Ashworth, A. 1995. *Sentencing and Criminal Justice*. 2nd ed. London: Butterworths.

Bennett, C. 2008. *The Apology Ritual: A Philosophical Theory of Punishment*. Cambridge: Cambridge University Press.

Bennett, C. 2012. "Do Multiple and Repeat Offenders Pose a Problem for Retributive Sentencing Theory?" In C. Tamburrini and J. Ryberg (eds.), *Recidivist Punishments: The Philosopher's View*, pp. 137–156. Lanham, MD: Lexington Books.

Bottoms, A. E. 1998. "Five Puzzles in von Hirsch's Theory of Punishment." In A. Ashworth and M. Wasik (eds.), *Fundamentals of Sentencing Theory: Essays in Honour of Andrew von Hirsch*, pp. 53–100 Oxford: Clarendon Press.

Duff, R. A. 2001. *Punishment, Communication, and Community*. Oxford: Oxford University Press.

Falls, M. M. 1987. "Retribution, Reciprocity, and Respect for Persons." *Law and Philosophy* 6(1): 25–51.

Frase, R. S. 2013. *Just Sentencing: Principles and Procedures for a Workable System*. New York: Oxford University Press.

Hart, H. L. A. 1968. *Punishment and Responsibility: Essays in the Philosophy of Law*. Oxford: Oxford University Press.

Hoskins, Z. 2011. "Deterrent Punishment and Respect for Persons." *Ohio State Journal of Criminal Law* 8(2): 369–384.

Hoskins, Z. 2013. "Punishment, Contempt, and the Prospect of Moral Reform." *Criminal Justice Ethics* 32(1): 1–18.

Jareborg, N. 1998. "Why Bulk Discounts in Multiple Offence Sentencing?" In A. Ashworth and M. Wasik (eds.), *Fundamentals of Sentencing Theory: Essays in Honour of Andrew von Hirsch*, pp. 129–140 Oxford: Clarendon Press.

Kaufman, W. 2008. "The Rise and Fall of the Mixed Theory of Punishment." *International Journal of Applied Philosophy* 22(1): 37–57.

Lippke, R. L. 2011. "Retributive Sentencing, Multiple Offenders, and Bulk Discounts." In M. D. White (ed.), *Retributivism: Essays on Theory and Policy*, pp. 212–231. New York: Oxford University Press.

Ross, W. D. 1930. *The Right and the Good*. Oxford: Oxford University Press.

Ryberg, J. 2005. "Retributivism and Multiple Offending." *Res Publica* 11(3): 213–233.

Wood, D. 2002. "Retribution, Crime Reduction and the Justification of Punishment." *Oxford Journal of Legal Studies* 22(2): 301–321.

6

Parsimony and the Sentencing of Multiple Offenders

RICHARD L. LIPPKE

Theories of sentencing understandably focus on individuals being sentenced for single offenses.[1] To begin with, controversy exists about the aims of punishment and the priorities among those aims. Then there are the problems with translating a plausible account of those aims into a systematic sentencing scheme, one which will accommodate a broad array of offense types. Some of these problems are borne of information deficits. If one believes that crime prevention plays a crucial role in justifying the punishment of criminal offenders, limitations on what we know about its magnitude across the broad spectrum of crime and sanction types are well-known (Doob and Webster, 2003; Nagin, 1998; von Hirsch, et al., 1999). So are the difficulties in evaluating the benefits of criminal sanctions against their varied costs (Lippke, 2007). With retributive penal aims, the challenges are no less daunting, though they tend to be more conceptual or normative than empirical. In particular, our notions of cardinal proportionality seem too vague or variable to be readily translated into precise sentence ranges for the various crime types (Walker, 1991; Ryberg, 2004).

The challenges are compounded with multiple offenders; individuals being sentenced all at once for numerous criminal offenses. We might be tempted to refuse these further challenges, insisting that multiple offenders should be treated as we treat sequential nonmultiple offenders, by which I mean ordinary recidivists being sentenced for their most recent offenses. Recidivists are not given any sort of discount for having served previous sentences. Indeed, recidivists are typically given sentence enhancements for already having criminal histories (Roberts, 2008; Frase, 2013; Reitz, 2014). Yet many theorists balk at simply adding up the sentences appropriate for each of a multiple offender's crimes, thereby assigning them, in some cases, spectacularly long sentences. Instead, it is thought that multiple offenders should be given some kind of bulk discount at sentencing, to reduce the potentially devastating impact of the summation of the sentences for each of their various crimes (Ryberg, 2005). Such discounts are often grounded in one or another version of the totality principle, which caps sentences for multiple offenders so that they do not impose crippling penal losses on individuals (Ashworth, 2010). Further, as other essays in this volume show, it is important to distinguish among different kinds of multiple offenders, with some seemingly entitled to more in the way of bulk discounts than others. This suggests that no simple algorithm exists for the sentencing of multiple offenders.

It might therefore seem a dubious move to suggest that a further sentencing principle, widely known as the principle of parsimony (hereafter abbreviated PP), is worthy of our consideration in thinking about the sentencing of multiple offenders. Given that we already have enough to worry about in sentencing multiple offenders, it might be asked why we would seek to complicate matters further by introducing another sentencing principle. Yet the allure of the PP in this context is strong, as it is widely understood as a principle of moderation in sentencing, according to which offenders ought to be assigned sentences that are no longer or harsher than necessary to achieve legitimate penal aims (Frase, 2013; Tonry, 1992). If our aim is to prevent the sentences of multiple offenders from becoming too onerous, then the PP seems not only relevant to the debate about the sentencing of multiple offenders, but a principle that ought to be front and center in it.

Before we include it and further complicate the deliberative tasks associated with the sentencing of multiple offenders, I believe that we need to clarify what the PP means. My aim in the first two sections is to do precisely that. In the first section, I cast doubt on the PP as an independent, substantive sentencing principle. Though the PP seems more often associated with consequentialist crime reduction approaches to the justification of legal punishment, nothing in the usual abstract formulations of the principle preclude its use in retributive approaches to sentencing. However, the conclusion of the first section is that that PP seems little more than a derivative principle within both of the two main justificatory frameworks for legal punishment.

In the second section, I recast the PP as a second-order principle, that is, as a principle designed to help us better ensure that the traditional aims of sentencing are more fully realized. I distinguish crime reduction and retributive versions of the PP as a second-order principle, and consider how they might be integrated into a mixed theory of sentencing.

In the third section, I consider whether and to what extent the PP as a second-order principle is useful in thinking about the sentencing of multiple offenders. Initially, its role appears to be modest. The PP can be invoked to limit the sentences assigned to multiple offenders of certain kinds. But I argue that the PP might also play a role in determining sentence ranges for crime types, as well as in formulating broader penal and social policies. These implications of the PP might, in turn, help to alleviate some of the concerns about totaling up the sentences of multiple offenders, ones that push theorists toward supporting bulk discounts.

The Puzzle of Parsimony as an Independent Sentencing Principle

In spite of the high regard with which the PP is held by many sentencing theorists, it is more often invoked than carefully analyzed. Again, the PP says that we ought to punish persons for their crimes no more than is necessary to achieve appropriate penal aims. If we can punish offenders less and still achieve the aims of sentencing, then we ought to do so. The sentiment behind the PP seems to be this: legal punishment is a costly and damaging practice; the less of it we can get by with, the better. If we can "go low" or "go lower" and still accomplish whatever it is we hope to accomplish by inflicting criminal sanctions, then we ought to do so. This might especially be true if there are two or more sanctions that seem appropriate for a crime and one of them is less harsh or onerous. The PP tells us to err on the side of assigning less rather than more punishment if it is not clear that more is needed to achieve our penal purposes.

Initially, it might seem that the PP coheres better with consequentialist crime reduction approaches to the justification of legal punishment than with retributive ones. The former focus on the benefits of legal punishment, in the forms of deterrence, incapacitation, and rehabilitation, while taking into account its many costs and burdens. It seems fair to say that theorists who embrace crime reduction as the aim of legal punishment, or who are uneasy with retributivism, have more often cited the PP than those who whole-heartedly embrace retributive logic (Bentham, 1970; Tonry, 1992). If we can get as much crime reduction out of legal punishment from reduced sentences, then given its considerable negative consequences, we should opt for such sentences. Retributive theorists, by contrast, are not concerned to weigh the costs and benefits of legal punishment in figuring out how much to punish offenders. For them, the principle of proportionality is the primary guide to sentencing. Once we have figured out which sentences are proportional with what crimes, it would not seem that there is anything left to consider. Subsequently, I will suggest that there is a way to understand how the PP might play a role in a retributive sentencing scheme, although it is not one based on lowering the costs of legal punishment while preserving its benefits.

In spite of the seemingly natural fit between the PP and crime reduction logic, I believe that it is far from clear whether the PP can be shown to be a distinct principle within that logic. It will be useful to distinguish three levels at which the PP might apply. First, there is the distinction between offense types and offense tokens (Moore, 1993). Armed robbery, first-degree homicide, and embezzlement are all offense types. Particular armed robberies, first-degree homicides, and embezzlements are offense tokens. One plausible kind of sentencing scheme is one in which offense types are assigned sentence ranges based on whatever factors are deemed relevant by a theory of legal punishment. Judges who are given the task of setting the sentences for tokens then determine where, in the relevant sentencing range, the sentence for a token ought to fall. Yet to which task does the PP apply? To the determination of sentence ranges for offense types or to the determination of a sentence for an offense token? Or might the PP apply to both? My sense is that the PP is most often conceived as a principle for determining sentences for offense tokens. In that context, it encourages judges to search for and select shorter sentences if doing so will equally serve the aims of the sentencing scheme. As between two (or more) sentences that seem equally suitable with a view to crime reduction, the PP might counsel sentencing judges to select the mildest one.

Still, there seems no a priori reason why the PP cannot be used in setting sentence ranges for offense types. At that level, it might tell the agency responsible for setting sentence ranges—whether that agency consists of legislators or specially appointed sentencing commissions—to opt for lower sentence ranges so long as doing so will equally serve the aims of crime reduction. A third level at which the PP might play some role also should be distinguished (Ashworth, 2010). We might adopt broad social policies related to sentencing, ones that could be spurred, in part, by the PP. We could decide, for instance, to try to make less use of the harshest and most expensive kinds of legal sanctions, such as imprisonment, at least so long as doing so is consistent with furtherance of the aims of punishing offenders in the first place. Similarly, we might prefer less stigmatizing or exclusionary sanctions to ones that are more so, so long as employing the former does not detract from the attainment of legal punishment's purposes.

Armed with these distinctions, the puzzle concerning how the PP is a distinctive sentencing principle can be explained. Start with the consequentialist crime-reduction approach to legal punishment's justification. At the level of offense types, the logic of that approach tells us to adopt sentence ranges that maximize the benefits of legal punishment (in the forms of deterrence, incapacitation, or rehabilitation) while minimizing its burdens and drawbacks. By this logic we should bring sentence ranges down, thereby minimizing the burdens and drawbacks of sentences for offense types, if we can do so without sacrifice of the benefits of longer or harsher sentences. It is hard to see how the PP plays any distinctive role in this; it already seems incorporated into the logic of maximizing benefits and minimizing costs. Similarly, at the level of determining sentences for offense tokens, sentencing judges should weigh the benefits of sentences higher or lower in the relevant sentencing range against their costs or drawbacks. Once they have done so, and arrived at sentences for offense tokens that maximize benefits and minimize costs, what role remains for the PP to play? Is the idea that it tells us to go lower still? Perhaps, but not if doing so would sacrifice more-than-compensating benefits of legal punishment. Finally, at the level of social policy, we might indeed seek to use imprisonment less often or adopt more rehabilitative sanctions. Consequentialist logic supports doing so if (but only if) such policies could be expected to maximize the benefits of legal punishment while minimizing its costs. Once we make this explicit, it is not clear how the PP adds anything to the consequentialist approach to thinking about what social policies to adopt with respect to legal punishment. At most, it seems to be a derivative principle within the larger consequentialist, crime reduction framework.

Next, consider positive retributive approaches to sentencing. According to them, we are to adopt sentences that proportion legal punishment to the criminal deserts of offenders. At the level of offense types, positive retributivists can admit that we ought to have sentence ranges. After all, offense types are broad enough to encompass differences among offenders that retributivists recognize as relevant to sentencing, such as the harms produced by their crimes or the culpability of offending agents. Of course, sentence ranges should probably have firm upper and lower bounds, presumably set with an eye to keeping penal harms commensurate with the harms caused by the different types of offenses (Lippke, 2012). For positive retributivists, maintaining proportion in sentencing is the be-all and end-all; it is not apparent how looking to reduce sanction levels further, as the PP would seem to mandate, makes any sense unless doing so is necessary to achieve proportionality (Ryberg, 2005).

Similar considerations hold for the sentencing of offense tokens. The sentencing judge's task is to determine where, in the relevant range, a particular offender's crime falls, taking into account such things as the harm done by the token (or threatened or attempted by it) and the offender's degree of culpability in inflicting it. Once the appropriate sentence for an offense token is determined in this way, seeking to "go lower" still, as the PP appears to advise, would make little sense within positive retributivist logic. At the social policy level, it is not immediately apparent what guidance a positive retributivist approach would offer, since it is focused on giving offenders what they deserve, rather than on reducing the financial costs or negative effects of legal punishment. But one possibility is this: some forms of legal punishment might not sit well with retributive commitments to ensuring that criminal sanctions comport with the dignity of persons. Lengthy imprisonment, or imprisonment under conditions of solitary confinement, might degrade offenders by eroding their capacities for moral self-governance. Positive retributivists could support social policies aimed at reducing prison terms or ameliorating the conditions of confinement for this reason (Lippke, 2007; Lippke, 2009). However, retributivist support for such policies seems more a matter of attempting to bring the institutions or practices of legal punishment in line with the deeper logic of the theory. The PP, as a distinct principle, adds little to the case for doing so.

Lastly, things might appear more hopeful with limiting retributivism, which can be understood as setting upper and lower limits to penal sanctions, determined by desert considerations, while permitting other sentencing aims to be pursued within those limits (Morris, 1982; Frase, 2013). The PP would not appear to have much, if any, role to play in setting the upper and lower limits of sentence ranges for offense types. Those are to be determined by retributive logic. However, when it comes to the sentencing of offense tokens, judges would usually not be permitted to exceed the limits, especially at the upper end of the range, but also would not be required or expected to assign sanctions up to them. They could take into account the other sentencing aims, typically, ones aimed at crime reduction. If a particular offender seemed less dangerous than most who committed the type of offense in question, or more susceptible to rehabilitation, then a sentence lower in the relevant range should be assigned. Although this looks like it leaves room for parsimony in sentencing, it really does not. The lowering of the sentence is dictated by the logic of limiting retributivism. Once the sentence for an offense token has been determined by the combination of desert limits and the other relevant sentencing considerations, whatever they turn out to be, the PP seems left with no role to play. Are we to look for a lower sentence still, even if it does not serve any legitimate penal aims? It is unclear why we would want to do that.

Some limiting retributivists propose sentencing schemes with upper limits set by desert considerations but no lower ones (Frase, 2013). On such approaches there be can be too much punishment assigned to offenders, but never too little. This might seem to comport with the PP. Although sentencing judges should never (or rarely) assign sentences that exceed the upper limits of the sentence range for an offense type, they should not worry about going too low if no other sentencing purpose, usually in the form of crime reduction, is thereby disserved. Yet I do not see how such an approach gains much from the PP. If one rejects lower limits, then one is left with crime reduction considerations in determining sentences for offense tokens. That means, as we have already seen, that the sentencing judge should simply look to maximize the benefits and minimize the costs of sanctioning the offender. The logic of consequentialism tells us that; what the PP tells us, distinct from that, is unclear.

In any case, I doubt that limiting retributivism is reasonably interpreted as eschewing lower limits to sentence ranges for offense types. Consider offense types that have identifiable victims whose interests were harmed by the crimes committed against them. It would seem that minima of punishment ought to be assigned the culpable perpetrators of such harms, which minima should vary by the extent of the standard harms the offense types inflict, or else the rights of the victims will not be validated because the state does not symbolically stand for them (Hampton, 1991). Just as criminal sanctions can punish disproportionately by assigning sanctions the harms from which substantially exceed the harms perpetrated by offenses, so they can punish disproportionately by imposing insufficient censure and hard treatment on individuals who harm others unjustifiably.

Making a New Start: Finding a Role for Parsimony

In the previous section, I argued that it is unclear how the PP makes a distinctive contribution to sentencing theory, at least with respect to what I take to be the main contending sentencing approaches. Before abandoning the PP entirely, however, I want, in this section, to see if I can find and defend a role for it. I believe that its most defensible role is as a second-order sentencing principle, one designed to help us devise and implement sentencing schemes that comport more fully and deeply with the logic of crime reduction and retributive approaches to sentencing.

Maybe the way to think about the PP in relation to the crime reduction approach to sentencing is this: it is a reminder, of sorts, that we consistently underestimate the costs and harms flowing from legal punishment, while simultaneously overestimating its benefits. Hence, we should look for ways to reduce the length or harshness of criminal sanctions, with some confidence that in doing so, we will arrive at sanctions that come closer to the aims of maximization. We overestimate the benefits of criminal sanctions because we tend to rely on simple heuristics about offenders—that they are rational beings responsive to the "price" of offending. Or, if offenders do not so respond, we think that by getting them off the streets for some period of time, we make the streets safer. The evidence about the limited deterrent and incapacitation impact of criminal sanctions reveals the complexity of offenses and offending, and thus the doubtful nature of the heuristics on which we tend to rely, but those heuristics retain powerful intuitive appeal. We underestimate the negative consequences of legal punishment because we tend to focus solely on the immediate and most salient ones. Offenders locked in prison lose their freedom and we all admit that such a loss is painful. However, the further psychological, social, and economic costs of legal punishment for offenders are more subtle and might dog them for years after the completion of their formal sentences. Thus we discount them, or do not know quite how to count them. The same goes for the effects of legal sanctions on offenders' families and the broader communities from whence they came and to which they will return. In light of this tendency toward asymmetry in our consequentialist accounting, the PP performs a useful role in urging us to consider less harmful or costly sanctions than the ones upon which we might initially hit, whether at the type or token level. It could also be employed at the level of social policy, counseling us to consider alternatives to legal punishment (e.g., improved educational opportunities for poor children) that might reduce offending as much if not more and have fewer damaging effects on persons. So interpreted, the PP is not an independent sentencing principle, but a corrective one designed to get us closer to the goal of optimal crime reduction.[2]

Is there a way to interpret the PP to give it a role in retributive approaches to sentencing (and by extension, in mixed approaches)? Elsewhere, I have argued that there is, though again, that role is not as an independent sentencing principle (Lippke, 2009). Instead, a retributive PP might perform two functions. First, it could draw our attention to the myriad ways in which offenders, sanctions, and the larger social order fail to robustly satisfy the conditions for just punishment. Retributive theories of punishment make sense only against a complicated normative and conceptual backdrop: those liable to legal punishment must be morally self-governing beings who freely chose to violate the criminal law, though they had reasonable opportunities to avoid doing so and no excuse or justification for doing so. When they are punished for their transgressions, they are to be treated as beings who can grasp the wrongness of what they have done and the rebuke to their conduct of which legal punishment consists. To put it mildly, legal punishment in the real world often occurs in ways and against individuals who fail to satisfy one or more of these conditions.

Many criminal offenders are youths and so still works in progress when it comes to their capacities for moral self-governance (Zimring, 1998; Feld, 2008). Also, many offenders have forms of mental illness or mental disability that compromise their capacities for moral self-governance (James and Glaze, 2006). Some are psychopaths and so might lack the capacity for moral self-governance altogether (Harris, Skilling, and Rice, 2001). Many more are poor and sometimes desperately so; though their offending is not entirely involuntary, it seems plausible to say that diminished opportunities undermine the voluntariness of their choices to offend (Lippke, 2011a). Social deprivation might also stunt or warp their capacities for moral self-governance, making them too focused on short-term gratification or hostile to the established social and legal order. Note also that the collateral consequences of legal punishment will make the socially deprived even more desperate than they were before their arrests and convictions (Travis, 2002).

Second, retributivists must be concerned about more than maintaining proportionality in sentencing. They must also worry about the potential for penal sanctions to degrade individuals, thereby turning them into beings who are no longer attuned to the censure of their acts that legal punishment is designed to communicate. Imprisonment that goes on for too long, or that imposes harsh conditions on inmates regardless of their duration, can erode or destroy the capacities of individuals for moral self-governance. Other criminal sanctions besides imprisonment, especially highly stigmatizing ones, might do so as well, by making it nearly impossible for ex-offenders to find work and reintegrate into communities.[3] Yet there seems some tendency to ignore or sleight the ways in which criminal sanctions undermine the conditions for responsible agency, perhaps because it is tempting to demonize offenders or let our resentment of their crimes blind us to the effects of our penal institutions upon them. A retributive PP might serve as a corrective in this regard, prompting us to search for forms of punishment that do not contravene fundamental retributive limits on legal punishment.

In short, the retributive PP plumbs the deeper logic of retributive punishment and, in light of real-world shortcomings or the destructive tendencies of criminal sanctions, urges mildness in sentencing. How much it does so depends on the divergence between retributive assumptions about the appropriate subjects and structure of legal punishment and real-world conditions and the actors in it. Some forms of parsimony in retributive punishment might be implemented most usefully at the sentencing of specific offenders (based on their youthfulness or struggles with mental illness). Other forms might be implemented as we devise sentence ranges for offense types. If we are convinced that imprisonment subtly erodes the moral responsiveness of offenders, we might reduce sentences ranges generally for the more serious types of offenses. Finally, other aspects of retributive parsimony might support the need for broader social policy changes, in particular ones designed to address the worrisome effects of social deprivation.

Mixed theories of sentencing, such as negative retributivism, could call upon both the retributive and crime reduction versions of the PP. The former could be invoked to motivate reductions in the sentence ranges for imprisonable offense types, thereby limiting their degrading tendencies, as well as to motivate lower sentences within a range for offense tokens, based on such reduced culpability factors as youthfulness, addiction, or mental illness. The crime reduction version of the PP would be most plausibly invoked in the sentencing of offense tokens. It would remind sentencing judges to assign sentences lower in the relevant range given the seemingly natural tendency to inflate the benefits of sentences and discount or ignore their costs.

Elsewhere in this volume, Richard Frase suggests another way of understanding the PP, one that also seems to treat it as a second-order sentencing principle (Frase, 2017). On Frase's account, sentencing judges might sometimes be unsure about which of two sentences to assign an offense token, one that possibly overpunishes the token or one that possibly underpunishes it. In such situations, Frase urges judges to err on the side of parsimony and thus possible underpunishment. We should give offenders the benefit of the doubt in the face of uncertainty about how much to punish them, much as we give possibly guilty offenders the benefit of the doubt by refusing to convict them unless the evidence against them is convincing beyond a reasonable doubt.

Frase's version of the PP as a second-order principle would seem to have more limited applicability than either of the versions I have proposed. It will apply only in sentencing offense tokens and then only when judges are unsure about which of two (or perhaps more) sentences optimally serve appropriate penal aims. The versions I propose can apply to the sentencing of tokens, to determining sentence ranges for offense types, and to determining broader penal policies. Also, there seems a difference between being innocent and suffering punishment and being guilty and suffering slightly too much punishment, as might be the case if the sentencing judge eschewed Frase's version of the PP. It is especially awful to be punished at all if one is innocent of offending, in ways that it is considerably less awful to be punished a bit more than one deserves or that crime reduction considerations require if one is, in fact, guilty. Notice also that one of the things that makes punishment of the innocent so bad is that not only are the innocent wronged, but the guilty get off scot free. There is no analogous problem in cases of slight overpunishment. Finally, Frase's version of the PP seems somewhat unmotivated compared with the two versions I propose. It makes sense to reduce penal sanctions if we systematically overestimate their benefits while ignoring their many costs and burdens, or if we consistently exaggerate the extent to which offenders are fully and solely responsible for their crimes. By contrast, Frase's version tells us to prefer slight underpunishment of the guilty to slight overpunishment of them. But why? The analogy with preferring nonpunishment of the innocent to punishment of the guilty is all that Frase offers, yet it seems less than fully convincing.

Parsimony and Multiple Offenders

Now that we have uncovered some useful role for the PP to play in sentencing, the next question is what, if any, role might it play in the sentencing of multiple offenders. As many of the other essays in this volume make clear, there are intuitively attractive grounds for limiting the overall penal bite of multiple-offense sentences. Moreover, judges in many legal jurisdictions seek to limit the impact of multiple sentences, whether any discernible theoretical basis for their practices can be identified and defended or not. In other words, there seems both intuitive and practical support for finding some middle ground between "pure consecutivism," according to which the sentences for a multiple offender would simply be totaled up, and "pure concurrentivism," according to which multiple offenders would serve the sentence for the worst of their crimes, with the rest folded in and thus not allowed to add to the sentence assigned for their worst crime.

Pure concurrentivism is not without its attractions, as it would set definite upper limits on the sentences to be meted out to multiple offenders. Yet its logic seems dubious on both crime reduction and retributive grounds in relation to certain kinds of multiple offenders. Even if we are skeptical about the magnitude of the deterrent effects of marginally longer sentences, as we should be, there seems wisdom in providing some multiple offenders with incentives to desist from further offenses. Consider individuals who undertake temporally extended sequences of crimes. By punishing those who continue offending more than those who leave off earlier, we create incentives for persons to desist from further offending once they have begun. Granted, some multiple offenses occur all at once, as it were, as when someone kills or injures numerous people by exploding a bomb. Such multiple offenders cannot be deterred, once they have killed or injured one or two or five people, from killing or injuring more. Nonetheless, the prospect of longer sentences for their planned crimes, based on the accumulation of victims, might give them pause. Further, some multiple offenders will appear to be quite dangerous because of the severity or frequency of their crimes. We might therefore seek to incapacitate them for longer periods of time than concurrent sentencing would permit.

For retributivists, concurrent sentencing seems most problematic when an offender injures or kills numerous victims over an extended period of time but is to be sentenced, all at once, for his multiple offenses. Intuitively, a person who rapes or kills five people ought to be punished more than an offender who rapes or kills one. I have referred to this as the "each victim counts" principle (or EVC) (Lippke, 2011b). The EVC principle need not be construed as requiring consecutive sentences in multiple victim cases, only something more than concurrent ones.

The reasons for rejecting concurrent sentences in some cases must be balanced against those for not permitting sentences for multiple offenders to become, in total, too harsh. At least three different versions of the so-called totality principle can be identified, two of which are retributive or desert-based, and one of which is consequentialist.[4] On one retributive version, we should not let the sentences assigned to multiple offenders become comparatively (or ordinally) unjust.[5] Comparative injustice will occur if a multiple offender, all of whose crimes were at or below a given level of seriousness, is assigned an overall sentence that is appropriate only for a much more serious offense or group of offenses. For instance, we should not punish a person being sentenced for multiple frauds or embezzlements as we would a person for even a single violent rape or homicide. If we are to avoid doing so, we must not only give the multiple offender a bulk discount but perhaps an escalating one, so that once he receives a sentence for a first offense, each subsequent offense adds increasingly little to his overall sentence. Of course, if among a multiple offender's several crimes was one or more quite serious ones, then this version of the totality principle might not function to constrain his sentence very much.

A second retributive version of the totality principle focuses more on the absolute severity of sentences than their relative severity. It advises us to not assign sentences to multiple offenders that are absolutely, as it were, disproportionate with the harms they inflicted on any single victim. Even if, for instance, an individual has perpetrated numerous frauds over a period of time for which she is now to be sentenced, she should not be assigned a sentence that inflicts penal harms on her that greatly exceed the harms done to any one of her victims. Again, this version of the totality principle might require not only bulk discounts but escalating ones, to ward off an accumulation of penal harms that swamps the harms done to any one victim. However, this second version of the totality principle might do little to shield an individual from a lengthy sentence if all of her crimes were quite serious, since any one of her offenses might have inflicted devastating harm on some victim.

A third version of the totality principle encourages us to weigh the good and bad consequences of assigning multiple offenders longer sentences, and to seek to maximize the former relative to the latter. Suppose that we believe it is necessary to assign certain kinds of multiple offenders longer sentences than the sentences we assign nonmultiple offenders in order to promote deterrence or effect incapacitation. Nonetheless, both of these benefits of longer sentences tend to have diminishing marginal utility. Most offenders "age out," even many serious offenders (Nagin, 1998). Keeping them in prisons past the aging out point is costly to them and to the rest of us and produces few benefits. This suggests that bulk discounts are in order, and perhaps escalating ones if the crimes in question are quite numerous or serious. Likewise, we do not want to exaggerate the deterrent effects of longer sentences or ignore their negative consequences. Perhaps longer sentences will give some multiple offenders incentives to cease offending sooner rather than later, but there is little reason to believe that the power of such incentives progressively rises or is effective beyond a certain point. Meanwhile, the costs and burdens of lengthy sentences do not tend to diminish as rapidly, if they diminish at all. All of this should lead us to endorse bulk discounts, whether steep or escalating ones.

Let us suppose that the various versions of the totality principle give us grounds for rejecting consecutivism in the sentencing of multiple offenders, and therefore that some policy of bulk discounting is the most plausible approach to their sentencing. Obviously, hard questions remain about what is the most defensible form of bulk discounting. As we undertake finding it, how, if at all, might the PP come into the mix of conflicting considerations that pull us one way or the other in thinking about the sentencing of multiple offenders?

Consider, first, the crime reduction version of the PP that I have sketched. Again, I have cast it as a second-order principle, one that helps us to arrive at optimal sentences by reminding us of our tendency to overestimate the benefits of punishment while downplaying its negative consequences. One way in which the PP, so understood, might usefully come into play in thinking about the sentencing of multiple offenders is by curbing our enthusiasm for deterrence-based or incapacitation-based add-ons for multiple offenders. True, we might think it useful sometimes to assign some multiple offenders longer sentences than we assign nonmultiple ones in order to maintain incentives to discontinue crime sprees sooner rather than later. But not only is our evidence concerning the deterrent effects of marginally harsher sentences less than impressive, the PP tells us that there is a tendency to exaggerate them while ignoring their costs and burdens. This would seem to point us in the direction of modest enhancements over and above the sentence appropriate for a multiple offender's most serious offense. In other words, steep bulk discounts for multiple offenders are apt to be good-to-bad consequence maximizing, compared with modest or slight ones. Similar considerations hold with regard to sentence enhancements for multiple offenders that aim at incapacitating them. Not only is there the aging out effect noted previously, but some kinds of offenses (e.g., drug sales) are not reduced in society by sentencing offenders to lengthy prison terms (Zimring and Hawkins, 1997). The PP might work to remind us that, in some cases, sentencing multiple offenders to lengthy prison terms is very costly not only to them but to society and produces few crime reduction benefits. Even if the totality principle should produce bulk discounts in sentencing, the PP might push us toward larger or escalating ones.

Next, consider the retributive version of the PP. The ways in which many criminal offenders or the social conditions in which they live fall short of satisfying the demanding criteria for retributively just punishment should lead us to assign them less than their fully deserved sentences. Presumably, this will be true when they are being sentenced for multiple offenses. The PP-based discounts for any given offense should be aggregated for multiple ones, thereby reducing overall sentences. Also, consider how the cumulative effects of multiple sentences imposed without any bulk discounting might run afoul of the retributive nondegradation constraint. Even if the sentence for each of several offenses is reduced based on the failure of society to satisfy the conditions of just punishment, collectively they might add up to a total sentence that, in the absence of some further discounting, could consign individuals to such lengthy terms of imprisonment as to cripple their prospects for having and exercising responsible moral agency. Lengthy imprisonment, even under more humane conditions than are currently the norm in many countries, has a decided tendency to gradually erode inmates' capacities for self-governance and self-control (Haney, 2006). Individuals who, for many years, are told what to do and when to do it eventually come to rely on external control and direction. Not only does this degrade them, it sets them up for failure once they are allowed to return to civil society. The retributive PP might therefore support bulk discounts for multiple offenders to ensure that their overall sentences do not run afoul of the nondegradation constraint.

If we move away from the sentencing of particular multiple offenders, to the construction of sentence ranges for offense types, the versions of the PP I have identified might support shorter sentences in general, and thus reduce the problematic character of multiple offender sentencing. It is tempting to presume the sentencing status quo, which in some countries (the United States foremost among them) is rather dispiriting. If we assume lengthy sentences for all crimes, or for most of them, with jails and prisons that are squalid and damaging, then the prospect of having to assign multiple offenders very long sentences, based on their accumulation of crimes, is daunting. Substantial bulk discounts will seem the only way to avoid the imposition of catastrophic penal harms on such individuals. Yet it is far from clear that either crime reduction or retributive logic supports existing sentences or confinement conditions, and the two versions of the PP can be called upon to help explain why this is so.

If there is a tendency on the part of legislators or sentencing commissions to overestimate the crime reduction benefits of longer sentences, while systematically underestimating the negative effects of longer sentences, then the consequentialist version of the PP will encourage them to go back and recalculate sentence ranges for crime types in ways that should bring those ranges down. This would then mean that each of the distinct sentences that multiple offenders faced would be shorter, even without bulk discounts motivated by the PP or the totality principle. Also, there might be some tendency for lawmakers to focus on deterrence and incapacitation as the main components of a crime reduction approach to sentencing. Yet this ignores the role of rehabilitation in sentencing and its potential for significant costs savings. As consequentialists have long understood, we will be better off, in the long term, if those prone to criminal offending desist on their own due to enhanced self-control or strengthened commitments to social responsibility. Deterrence and incapacitation are costly ways in which to reduce offending, compared with rehabilitation, and the consequentialist PP might remind legislators and sentencing commissions of this important point as they devise sentences for offense types. Notice how less harsh and more rehabilitative sentences would alleviate some of the concerns raised by the accumulated sentences of multiple offenders. Simply put, the aggregation of sentences each one of which aims at rehabilitation is less worrisome than the aggregation of sentences each one of which emphasizes hard treatment and little else.

In similar ways, the retributive version of the PP should remind those who determine sentence ranges for offense types that the length of sentences, or the harshness of prison conditions, can both work to compromise the moral capacities of offenders in ways that do not cohere with retributive presuppositions about the appropriate subjects of legal punishment. Also, if we could convince legislators and sentencing commissions that most offenders tend to not fully satisfy the conditions of just punishment, they might be persuaded to reduce sentence ranges for offense types for that reason. Even if retributivists must endorse the consecutive sentencing of multiple offenders, as some in this volume argue, the implications of doing so might not be as ominous as they think if retributive parsimony strongly counsels against the lengthy sentences and prison conditions that are currently the norm in some countries.

Both versions of the PP might also have implications at the social policy level that would indirectly help with the problems raised by multiple-offense sentencing. Both could conceivably support efforts to reduce social deprivation, ensure universal and fully adequate mental healthcare, and undertake more pro-active social efforts to ensure occupational training and decently paying jobs for those who have traditionally been disadvantaged or to those left unemployed by business closings or relocations. Consequentialist crime reductionists would support measures such as these on different grounds than retributivists. The former would emphasize the long-term cost savings of reduced crime and the inevitable punishment outlays that follow; the latter would emphasize the background conditions of justice and support for individual responsibility that make legal punishment fully defensible. On either account, it is conceivable that social orders that were more attentive to reducing criminogenic social conditions would have fewer offenders to sentence, including fewer multiple offenders.

Conclusion

The conclusions to be drawn from the preceding discussion with respect to the PP are mixed, though more positive than negative. I have argued that the PP is not an independent sentencing principle. Instead, it is better understood as a second-order principle designed to encourage judges, sentencing commissions, and legislators to more carefully craft sentencing practices so as to ensure that they comport fully with the aims and logic of crime reduction and retribution. If state officials take the PP seriously, they will be more apt to adopt sentences, punishment practices, and social welfare schemes that are less costly, damaging, and criminogenic. These salutary effects will percolate down, in a variety of ways, to the sentencing of multiple offenders.

Notes

1. My sincere thanks to the many participants in the Oxford Multiple Sentencing Seminar who offered helpful comments concerning an earlier draft of this chapter.
2. There might be other second-order principles of particular relevance to consequentialists. For instance, we might, in general, overcount short-term consequences while consistently undercounting longer-term ones. This suggests the need for a second-order principle that reminds us not to ignore or unreasonably discount long-term consequences. Such a second-order principle would be relevant in numerous contexts, including the criminal justice context. The particular salience of the PP, as a second-order principle in the criminal justice context, might be traced to our tendency to ignore or discount the negative effects of legal punishment on persons whose interests we have less regard for precisely because they are stigmatized by punishment practices.
3. Massaro (1991) expresses these concerns about the exclusionary effects of so-called shaming sanctions.
4. Anthony Bottoms (1998) identifies a fourth version of the totality principle, according to which multiple offenders should not be sentenced in ways that deprive them of "high proportion of the prime years of his life." However, Bottoms's version of the principle seems unattractive in cases in which offenders have deprived victims, and perhaps numerous ones, of their entire lives or a high proportion of the prime years of them.
5. Von Hirsch (1993) distinguishes between ordinal and cardinal proportionality.

References

Ashworth, A. 2010. *Sentencing and Criminal Justice*. 5th ed. Cambridge: Cambridge University Press.

Bentham, J. 1970. *An Introduction to the Principles of Morals and Legislation*. In J. H. Burns and H. L. A. Hart (eds.), *The Collected Works of Jeremy Bentham*. London: The Athlone Press.

Bottoms, A. E. 1998. "Five Puzzles in von Hirsch's Theory of Punishment." In A. Ashworth and M. Wasik (eds.), *Fundamentals of Sentencing Theory: Essays in Honour of Andrew von Hirsch*, pp. 53–100. Oxford: Oxford University Press.

Doob, A. N., and C. M. Webster. 2003. "Sentence Severity and Crime: Accepting the Null Hypothesis." In M Tonry (ed.), *Crime and Justice: A Review of Research* 30: 143–195. Chicago: University of Chicago Press.

Feld, B. C. 2008. "A Slower Form of Death: Implications of *Roper v. Simmons* for Juveniles Sentenced to Life without Parole." *Notre Dame Journal of Law, Ethics, and Public Policy* 22(1): 9–65.

Frase, R. S. 2013. *Just Sentencing: Principles and Procedures for a Workable System*. New York: Oxford University Press.

Hampton, J. 1991. "A New Theory of Retribution." In R. G. Frey and C. W. Morris (eds.), *Liability and Responsibility: Essays in Law and Morals*, pp. 377–414. Cambridge: Cambridge University Press.

Haney, C. 2006. *Reforming Punishment: Psychological Limits to the Pains of Imprisonment*. Washington, DC: American Psychological Association.

Harris, G. T., T. A. Skilling, and M. E. Rice. 2001. "The Construct of Psychopathy." In M. Tonry (ed.), *Crime and Justice: A Review of Research* 28: 197–264. Chicago: University of Chicago Press.

James, D. J., and L. E. Glaze. 2006. "Mental Health Problems of Prison and Jail Inmates." *Bureau of Justice Statistics Special Report*. Washington, DC: US Department of Justice.

Lippke, R. L. 2007. *Rethinking Imprisonment*. Oxford: Oxford University Press.

Lippke, R. L. 2009. "Retributive Parsimony." *Res Publica* 15: 377–395.

Lippke, R. L. 2011a. "Social Deprivation as Tempting Fate." *Criminal Law & Philosophy* 5(3): 277–291.

Lippke, R. L. 2011b. "Retributive Sentencing, Multiple Offenders, and Bulk Discounts." In M. D. White (ed.), *Retributivism: Essays on Theory and Policy*, pp. 212–231. New York: Oxford University Press.

Lippke, R. L. 2012. "Anchoring the Sentencing Scale: A Modest Proposal." *Theoretical Criminology* 16(4): 463–480.

Massaro, T. M. 1991. "Shame, Culture, and American Criminal Law." *Michigan Law Review* 89(7): 1880–1944.

Moore, M. 1993. *Act and Crime: The Philosophy of Action and Its Implications for Criminal Law*. Oxford: Oxford University Press.

Morris, N. 1982. *Madness and the Criminal Law*. Chicago: University of Chicago Press.

Nagin, D.S. 1998. "Deterrence and Incapacitation." In M. Tonry (ed.), *The Handbook of Crime and Punishment*, pp. 345–368. New York: Oxford University Press.

Reitz, K. 2014. "The Illusion of Proportionality: Desert and Repeat Offenders." In J. V. Roberts and A. von Hirsch (eds.), *Previous Convictions at Sentencing: Theoretical and Applied Perspectives*, pp. 137–159. Oxford: Hart Publishing.

Roberts, J. V. 2008. "Punishing Persistence: Explaining the Enduring Appeal of the Recidivist Sentencing Premium." *British Journal of Criminology* 48(4): 468–481.

Ryberg, J. 2004. *The Ethics of Proportionate Punishment: A Critical Investigation*. Dordrecht: Kluwer Academic Publishers.

Ryberg, J. 2005. "Retributivism and Multiple Offending." *Res Publica* 11(3): 213–233.

Tonry, M. 1992. "Proportionality, Parsimony, and the Interchangeability of Punishments." In R. A. Duff, S. Marshall, R. E. Dobash, and R. P. Dobash (eds.), *Penal Theory and Penal Practice*, pp. 59–83. Manchester: Manchester University Press.

Travis, J. 2002. "Invisible Punishment: An Instrument of Social Exclusion." In M. Mauer and M. Chesney-Lind (eds.), *The Collateral Consequences of Mass Imprisonment*, pp. 15–36. New York: The New Press.

Von Hirsch, A. 1993. *Censure and Sanctions*. Oxford: Clarendon Press.

Von Hirsch, A., A. E. Bottoms, E. Burney, and P-O. Wikström. 1999. *Criminal Deterrence and Sentence Severity: An Analysis of Recent Research*. Oxford: Hart Publishing.

Walker, N. 1991. *Why Punish? Theories of Punishment Reassessed*. Oxford: Oxford University Press.

Zimring, F. 1998. "Towards A Jurisprudence of Youth Violence." In M. Tonry (ed.), *Crime and Justice: A Review of Research* 24: 477–501. Chicago: University of Chicago Press.

Zimring, F., and G. Hawkins. 1997. *Incapacitation: Penal Confinement and the Restraint of Crime*. New York: Oxford University Press.

7

Multiple Offenders and the Question of Desert

YOUNGJAE LEE

Introduction

The headlines are staggering: "Justices Decline Case on a 200-Year Sentence for Man Who Possessed Child Pornography" (Greenhouse, 2007); "Life Sentence for Possession of Child Pornography Spurs Debate Over Severity" (Goode, 2011); "Ex-Headmaster Sentenced to 50 Years for Child Porn" (Barrish and Reyes, 2015). To be sure, people are not exactly lining up to defend the practice of viewing recordings of child sex abuse for pleasure. Nevertheless, it is a commonly held belief that these are disproportionate punishments for possessing child pornography, especially compared to similar sentences handed down for crimes like murder (Goode, 2011; Sulzberger, 2010).

If such heavy punishments are being imposed by the system, why is it happening? There are many proposed explanations: prosecutorial abuses of power, harsh judges, tough-on-crime lawmakers, mandatory sentencing laws, unfair plea bargaining practices, weak constitutional protections against excessive punishments, and so on. In order to identify, though, whether these features of our criminal justice system are producing excessive punishments, we first need a standard to measure whether these punishments are indeed excessive.

Punishments in child pornography possession cases often appear excessive for two reasons. First, there is controversy surrounding how serious the crime of possession of child pornography actually is (Bazelon, 2013; Hessick, 2011). Second, punishments can quickly reach sky-high levels due to the ease of amassing hundreds of images on one's computer and the practice of determining punishments by the number of images in one's possession. This article focuses on the latter issue—the problem of multiple offenses committed by a single offender.

In all the headline stories mentioned above, the offenders violated laws banning possession of child pornography multiple times by having multiple images, and the fact that they were facing multiple counts at least partially explains the kinds of punishment they ended up facing. For instance, Morton Berger received a 200-year sentence by receiving 10 years per image (*State v. Berger*, 2006). Daniel Enrique Guevara Vilca was charged with 454 counts of possession of child pornography, one count per image found on his computer, and received a life sentence without parole (Goode, 2011). Christopher Wheeler had more than 2,000 images, was charged with 25 counts of possession of child pornography, and received a 50-year sentence, two years per count (Barrish and Reyes, 2015).

Even though the problem of sentencing multiple offenders is unusually starkly raised in child pornography possession cases for the reasons mentioned, it is of course not unique to that context, as the problem is much more general. Should it make a difference not only what crimes people commit, but how many times they commit them? If so, what is the appropriate way of thinking about what each instance of lawbreaking is worth? Should every instance of lawbreaking be worth the same amount of time in prison? Should we simply add up the punishment for each charge to arrive at the final sentence, or should there be, as some theorists have dubbed it, a bulk discount for multiple offenders through concurrently imposed sentences (Jareborg, 1998)? If the punishment for each offense is set at an appropriate level, would simply adding them up ever lead to an excessive punishment? If so, why, and is there a different way of thinking about multiple offenses?

According to a number of scholars, theories of sentencing that use principles of desert and proportionality to determine sentences have trouble arriving at a view other than the consecutive approach of adding the punishment for each offense and arriving at the final number. Anthony Bottoms, for instance, has remarked that "for the desert theorist, . . . the 'discount for bulk offending' . . . clearly presents potentially quite severe theoretical difficulties" (Bottoms, 1998). Martin Wasik, too, has observed that the desert theory "at face value . . . suggests that for multiple offenders each offence should receive its appropriate sentence and it is simply a matter of adding up the individual terms" (Wasik, 2012). Andrew Ashworth, who is committed to the proportionality theory yet rejects the consecutive approach, has acknowledged that a "logical approach, following desert theory and the principle of proportionality, would be to ensure that each offence receives its appropriate sentence" (Ashworth, 2010).

This essay argues that, contrary to these initial impressions, bulk discounts are appropriate—and even mandatory—from the just deserts perspective and that, as a general matter, there should be a substantial reduction in sentence for each additional offense when sentencing multiple offenders. Briefly stated, this essay argues as follows: punishment and conviction send the message not only that a person has acted wrongfully but that he has acted wrongfully in a way that reflects poorly on him as a person. If multiple offenses simply add up to produce a sentence, the system could end up sending a message about how "bad" the offender is, and such a message could be unfair, if a person who steals, for instance, is described to be as "bad" as a person who kills. Consecutive sentencing as a way of determining punishment is wrong, then, because it would permit such unfair messages. However, this does not mean that single-crime offenders and multiple offenders should be treated the same way; multiple offenders are more culpable than single-crime offenders and their sentences should reflect that. Such sentences, though, should not exceed the limit set by the aforementioned fairness considerations.

Although this essay thus defends a sentencing practice that is familiar and has been defended by others (Ashworth, 2010; Bennett, 2011; Bottoms, 1998; Jareborg, 1998; Lippke, 2011), the idea of a "discount" for multiple offenders is mysterious. Bulk discount is a tactic that commercial enterprises offer to encourage large purchases, and, in the criminal context, of course, multiple offending is not something to be made attractive. In addition, some argue that bulk discounting for repeat offenses is in considerable tension with another common sentencing practice, the recidivist premium, which refers to the harsher punishment that the criminal justice system gives to offenders with previous convictions (Reitz, 2010). Thus, one question this essay asks is whether we can give a theoretical account of sentencing discounts for multiple offenders and articulate how it relates to the recidivist premium.

The topic of this essay is not merely of theoretical interest, however. First, as the examples given above illustrate, not having a clear understanding of how to treat multiple offenders fairly could lead to excessively harsh punishments through consecutive sentencing of multiple offenses. Second, the problem of injustice due to consecutive sentencing may be more serious and widespread—and the theoretical issue thus more urgent—than it may appear from the actual sentences handed down. Several contributions in this volume assume that the discount for bulk offending is both widespread and just, which gives the impression that the status quo is more or less unobjectionable and that the main task left for scholars is to give a theoretical account to rationalize and improve upon the status quo (Ashworth and Wasik, this volume; Frase, this volume; Roberts and de Keijser, this volume). It seems to me that it is a mistake to make such an assumption given the practice of plea bargaining (Stuntz, 2011). As long as a genuine threat of a lengthy sentence looms, enabled by the possibility of consecutive sentencing of multiple offenses, prosecutors' hands are strengthened at the plea bargaining stage. Defendants, facing a choice between fighting the charges and facing massive sentences upon a loss at trial and entering a guilty plea and having a discounted sentence from dropped charges in exchange, may be pressured into admitting guilt. Even if these defendants thus end up with sentences that look reasonable, they may still be victims of artificially engineered sanctions prosecutors use to bludgeon them into submission. If certain consecutive sentences can be taken simply off the table on fairness grounds, such abuses of power can be prevented.

Overview of Essay

This essay proceeds as follows. In the first part of the essay, I give and overview of different types of multiple offenders with specific examples. I then discuss the relationship between culpability and character from the just deserts, or retributivist, perspective. Next, I apply the development of that insight to argue that sentences for multiple offenders should not reach the level at which the state would be communicating an unfairly and inappropriately harsh assessment of the character of each multiple offender. I then describe the ways in which multiple offenders are nevertheless more culpable than single-crime offenders. Finally, I argue that discounts for multiple offenders and premiums for repeat offenders are not inconsistent.

Multiple Offenders: Some Examples

The problem of multiple offenses shows up in—naturally—multiple ways. Here is a typology with categories and subcategories.

One Offense Type, Multiple Instances

Multiple Transactions, Single or Multiple Victims

One example we already saw is possession of child pornography. In *State v. Berger* (2006), the defendant possessed "numerous videos and photo images of children . . . being subjected to sexual acts with adults and other children" and was convicted of 20 counts of "knowingly . . . possessing . . . any visual depiction in which a minor is engaged in exploitive exhibition or other sexual conduct." He was convicted of 20 counts, one count per image (though he had many more than that), and sentenced to 200 years in prison—20 consecutive 10-year prison terms. In these sorts of cases, there is one criminal prohibition at issue, and the offender is charged with multiple instances of breaking the same law over time.

Child pornography cases often have offenders with only indirect links to victims. But sometimes there are multiple counts because one identifiable person is directly victimized repeatedly by an offender. In *State v. Boudreaux* (2006), the defendant installed a video camera in his 18-year-old stepdaughter's room and secretly videotaped her in various states of undress over a four-month period. He was convicted of 14 counts of video voyeurism, or "the use of any camera . . . for the purpose of . . . videotaping a person [without consent] and it is for a lewd or lascivious purpose" and was initially sentenced to 56 years—14 consecutive four-year prison terms.[1] *Smith v. State* (2008) follows a similar pattern of one offender, one victim, and multiple offending over time. In *Smith,* the defendant had sexual intercourse with his stepdaughter four times when she was between the ages 10 and 14. He was originally sentenced to 120 years in prison—four consecutive terms of 30 years in prison, one per incident.[2]

Single Transaction, Single or Multiple Victims

Multiple counts, though, do not require multiple transactions over time. For instance, according to *State v. McPherson* (2012), another Arizona child pornography possession case, sometimes those multiple instances can happen in one transaction, as it upheld a 70-year sentence—seven consecutive 10-year prison terms—for a defendant who had seven images on a single DVD, which the court assumed was acquired in one transaction for the purposes of its analysis. Sometimes one transaction can give rise to multiple crimes because of the number of victims affected. In *Johnston v. State* (2012), the defendant was sentenced to 90 years in prison—three consecutive terms of 30 years in prison—for an act of armed robbery in which three separate individuals were robbed.

Multiple Offense-Types, Multiple Instances

Single Transaction

One activity in one evening can implicate not only multiple violations of one prohibition but violations of multiple prohibitions. In *Oregon v. Ice* (2009), the defendant, a building manager, went into an apartment of a family in his building and touched an 11-year-old girl's chest and vagina on two occasions. He was sentenced to 80 months for the first burglary, 80 months for the first sexual abuse, 90 months for the second burglary and 90 months for the second sexual abuse, all to be served consecutively, for a total of 340 months. In this case, each transaction gave rise to two violations.

Multiple Transactions

A person can face a long sentence for breaking multiple laws over time. In *United States v. Cruz-Rodríguez* (2008), one of the defendants in the case was convicted of 1) conspiring to possess with the intent to distribute cocaine, crack cocaine, and heroin within 1000 feet of both a school and a public housing facility; 2) conspiring to use, carry, or possess a firearm in furtherance of a drug trafficking crime; and 3) possessing a firearm at a place he knew or had reasonable cause to believe was a school zone. For the first and second conspiracy charges, which the trial judge combined as one crime, the defendant was sentenced to 202 months in prison and for the third, possession, charge, he was sentenced to 60 months in prison. The sentences were to be served consecutively.

Another example with a similar pattern is *State v. Hairston* (2009), in which the defendant was sentenced to 134 years for robbing four homes in a three-month period (and incapacitating an occupant in each house during the robbery). He was convicted of four counts of aggravated robbery, three counts of aggravated burglary, four counts of kidnapping, and three counts of having a prohibited weapon, and sentences for all 14 counts were imposed consecutively.

Note on Consecutive and Concurrent Sentencing

All the examples discussed are examples of multiple offenders who were sentenced consecutively, but, of course, not all multiple-offense cases end with consecutive sentences. There is a plenty of examples of concurrent sentencing of multiple counts. For instance, in *Commonwealth v. Jefferson* (2012), the defendant was convicted of six counts of production of child pornography and was sentenced to six six-year terms, to run concurrently, despite the government's argument that they should run consecutively. In *State v. Quan* (2015), the defendant, participating in a credit card scam, was convicted of 18 counts of four different types of crimes, including identity theft and illegal transmission of monetary funds, and he was sentenced to six months for four counts, seven years for four counts, seven years for six counts, and five years for four counts, all to run concurrently. Similarly, in *State v. Jones* (2013), the defendant was convicted of production and manufacture of an illicit drug and creation and operation of a clandestine laboratory and received two sentences, 18 years and 15 years, to run concurrently.

Summary

As these examples show, one can end up a multiple offender by breaking the same law multiple times over time, by breaking the same law multiple times in a single transaction, by hurting multiple victims in one transaction, by breaking multiple laws in one transaction, by breaking multiple laws over time, and so on. And these crimes are at varying levels of seriousness and patterns of victimization. There are multiple approaches to dealing with these situations, and sentences imposed can differ dramatically depending on which approach is taken. Sentences can be imposed consecutively, concurrently, or with a bulk discount, which may take the form of concurrent sentences or at least a smaller prison term for each additional crime. The question is how to think about these different approaches theoretically.

Desert and Character

Before we consider the question of what the desert theory says about multiple offenders, we need a working definition of the desert theory of punishment. The basic idea is that persons should get what they deserve, and that those who commit wrongdoing deserve punishment. Under this view, the amount of punishment should vary according to the seriousness of the crime; therefore, the more serious the crime, the harsher the punishment ought to be, and no more than that (von Hirsch and Ashworth, 2005). This bare-bones formulation by itself says little about what should be done in situations where a person commits multiple offenses, but as some have pointed out (Bottoms, 1998; Wasik, 2012; Lippke, 2011; Ashworth, 2010), one tempting reading of this principle is that we should take the punishment for each offense and add them up in order to generate the punishment that a multiple offender deserves. But once we take a closer look, we can see that the desert theory need not imply such a thing.

We should start with what it means to deserve something. According to Joel Feinberg's formulation, desert statements have the form "*A* deserves *X* in virtue of *Y*," where *A* is the person deserving, *X* is what that person deserves, and *Y* is the desert basis, or whatever serves as the basis for *X* (Feinberg, 1970). To understand how it is that a person deserves something, we must understand two relationships: the relationship between the person who is deserving and the desert basis (*S* and *F*), and that between what is deserved and the desert basis (*X* and *F*). The person who is deserving and the desert basis (*S* and *F*) are related in that the desert has to be an attribute of the deserving person (Feinberg, 1970). The focus of the desert inquiry is thus on the person. In the relationship between what is deserved and the basis for desert (*X* and *F*), the key concept is "fittingness" or appropriateness (Feinberg, 1970). In the punishment context, a response is "fitting" or "appropriate" only if it takes a form that symbolizes or expresses the society's condemnatory attitude toward the person and his or her desert basis (Feinberg, 1970). The harshness of the punishment thus should reflect our level of condemnation or disapproval, and a punishment would be excessive if the degree of condemnation symbolized by the amount of punishment were too high relative to the criminal's blameworthiness.

For our purposes, an important feature of desert in the punishment context is the essential role of an actor as a recipient of blame and punishment (Sher, 2006; Williams, 1995). Our criminal justice system focuses on crimes and punishes people for crimes that they commit and not primarily for who they are, and nothing in the discussion that follows here contradicts that fundamental feature of our system. Nevertheless, we cannot make any sense of the practice of blaming if we try to think about it exclusively in terms of wrong acts, detached from actors. Blaming actors for what they have done implies that the acts that they have engaged in reflect badly on them, and to blame them for what they have done thus requires that we see a tight relationship between the actors and the acts. As Antony Duff puts it, "we are responsible for our actions, and are justly blamed for them, insofar as they do indeed reflect or flow from our characters" (Duff, 1993). Similarly, Victor Tadros argues that "the imposition of criminal responsibility .... says something *personal* about the agent *qua* agent" in that such imposition, "at least within the range of relatively serious offences, necessarily involves moral criticism of the defendant as a person" (Tadros, 2005).[3]

This proposition—that blaming a person *for an act* entails a judgment that the act reflects badly *on that person*—implies that a criminal justice system may punish people only for "actions which are in a real sense *their own*" (Lacey, 1988). Only when actions are their own can we justify blaming persons for what they do (Duff, 1993). Theories of culpability that bridge the gap between an actor and an act through the notion of character derive some of their persuasive force from this idea of one's ownership of one's acts. According to this account, character plays both inculpatory and exculpatory roles in criminal culpability. It is appropriate to blame persons for their acts if the bad acts can be traced to their character defects (Nozick, 1981). It is inappropriate to blame persons for their acts if the circumstances surrounding their actions are such that the acts cannot be explained as resulting from their character defects (Tadros, 2005).

More specifically, what does imposition of criminal responsibility say about these offenders and their character defects? Answers may vary, but here is Tadros's explanation: "The criminal justice system communicates publicly both about the act that the agent has performed, and about the agent in performing that act. The content of the communication is at least moral indignation" (Tadros, 2005). "Moral indignation," in turn, has the following feature according to Tadros: "It is a necessary condition of moral indignation that the agent has displayed an appropriate kind of vice, the kind of vice that displays a failure to have proper regard for a significant interest of others" (Tadros, 2005). It follows that it is "only when an agent has shown himself not properly to be motivated by the interests of others that indignation becomes appropriate," and it is "only when the defendant has displayed such a vice that the imposition of criminal responsibility is appropriate" (Tadros, 2005). Others have made similar arguments (Horder, 1993).

The defense of duress can be explained this way for instance. Under the Model Penal Code formulation, the duress defense requires that the kind of threat that has brought about the crime be something "a person of reasonable firmness in his situation would have been unable to resist."[4] According to this standard, even if a person genuinely feels that he has no choice other than to commit a crime to prevent a serious harm to himself by someone else, the duress defense would not be available to him if he did not live up to the standard of behavior set by the hypothetical "person of reasonable firmness." Persons of reasonable firmness are those who recognize the wrongness of the crime they are being pressured to commit and are courageous enough to resist the pressure (Duff, 1993). If someone who commits a crime meets the requirement of the duress defense, the message the legal system communicates is that the crime does not reflect badly on the offender because the source of the criminality is something external to the offender's self, and giving in to the threat of harm is not to be condemned because the offender has behaved in the same way a reasonable person would have (Duff, 1993).[5]

Conversely, if the duress defense is not applicable in a particular offender's situation, the legal system judges the offender for being the sort of person who either does not live up to the society's expected standard of fortitude and resistance to criminal temptations or threats, or does not care sufficiently about the seriousness of the values that the law protects, or both (Duff, 1993).[6] Of course, this is not to say that the law is punishing the offender *for* being a coward; rather, the punishment is for the crime itself. Implicit in the punishment, however, is the proposition that whatever pressure the offender might have felt to commit the crime is something that should have been resisted, and the failure to resist it shows a character defect.

We must be careful here, of course. There is a difference between treating bad character as a necessary condition of liability and treating it as a target of condemnation (Duff, 2002b). The formulation that we punish people for actions only when they reflect their character defects can imply one of two things. First, it may be argued that it is unfair to hold persons responsible for actions not flowing from their character defects. Alternatively, it may be argued that the legal system is interested in character defects as a target of condemnation. The account of the role of character in criminal culpability I have given thus far does not appear to go beyond the former formulation, in which case we punish people only for what they do, but only to the extent that what they do reflects who they are. Character, under this account, is only a condition of liability and nothing more.

However, even if character is only a condition of liability, it is doubtful that we can neatly separate out different messages sent by the state as it punishes an offender. Once character defects are thought to be behind the bad actions condemned by the criminal justice system, and it is this link that satisfies the condition of liability, then it is difficult to imagine how the character defects can escape the reach of condemnation. The reasons we take character defects seriously as conditions of liability do not suddenly cease to operate when it comes to understanding them as the target of the state's condemnation as if there were some on–off switch. Therefore, once an act is condemned because of the vices it reflects, there is no way for the criminal justice system to avoid commenting on the actor's bad character traits as well as the bad act.

This account raises many questions, and an extensive literature on the relevance of character to criminal culpability has grown around the debate among "choice," "character," and "capacity" theories of culpability (Fletcher, 1978; Hart, 1968; Horder, 2004; Lacey, 1988; Nozick, 1981; Tadros, 2005; Arenella, 1990; Duff, 1993; Duff, 2002b; Finkelstein, 2002; Gardner, 1998b; Horder, 1993; Sher, 2006; Alexander and Ferzan, 2009). The theory remains controversial and has attracted a number of criticisms (Brudner, 1987; Horder, 1993; Horder, 2004). Despite the controversies, it seems to me that character theorists are correct when they argue that criminal law punishes persons *for their actions only when those actions reflect badly on the actors* in the sense that the actions display their character defects. Without an account along these lines, it is difficult to explain what makes up the relationship between actors and their acts, and why it is that we have no trouble connecting our condemnation of a bad act to the agent who performed it. It should also be emphasized here that the focus remains on actions. The crucial idea is that once an act is condemned because of the vices it reflects the criminal justice system expresses a message about the actor's bad character trait as well as the bad act. The question for us is what this has to do with the problem of sentencing multiple offenders.

Desert, Character, and Multiple Offenders

Why Multiple Offenders' Sentences Should Be Limited

What the account given in the previous section suggests is that when an offender is convicted and punished, he is blamed not just for what he has done but also for the kind of person he is. A person convicted of murder is not just a person who has committed the crime of murder but is also a murderer. A person convicted of rape is not just a person who has committed the crime of rape but is also a rapist. A person convicted of theft is not just a person who has committed the crime of theft but is also a thief. By labeling a person a "rapist" the state would then be commenting on a set of traits that the person has that has generated the wrongful act of rape, and that set of traits would be different from the set of traits that has generated the wrongful act of theft both in kind and in degree of badness. To see the relevance of this observation to the question of multiple offenders, we need to go back to the concept of desert.

As we saw earlier, desert statements have the form "*A* deserves *X* in virtue of *Y*," where the relationship between what is deserved and the basis for desert (*X* and *F*) is characterized by the concept of "fittingness" or appropriateness. As many have pointed out, fittingness has both comparative and noncomparative aspects.[7] The latter demands that a person convicted of a given crime receive a certain amount of blame, no matter how other people are treated, while the former focuses on what the punishment for a given crime is compared to punishments for different crimes of varying degrees of blameworthiness.

No theory of retributivism is complete without an account of the role of comparative desert because what one deserves is sometimes determined in reference to what others deserve. The reason for this is that the institution of punishment has an expressive dimension. When it punishes, it condemns the behavior and the person, and the degree to which the behavior and the person are condemned is expressed by varying the amount of punishment. In other words, when the state punishes, how one's punishment stands in relation to punishments for other crimes supplies a crucial piece of information as to how wrong the behavior punished is viewed by the society. This means that a punishment imposed on a criminal would be "undeserved" if it is more severe than or as severe as the punishment imposed on those who have committed more serious crimes, because the judgment it expresses about the seriousness of the criminal's behavior would be inappropriate (Feinberg, 1970; Duff, 1993; Feinberg, 1988; von Hirsch, 1993; von Hirsch, 1985).

From this account it also follows that it would be unjust to punish, as a general matter, thieves more than or similar to robbers, robbers more than or similar to rapists, rapists more than or similar to murderers, and so on. This is because the amounts of punishment send the message about character traits of the offenders. A rapist and a thief may not only have different sets of character traits, but a rapist's set of character traits compares poorly to a thief's set of character traits. If the state, however, punishes a thief as much as it punishes a rapist, it would be sending the message that the character make-up of a thief, as a whole, is roughly equivalent in terms of seriousness of defectiveness to the character make-up of a rapist. Such a message would be unduly stigmatizing and unfair.

For example, the defendants in *State v. Berger* and *State v. McPherson* were convicted of possession of child pornography and sentenced to 200 years in prison for 20 counts in *Berger* and 70 years in prison for seven counts in *McPherson*. We may argue about the culpability of those who consume child pornography, but

200 years in prison or 70 years in prison far exceeds the amount of punishment that seems appropriate for someone who is guilty of possessing child pornography, as it exceeds or is equivalent to the typical punishment for other more serious offenses.[8]

Now it is true that in these two cases the punishment per image was very high—ten years per image, and the two cases may have been illustrations of excessive punishments even if each received just 10 years for a single count. But it is easy to imagine each defendant having far more images on his computer. As anyone with a computer and a high-speed Internet connection knows, it is not difficult for one to collect thousands of images on a computer. So each defendant could have been punished one month per image with two thousand images, and that would add up to nearly 170 years. Even if we reduce the punishment for each image to one week, for 2,000 images, we would have 38 years in prison. Under these scenarios, even if the punishment per image seems reasonable, assigning the amount of punishment per image and adding them all up would generate an excessive punishment, as the final amount of punishment would send the message that these consumers of child pornography are as bad as those who have committed far more serious crimes.

We may say something similar about the voyeur in *State v. Boudreaux*, who was initially sentenced to 56 years for 14 counts of the crime of video recording his 18-year-old stepdaughter in her bedroom. While he invaded her privacy this way multiple times, his criminality never went beyond that of a voyeur perhaps with an enhancement in culpability for the way in which he violated her trust. Fifty-six years in prison is much higher than what a person like that probably ought to receive, compared to the seriousness of other crimes that carry similar punishments.[9]

These are relatively easy cases, of course, since there is only one type of offense involved in each case. How should we deal with fact patterns like *Oregon v. Ice*, where the defendant sneaked into someone's home and touched an 11-year-old girl on two different days? In the actual case, he was sentenced to 80 months for the first burglary, 80 months for the first sexual abuse, 90 months for the second burglary and 90 months for the second sexual abuse, all to be served consecutively, for a total of 340 months.

To simplify, let's assume that he stopped after the first time. He would then have to be punished for burglary and sexual abuse, and the question would be whether the sentences for the two should be added to each other. One should not generalize for all types of sexual abuse cases as compared to burglary, but burglary is an inchoate offense and is a property crime whereas sexual abuse is an offense against a person, so it seems that, as a general matter, sexual abuse is an offense more serious than burglary. And to the extent that the idea here is that the punishment sends a message about the offender as a person, then it would be accurate to punish this person as a person who sexually abuses girls and not just as a person who burglarizes.

But should the punishment reflect the fact that he is a person who sexually abuses *and* burglarizes? Perhaps, but I would argue that adding up the sentences for the two crimes would be unfair. When a person commits a crime, it can be assumed that he is not only capable of committing the crime but is also capable of committing crimes that are less serious than the actual crime committed. This means that the fact that the person has committed the less serious crime in addition to the more serious crime adds little additional information about the character make-up of the person, as the greater includes the lesser.

The assumption that people who commit serious crimes are capable of committing less serious crimes may easily be questioned. A person may molest children but would never hit another person; a person may rape but would never defraud another; a person may kill but would never steal; and so on. It is also easy to imagine an employer who is willing to hire a person who the employer knows can be violent to one's spouse because the employer has judged the person to be someone who would never steal from work, despite his failings as a person at home. In other words, in everyday interactions with people, we might trust people with some things but not with others and place them in different spheres of our lives depending on how we judge the character make-up of a person. And in such interactions, we may trust a person who is capable of doing a great evil to be incapable of committing a lesser evil.

But the topic of this essay is not how people generally interact with one another but about the institution of punishment, where we are, as noted earlier, engaged in the project of assigning comparative deserts by lining up offenders in order of seriousness along a single scale.[10] Once we conduct this lining up exercise, the assumption that those who are capable of greater wrongs are capable of lesser wrongs naturally follows. Even if we firmly believe that a particular person who has committed a crime of rape would never steal from others, when we judge a person in the criminal justice system we insert him into an institutional setting in which we increase the harshness of punishment according to the seriousness of crime, and the measure of badness as we go from, say, level 1 to level 5 necessarily hits each level as it goes past levels 2, 3, and 4. So, by the time the person has hit level 5, we have already been informed that he has hit all the levels below level 5.

Therefore, as a general matter, it seems that there is little loss in expressive meaning about the character of the offender who commits two different crimes of varying seriousness when he or she is not punished beyond the level warranted for the more serious crime. It is not only that because of the assumption that the greater includes the lesser, adding the two punishments would result in an excessively harsh punishment. The condemnation of the person for the kind of person he is for committing the less serious crime has already been included in the condemnation of the person for the kind of person he is for committing the more serious crime. This means that punishing him for the less serious crime in addition to punishing him for the more serious crime would amount to a double punishment of the less serious crime. The punishment for him that respects fairness considerations, all other things being equal, would be the punishment for the more serious crime and no more than that. Moreover, once the fairness considerations limit the appropriate punishment to the level specified by the more serious crime, it follows that if the two punishments are added and the offender ends up being punished, say, at the same level as a person who has committed a crime that is more serious than the most serious crime the offender in question has committed, we would be treating the offender unfairly.[11] All of this suggests that when considering the correct sentence for a person who has committed multiple offenses of different types, it would be appropriate to use as the baseline the punishment level for the more serious crime and not depart from it significantly.

The discussion thus far shows that the character theory of culpability can place restrictions on amounts of punishment for multiple offenders. It would be unjust to devise the punishment by adding up the sentence for each offense because the resulting punishment would place some offenders in the same category of bad actors as those who have committed much worse crimes. However, there is still the question whether the fact of multiple offending should play any role in sentencing. That is, are multiple offenders at the same level of seriousness as single-crime offenders, all other things being equal? Probably not, and the question is why and how.

Why Multiple Offenders Are More Culpable than Single-Crime Offenders

As the previous section argued, the character theory of culpability places limitations on amounts of punishment for multiple offenders and articulates a reason not to sentence consecutively in cases of multiple offenses. But can we say more than that about the significance of multiple offenses?

The next part will discuss how multiple offenders differ from repeat offenders, but some of the thoughts expressed in the repeat offender literature are relevant here. In a series of writings, Andrew von Hirsch has argued that first-time offenders should receive sentencing discounts because even well-intentioned, law-abiding citizens may at times come across opportunities to commit crimes and may give in to the temptation at moments of weakness (von Hirsch, 1985; von Hirsch, 1991; von Hirsch, 1981). I have in previous writings raised some difficulties of this account as a way of explaining the recidivist premium (Lee, 2009; Lee, 2010), but the central insight regarding human frailty is relevant in thinking about multiple offenses.

That is, when a person offends for the first time, we might attribute it to a temporary breakdown of self-control, but if the same person commits another offense afterward and then another, we can no longer attribute the subsequent offenses to a moment of weakness, and accordingly we may think less of him as a person. Of course, it is true that those who offend only once and those who offend multiple times may have the identical character make-up, but the criminal justice system is not able to tell whether those who offend only once have acted out of character, in the sense of having a one-time slip, or whether they have permanent, bad character traits that happen to have manifested themselves only once. But if that person continues to commit crimes over time we could be more confident in the judgment that the offender is a criminal with a pattern of offending over time, and not just a law-abiding citizen who slipped in a moment of weakness. So this suggests one reason to think that those who offend only once and those who offend multiple times ought to be treated differently.

We could go even further with the following observation. It may be the case that everyone knows that stealing is wrong in the abstract, but once a person in fact steals, he has, or at least ought to have, from feelings of guilt, an advanced knowledge of what it is like to transgress. That is, there may be a difference in quality between knowledge based on direct experience and knowledge based on indirect experience. A multiple offender's knowledge of what it is like to commit a crime would be held not just in some intellectual sense, but also in a deeper, experiential, affective sense. And it is *that* deeper, more personal, individualized sort of knowledge—perhaps analogous to the phenomenon of muscle memory— one had or ought to have had and multiple offenders' continued willingness to keep offending despite such advanced knowledge render multiple offenders more culpable and reveal character defects that single-crime offenders lack.

We could apply this insight to *Berger* and *McPherson*. A person who accesses child pornography might do so at first by being attracted to the abstract idea of child pornography and being driven by curiosity and temptation to give it a try, but once the person experiences looking at child pornography, he should have further thoughts about what he has done. To say the very least, it is a highly private image of a person engaging in acts that require consent when the person in question lacks the capacity to consent and is in fact being sexually exploited. If the full ramification of the act of participating in the market for creation of child pornography was not apparent before he accessed it for the first time, it should be more apparent after accessing it once. And a person who continues to collect child pornography after experiencing it once is disregarding such advanced knowledge of the badness of the act, and such willingness to continue to offend reflects poorly on him.

We might say the same about *State v. Boudreaux*, the case of the person who video recorded his stepdaughter surreptitiously multiple times over a four-month period when she thought she was alone in her bedroom, and *Smith v. State*, the case of the person who had sexual intercourse with his stepdaughter four times over a four-year period. In both cases, the fact that the offenders were willing to engage in these acts more than once reveals their willingness to continue to offend even after they have had a chance to face the full ramifications of what they have done.

This discussion also suggests that if multiple offenses are committed in a single instance, such offenders are to be considered less culpable than those who commit multiple offenses over time.[12] So in *State v. McPherson*, which was a seven-count child pornography case because of multiple images in a single DVD, the fact that all images were acquired at once should mean that the defendant should not be considered as culpable as those who acquire these images over time.[13]

But is that all there is to it? Take the two robbery cases discussed earlier. In *Johnston v. State*, there was one robbery event in which three separate individuals were robbed, whereas in *State v. Hairston*, the defendant robbed four different homes in a three-month period. Is the defendant in *Hairston* more culpable than the defendant in *Johnston* because he committed his crimes over time and had more time to deliberate about the ramification of his act after the first robbery? That seems plausible as far as it goes.

At the same time, the account is incomplete because the fact that there were three separate victims in *Johnston* should matter even though the deliberation account of additional culpability for subsequent offenses cannot do the explaining. That is, if the *Johnston* case were to be compared to a robbery case involving a single victim, would we say that there is no difference between the two cases because each robbery happens in a single transaction, giving the offender no time to reflect on the nature of his crime after each instance? That seems wrong. It seems that the fact that one is willing to produce multiple victims as opposed to just one makes the multiple offender more culpable.

Why should the number of victims matter, though? Let's reconsider *Boudreaux* and *Smith*. *Boudreaux* was about a man who video-recorded his stepdaughter multiple times whereas *Smith* was about a man who slept with his stepdaughter multiple times. It has been already mentioned that these men are more culpable than those who stop after the first time because they have had time to reflect on the nature of their acts after the first time. But the question on the table now is how they compare to a person who commits the same questionable act with four different individuals, once with each, over the same time period as opposed to with just one individual four times. The answer to the question is that while the number of victims matters, the number of times one wrongs another person matters as well, even if there is only one victim, aside from the additional culpability one acquires through offending over time.

All in all, then, it seems that multiple offenders are more culpable than single-time offenders for multiple reasons. First, multiple offenders are more culpable if they have had time to deliberate about their criminal acts after the first time, which does or should provide advanced knowledge of the nature of one's criminal act and its impact on other people. Second, multiple offenders are more culpable if they have multiple victims, even if the victims are victimized all at the same time with no additional time to reflect on the nature of one's criminal act. Third, multiple offenders who victimize the same person multiple times are no less culpable than those who victimize multiple people over time even though there is only one victim involved.

None of the marks that distinguish multiple offenders from single time offenders challenge the conclusion of the previous section that the character theory of culpability places limitations on how much multiple offenders can be punished because of the ways in which punishments make statements about not just what offenders have done but also what kinds of people they are. However, within those limitations, upward adjustments should be made for multiple offenders because there are good reasons to think that they are more culpable than single-crime offenders.[14]

Multiple-Offender Discount and the Recidivist Premium

A question that the argument made thus far raises is whether the practice of concurrent sentencing, or at least bulk discounts, for multiple offenders, is consistent with the practice of imposing the recidivist premium on repeat offenders.

The puzzle may be stated as follows: Offender A commits offenses A1, A2, and A3. Offender B commits identical offenses B1, B2, and B3. The only difference between Offender A and Offender B is that Offender A is a multiple offender (with no criminal history) who is being sentenced all at once for A1, A2, and A3, whereas Offender B is a repeat offender who offends once, is convicted and punished for it, offends again, is convicted and punished for the second offense, and then offends again and is convicted and punished for the third time. The two offenders are indistinguishable in terms of the type and number of offenses each commits, but the legal system treats them very differently. Offender A's punishment for A2 is smaller than his punishment for A1 and his punishment for A3 is smaller than the punishment for A2, whereas Offender B's punishment for B2 is larger than his punishment for B1, and his punishment for B3 is larger than his punishment for B2. Once the punishments for each offender are added up, we could easily end up with significantly different treatments for the two offenders (Reitz, 2010). Can this difference, which may appear arbitrary at first blush, be defended? It seems to me that the answer is yes, though how dramatic the difference can be would depend on how large the recidivist premium can be.

To understand why the two offenders ought to be treated differently, we need to examine the justifiability of the recidivist premium. I have given a theoretical account of the recidivist premium in previous work, and what follows is a quick summary of the argument (Lee, 2009; Lee, 2010). It seems to me that the recidivist premium stems from an omission—namely, what the repeat offenders have failed to do between the time of the previous conviction and the time of the new offense. That is, the recidivist premium is not directed at the moment a crime is committed by an offender; rather, the recidivist premium is additional punishment directed at the previous steps taken by him that *enabled* the later crime to be committed.

Of course, first-time offenders, too, have taken steps in the past that enabled the later crimes to be committed, so what is so special about repeat offenders? The answer is that there is a difference between a first-time offender and a repeat offender because a repeat offender has gone through the process of conviction and punishment and a first-time offender has not. When a person is convicted and punished for a crime, one thing we can say is that the relationship between that person and the state has changed in a way that makes that person different from others who have not had that kind of encounter with the state. This change in relationship changes the normative positions of offenders with regard to the state.

How does this change in the normative position exactly occur? To answer the question, we need to focus on the nature of the relationship between an offender and the state. When the state punishes, it condemns what the offender has done as blameworthy, and it communicates to the offender that what he has done is wrong. Implicit in that message, of course, is that the offender is being punished for what he has done, and after his punishment is complete, he shall not offend again. If the process of conviction and punishment communicates the message that what the offenders have done is wrong and they should not do it again, the process also should prompt a period of reflection on the part of offenders to determine how they ended up committing the prohibited act. This kind of self-diagnosis, aided by the institution of punishment, should identify what has gone wrong in an offender's life. People may end up committing crimes for different kinds of reasons, and those reasons differ for different types of offenses. Such diagnoses should lead to appropriate prescriptions for each offender, and each offender should follow those prescriptions while and after serving a sentence.

A repeat offense by someone who has or should have gone through this process of reflection, diagnosis, and prescription justifies the inference that, for whatever reason, the prescription was not followed, and the offender failed to prevent herself from reoffending by failing to organize her life in a way that steers clear of criminality.

Can we distinguish between multiple offenders and repeat offenders on such grounds? Some may still object that none of what I have said here about repeat offenders is unique to repeat offenders and that the same considerations apply to multiple offenders as well. Those without criminal histories also have the ability to know themselves and to understand the kinds of factors that lead people into situations in which they end up committing a crime. First-time offenders may have taken each step leading to their crimes knowing exactly what they were doing and understanding that each step was leading them closer to the commission of a crime. Plus, multiple offenders (at least the kinds we are assuming for the purposes of comparison with repeat offenders) are those who, while facing conviction and punishment for the first time in their lives, are not those who have committed only one crime in their lives. But if multiple offenders have a significant amount of experience in offending and reflecting on the significance of what they have done, those who are convicted of crimes probably know themselves well enough to know what kinds of things lead them down the path of the criminal. If so, shouldn't the argument I have given about repeat offenders apply to multiple offenders as well?

The answer is no. For one thing, this objection would apply only to multiple offenders whose offenses happen over time with time for reflection after each offense. Second, more importantly, this objection misses the point that the crucial difference between a multiple offender and a repeat offender is that the repeat offender has gone through a process with the state that has created a relationship with the state, and the point of that relationship was to ensure that whatever led the offender to the status of being a convict should be avoided in the future. It is *that* history of having had *that* relationship that multiple offenders lack. And once a person enters into a thick relationship with the state through the process of conviction and punishment, it is appropriate for the state to attribute blame to how a person has increased the risks of criminal wrongdoing over time. We cannot say the same about multiple offenders.

Of course, this argument by itself does not specify how large the differential in punishment between multiple offenders and repeat offenders can be. Nevertheless, it points at the way in which one may justify a differential treatment of these two types of offenders by focusing on and exploring the significance of the one thing repeat offenders have that multiple offenders lack: the history of having been convicted and punished.[15]

Conclusion

This essay has defended the proposition that while multiple offenders are more culpable than single-crime offenders and should thus be treated differently, multiple offenders should not be punished to such an extent that the state ends up treating an offender who has committed multiple offenses more harshly or in the same way as those who have committed more serious offenses, given the message each punishment communicates about the character defects about the recipient of the punishment. Following this principle would likely result in a presumption in favor of concurrent sentencing or at least bulk discounts, where even if an offender is guilty of committing multiple offenses, the punishment for each additional offense is smaller than that for the first offense. This essay has further argued that the practice of bulk discounts for multiple offenders is consistent with the practice of imposing the recidivist premium on those who, after having been convicted and punished, continue to reoffend.

Notes

1. After a successful appeal of this sentence, he was resentenced to 15 years—three consecutive five-year terms (*State v. Boudreaux*, 2009).
2. The appellate court later ordered that the sentence be reduced to 60 years in prison by letting two of the four prison terms run concurrently after it found a mix of aggravating and mitigating circumstances.
3. See also Gardner, 1998a; Redmayne, 2015.
4. Model Penal Code § 2.09(1).
5. For a more detailed and nuanced discussion of different situations in which the duress defense is available, see R. A. Duff, 2002a.
6. It is also possible that what the reasonable person test does in a particular context is serve as an evidentiary device—for example, to determine whether the report of fear of one's life is credible or is a mere exculpating story developed after the commission of the crime in order to avoid conviction.
7. There are many labels to describe the same distinction. In philosophy, following Joel Feinberg, the terms "comparative" and "noncomparative" are used. See, for example, Feinberg 1974; Miller 2003. In sentencing theory, the same distinction is often expressed as "cardinal" proportionality and "ordinal" proportionality. See, for example, von Hirsch 1985.
8. *Berger* and *McPherson* are Arizona cases. In Arizona, one can receive a life sentence, which is equivalent or practically equivalent to a 70- or 200-year sentence, for, for example, first degree murder (ARIZ. REV. STAT. ANN. § 13–752 (2012)) or sexual assault involving an intentional or knowing infliction of serious physical injury (§ 13-1406(D)). The sentence designated for second-degree murder, which requires an intentional killing, is between 10 and 25 years. §13-710; § 13-1104.
9. *Boudreaux* is a Louisiana case. Fifty-six years in prison is practically a life sentence. In Louisiana, life sentence is the punishment for second degree murder (LA. REV. STAT. ANN. § 14:30.1 (2015)) or for first degree murder unless the death penalty is imposed. The punishment for aggravated battery (battery committed with a dangerous weapon) is maximum 10 years (§14:34) and the punishment for forcible rape is maximum 40 years (§14:42.1).
10. One commentator has admonished me for having on typical American blinders in thinking of these problems in terms of a single measure, namely years in prison. I concede that this essay assumes that the harshness of punishment is primarily measured by the number of years in

prison, but I also note that all other contributors to this volume, who come from several different legal systems, make the same assumption in dealing with the question of multiple offenders.

11. Ice received 160 months for the first burglary and the first sexual abuse. The minimum sentence for rape in the first degree in Oregon is 100 months (unless the victim is under 12, in which case the minimum sentence is 300 months). OR. REV. STAT. § 137.700 (2016). The minimum sentence for arson in the first degree when there is a threat of serious physical injury is 90 months. *Id.*
12. For a similar conclusion, see Roberts and de Keijser, this volume.
13. This assumes that the core culpability of possession has to do with receiving or acquiring as opposed to failing to omit. If the culpability of possession includes failing to dispossess oneself of the materials in question, the culpability assessment of someone who possesses images over time would be different.
14. I note here that the proposition that multiple offenders are more culpable than single-crime offenders is not the same as the proposition that such multiple offenders ought to receive consecutive sentences.
15. As mentioned earlier, I previously defended the view that intervening convictions are morally significant in assessing the culpability of repeat offenders (Lee, 2009; 2010). In fact, Richard Frase has criticized my theory of repeat offenders for this very feature when he observed that "Lee's theory . . . only seems to explain prior-record enhancements involving an intervening conviction" (Frase, 2010). Kevin Reitz, similarly, has criticized the theory for its inability to explain the culpability of "repeat offending, in the absence of interruption by legal authorities" (Reitz, 2010). My response to these criticisms should now be clear. There *is* a significant difference between repeat offenders and multiple offenders having to do with the existence of intervening convictions or lack thereof, and it is a mistake to look for one theory to explain sentencing practices for both repeat offenders and multiple offenders. Michael Tonry has even gone further and disputed the moral significance of previous convictions when has he argued in response to my view that "it is unclear why a first conviction and punishment puts an offender into a position different from that of any other citizen" (Tonry, 2010). For other views broadly sympathetic to mine on the significance of intervening convictions, see Ashworth and Wasik, this volume; Frase, this volume; and Roberts & de Keijser, this volume.

References

Alexander, L., and K. Kessler Ferzan. 2009. *Crime and Culpability: A Theory of Criminal Law.* New York: Cambridge University Press.

Arenella, P. 1990. "Character, Choice and Moral Agency: The Relevance of Character to Our Moral Culpability Judgment." *Social Philosophy and Policy* 7(2): 59–83.

Ashworth, A. 2010. *Sentencing and Criminal Justice.* 5th ed. Cambridge: Cambridge University Press.

Bazelon, E. 2013, January 24. "The Price of a Stolen Childhood." *New York Times Magazine.*

Barrish, C., and J. M. Reyes. 2015, June 9. "Ex-Headmaster Sentenced to 50 Years for Child Porn." *USA Today.*

Bennett, C. 2011. "Do Multiple and Repeat Offenders Pose a Problem for Retributive Sentencing Theory?" In C. Tamburini and J. Ryberg (eds.), *Recidivist Punishments: The Philosophers' View*, pp. 137–156. Lanham, MD: Lexington Books.

Bottoms, A. 1998. "Five Puzzles in von Hirsch's Theory of Punishment." In A. Ashworth and M. Wasik (eds.), *Fundamentals of Sentencing Theory: Essays in Honour of Andrew von Hirsch*, pp. 53–100. Oxford: Clarendon Press.

Brudner, A. 1987. "A Theory of Necessity." *Oxford Journal of Legal Studies.* 7(3): 339–368.

Duff, R. A. 1993. "Choice, Character, and Criminal Liability." *Law and Philosophy* 12(4): 345–383.

Duff, R. A. 2002a. "Rule-Violations and Wrongdoings." In S. Schute and A. P. Simester (eds.), *Criminal Law Theory: Doctrines of the General Part*, pp. 47–74. Oxford: Oxford University Press.

Duff, R. A. 2002b. "Virtue, Vice, and Criminal Liability: Do We Want an Aristotelian Criminal Law?" *Buffalo Criminal Law Review* 6(1): 147–184.

Feinberg, J. 1970. *Doing and Deserving: Essays in the Theory of Responsibility*. Princeton, NJ: Princeton University Press.

Feinberg, J. 1974. "Noncomparative Justice." *The Philosophical Review*. 83(3): 297–338.

Feinberg, J. 1988. *The Moral Limits of the Criminal Law*. Vol. 4. New York: Oxford University Press.

Finkelstein, C. 2002. "Excuses and Dispositions in Criminal Law." *Buffalo Criminal Law Review* 6(1): 317–359.

Fletcher, G. P. 1978. *Rethinking Criminal Law*. Boston: Little, Brown.

Frase, R. S. 2010. "Prior-Conviction Sentencing Enhancements: Rationales and Limits Based on Retributive and Utilitarian Proportionality Principles and Social Equality Goals." In J. V. Roberts and A. von Hirsch (eds.), *Previous Convictions at Sentencing: Theoretical and Applied Perspectives*, pp. 117–136. Oxford: Hart Publishing.

Gardner, J. 1998a. "On the General Part of the Criminal Law." In R. A. Duff (ed.), *Philosophy and the Criminal Law: Principle and Critique*, pp. 205–255. Cambridge: Cambridge University Press.

Gardner, J. 1998b. "The Gist of Excuses." *Buffalo Criminal Law Review*. 1(2): 575–598.

Goode, E. 2011, November 5. "Life Sentence for Child Pornography Spurs Debate Over Severity." *The New York Times*. A9.

Greenhouse, L. 2007, February 27. "Justices Decline Case on 200-Year Sentence for Man Who Possessed Child Pornography." *The New York Times*. A3.

Hart, H. L. A. 1968. *Punishment and Responsibility: Essays in the Philosophy of Law*. New York: Oxford University Press.

Hessick, C. B. 2011. "Disentangling Child Pornography from Child Sexual Abuse." *Washington University Law Review* 88(4): 853–902.

Horder, J. 1993. "Criminal Culpability: The Possibility of a General Theory." *Law and Philosophy* 12(2): 193–215.

Horder, J. 2004. *Excusing Crime*. Oxford: Oxford University Press.

Jareborg, N. 1998. "Why Bulk Discounts in Multiple Offence Sentencing?" In A. Ashworth and M. Wasik (eds.), *Fundamentals of Sentencing Theory: Essays in Honour of Andrew von Hirsch*, pp. 129–140. Oxford: Clarendon Press.

Lacey, N. 1988. *State Punishment: Political Principles and Community Values*. London: Routledge.

Lee, Y. 2009. "Recidivism as Omission: A Relational Account." *Texas Law Review*. 87(3): 571–622.

Lee, Y. 2010. "Repeat Offenders and the Question of Desert." In J. V. Roberts and A. von Hirsch (eds.), *Previous Convictions at Sentencing: Theoretical and Applied Perspectives*, pp. 49–71. Oxford: Hart Publishing.

Lippke, R. L. 2011. "Retributive Sentencing, Multiple Offenders, and Bulk Discounts." In M. D. White (ed.), *Retributivism: Essays on Theory and Policy*, pp. 212–231. New York: Oxford University Press.

Miller, D. 2003. "Comparative and Noncomparative Desert." In S. Olsaretti (ed.), *Desert and Justice*, pp. 25–44. Oxford: Clarendon Press.

Nozick, R. 1981. *Philosophical Explanations*. Cambridge, MA: The Belknap Press of Harvard University Press.

Redmayne, M. 2015. *Character in the Criminal Trial*. Oxford: Oxford University Press.

Reitz, K. 2010. "The Illusion of Proportionality: Desert and Repeat Offenders." In J. V. Roberts and A. von Hirsch (eds.), *Previous Convictions at Sentencing: Theoretical and Applied Perspectives*, pp. 137–159. Oxford: Hart Publishing.

Sher, G. 2006. *In Praise of Blame*. New York: Oxford University Press.

Stuntz, W. 2011. *The Collapse of American Criminal Justice*. Cambridge, MA: Harvard University Press.

Sulzberger, A.G. 2010, May 22. "Defiant Judge Takes on Child Pornography Law." *The New York Times*. A1.

Tadros, V. 2005. *Criminal Responsibility*. New York: Oxford University Press.

Tonry, M. 2010. "The Questionable Relevance of Previous Convictions to Punishments for Later Crimes." In J. V. Roberts and A. von Hirsch (eds.), *Previous Convictions at Sentencing: Theoretical and Applied Perspectives*, pp. 91–116. Oxford: Hart Publishing.

Von Hirsch, A. 1981. "Desert and Previous Convictions in Sentencing." *Minnesota Law Review* 65(4): 591–634.

Von Hirsch, A. 1985. *Past or Future Crimes: Deservedness and Dangerousness in the Sentencing of Criminals*. New Brunswick, NJ: Rutgers University Press.

Von Hirsch, A. 1991. "Commentary: Criminal Record Rides Again." *Criminal Justice Ethics*. 10(2): 54–56.

Von Hirsch, A. 1993. *Censure and Sanctions*. New York: Oxford University Press.

Von Hirsch, A. and A. Ashworth. 2005. *Proportionate Sentencing: Exploring the Principles*. Oxford: Oxford University Press.

Wasik, M. 2012. "Concurrent and Consecutive Sentences Revisited." In L. Zedner and J. V. Roberts (eds.), *Principles and Values in Criminal Law and Criminal Justice: Essays in Honour of Andrew Ashworth*, pp. 285–305. Oxford: Oxford University Press.

Williams, B. 1995. *Making Sense of Humanity: and Other Philosophical Papers*. Cambridge: Cambridge University Press.

CASE LAW

Commonwealth v. Jefferson, 732 S.E.2d 728 (Va. App. 2012).

Johnston v. State, 172 So.3d 756 (Miss. 2012).

Oregon v. Ice, 555 US 160 (2009).

Smith v. State, 889 N.E.2d 261 (In. 2008).

State v. Berger, 134 P.3d 378 (Az. 2006).

State v. Boudreaux, 945 So.2d 898 (La. 2006).

State v. Boudreaux, 21 So.3d 1022 (La. 2009).

State v. Hairston, 888 N.E.2d 1073 (Oh. 2009).

State v. Jones, 2013 WL 616890 (La. App. 2013).

State v. McPherson, 269 P.3d 1181 (Az. 2012).

State v. Quan, 157 So.3d 1259 (La. App. 2015).

United States v. Cruz-Rodríguez, 541 F.3d 19 (1st Cir. 2008).

8

Sentencing the Multiple-Conviction Offender

Diminished Culpability for Related Criminal Conduct

JULIAN V. ROBERTS AND JAN W. DE KEIJSER

Across all jurisdictions, offenders convicted of multiple crimes benefit from what Ashworth first termed a bulk discount (1983, p. 260), a phrase later used by subsequent scholars (Jareborg, 2002, p. 64).[1] That is, the total severity of the sentences constitutes a fraction of that which would be imposed if each individual offense resulted in a separate sentence which were then simply aggregated. The contrast between the sentences imposed in multiple-offense cases and penalties imposed for the same offenses committed consecutively becomes even more striking when comparisons are made between serial offenders—convicted of multiple offenses over time—and concurrent offenders (Reitz, 2010).

This chapter addresses the punishment of offenders sentenced for multiple offenses that have not been separated by independent prosecution and sentencing. We distinguish such cases from multiple repeat offenders—those appearing for sentence with multiple prior convictions and sentences on their record. And, of course, there is a third category, namely offenders being sentenced for multiple current crimes, and who also have records of multiple prior convictions. Our primary focus is upon the first category of offender.

Most scholars believe that the striking discrepancy between sentences imposed on multiple and repeat offenders cannot be justified in retributive terms.[2] The existing solutions to the overpunishment of offenders convicted of multiple crimes invoke concurrent sentencing or the exercise of mercy by a sentencing court. Both approaches mitigate punishment but also create a number of problems which are discussed in this essay. The only principled retributive justification for a multiple-offense sentence discount that we are aware of draws on the concept of overall proportionality. While on the one hand, as Ryberg (this volume) shows, overall proportionality is subject to fundamental criticism, one may also question whether it should be conceived of as a true justification for multiple-offense sentence mitigation—or merely as a cap on cumulative sentences.

Many of the problems arise from the application of single-offense sentencing to cases of multiple crimes. Thus in this essay we advocate adoption of a clearer distinction between the two categories (single; multiple). When an offender is sentenced for multiple convictions, we invoke a separate regime, one which results in the imposition of a "global sentence." This regime highlights the importance of the multiple offender's diminished culpability, relative to single-crime cases.

Our contention here is that much of the gap between the repeat and the multiple offenders' sentences can be accommodated within a retributive framework. The multiple offender *deserves* less punishment than would be appropriate if his crimes had been committed (and sentenced) separately. This reduction is no less deserved than the first-offender sentencing "discount" (Roberts, 2010). Retributive accounts of sentencing accord primacy to the twin dimensions of harm and culpability; sanctions should be proportionate to the degree of harm and level of culpability. If each offense carries a separate quantum of punishment and these are accumulated in multiple-offense cases the result is retributive "overpunishment."[3]

We consider the components of culpability and harm to constitute *independent* elements of deservedness. The total harm of a series of offenses is simply the accumulation of the separate harms. Consequently, a lesser sentence in multiple-crime cases cannot be justified by reference to diminished harm. Our account therefore invokes and draws upon the culpability component of a proportional sentence. Under particular circumstances, multiple offenders *deserve* less punishment because they are less culpable than offenders convicted of the same crimes committed sequentially. We introduce and operationalize the concept of *relatedness* between multiple offenses. This resembles Lovegrove's (2004) notion of "connectedness." Our contribution provides a principled justification for differential sentencing in cases of related criminal conduct.

Related offenses are crimes for which the culpability is overlapping, rather than discrete culpabilities (for the individual offenses) that should be summed. Having articulated the retributive basis for a bulk discount we explore the practical implications of this approach. This principle alone is insufficient to justify the differential sentencing of multiple concurrent crimes, and therefore we note the need for an additional consideration, namely the application of mercy.

Our proposal is conceptually simple. If the offender is convicted of multiple counts, all for the first time, a discount should apply to all crimes—they are all subject to the first-offender discount. The court then determines whether the offenses are related, and applies a "culpability correction" to reflect the degree of relatedness. This accomplished, the court decides whether the provisional sentence is still excessive, and, if necessary, a portion of that total sentence is then suspended.

Overview of Essay

In the first part of this essay, we comment on the nature of the problem and the deficiencies of current approaches to sentencing offenders convicted of multiple crimes. This section includes our attempt to reconcile the gap between the multiple and serial offender within a retributive framework. We conclude by identifying the guiding determinant of any discount—the degree to which the offenses are related to each other in ways that have retributive significance. Next, we propose two justifications for reduced sentences when the offenses are related to one another: First, until prosecuted, convicted, and sentenced, the offender remains eligible for substantial first-offender mitigation. The offender who commits five burglaries in one evening should be treated as a first offender on each count (if he has a clean criminal record). Second, offenders convicted of related crimes are less culpable for each individual crime when the offenses arise from what may be broadly described as a shared state of culpability. We then describe the model in more detail and apply it to some specific examples, and conclude that relatedness alone will not justify reducing sentences sufficiently in multiple-crime cases. In light of current penalty levels, sentences in multiple-crime cases will still be excessive. Another principle or consideration is needed, and in this sense our solution to the problem of sentencing the multiple offender is hybrid in nature.

Preliminary Comments

The problem of multiple count sentencing arises from contemporary sentencing practices which impose such significant deprivations on liberty to reflect each individual offense. Prison time is measured in days, weeks, months, even years. The consequence is that offenders can quickly accumulate long periods of imprisonment as a result of a series of crimes. For example, the offender who commits a series of burglaries (and some related offenses, for example, assaulting the homeowner; stealing property; assaulting a police officer while resisting arrest) can easily attract a sentence of many years in prison within a single (albeit rather busy), evening's work—if the sentences for the individual crimes are simply totted up.[4] This is one cause of the problem. The second is less obvious.

Currently, sentencing in multiple-conviction cases mirrors sentencing in single charge cases. Criminal behavior is *unitized*: each conviction generates an independent quantum of liability which is then converted into a discrete period of time in prison (if the offenses warrant custody). Unitization implies independence, yet the offenses are more often related to each other. When a sentencing court adds up the time required for each specific conviction, it is required to impose a very lengthy sentence of custody—or adopt some remedial strategies to reduce the overall level of punishment. As noted earlier, these strategies, adopted to prevent the offender from being crushed by the onerousness of the sentence, create their own set of problems. The cure is worse than the disease.

Concurrent and Consecutive Sentencing

The most common sentencing response to the overpunishment of multiple offenders creates a legal fiction,[5] and constitutes a penal sleight of hand. A typical arrangement involves imposing a "proportionate" sentence for each separate conviction, and then allowing the offender to serve the terms of imprisonment concurrently. In other words, the offender discharges many sentences of imprisonment at the same time. Legal practitioners and scholars are familiar with concurrent sentencing but it seems unlikely that members of the public see the logic of letting offenders discharge multiple terms of imprisonment at the same time (e.g., Thomas, 1979).[6] While the public reject a cumulative model, they are also likely to oppose the solution of concurrent sentencing.

The principles underlying sentencing become obscured as a result of the concurrent execution of the sentences. For individual offenses there is a clear relation between sentencing goals and principles and the nature and severity of the specific sentence. Any such calculus will be either obscured or rendered meaningless when multiple sentences are collapsed into a single concurrent execution of its constituent sanctions. The only solution is for the sentencing judge who orders concurrent sentence to make explicit how the collapsed sentence relates to goals and principles of punishment in that particular instance. From a desert perspective it is impossible to maintain a clear link between principle and sentence when collapsing separate sanctions into a concurrent sentence. If penal pain is the currency used to express proportionate censure and desert for concrete acts of mischief, then once this currency is spent it cannot be used to respond to other crimes. Transpose the logic of concurrency to fines. A court orders an offender with two convictions to pay two fines of £5,000. Upon presentation of his credit card, the offender is informed that a single payment of £5,000 will suffice to clear the debt incurred to the state for both offenses simultaneously.

An alternative approach to concurrent sentencing is to make the sentences consecutive, but to reduce the length of each sentence to a more reasonable duration by "top slicing" each individual sentence.[7] An offender convicted of five burglaries, each worth six months in prison might be ordered to serve two months on each count, for a total of 10 months. This is more than a single conviction, yet still significantly less than a cumulative total. Although this solution avoids the fiction of currency, it is equally problematic. It requires the court to undersentence on each specific count or conviction. Again, the connection to sentencing principle is jeopardized by such a pragmatic solution to the problem.

Under a proportional sentencing model multiple crimes should attract multiple sentences and these should all be imposed, unless some reason can be found for distinguishing between an offender convicted of multiple crimes and one convicted of multiple crimes sequentially. An offender who commits an offense in 2015 and then reoffends in 2017 cannot claim a lesser sentence on the second occasion by virtue of the fact that he has also already committed a similar crime. On what basis therefore is the offender convicted of multiple, concurrent crimes entitled to mitigation?

Strict unitization of criminal conduct and the subsequent straightforward summation of liability is inappropriate for multiple-conviction cases. The reason for this is that it assumes a fixed quantum of punishment is required for each conviction, *as though the crimes were independent of each other*. Imagine an offender convicted of two assaults, first in 2010 and then in 2015. Assume that each assault warrants a sentence of six months. His liability is therefore for 12 months; the crimes are wholly independent of one another. Imagine instead that he punches someone in a pub, and then assaults a second person who intervenes. What is the offender's liability now? Intuition may suggest something more than six, but less than twelve. Such a position finds support in public opinion research which demonstrates that people do not simply sum the appropriate sentence for each crime. Robinson (2013) found that when sentencing multiple crimes, respondents "give a more extended sentence for two crimes than one, but generally not one that doubles the sentence that would be given for the first offence" (p. 398; see also Robinson and Darley, 1995). The critical challenge here, and the one we address directly in this essay, is how to move beyond mere intuition and define the principle which determines where the liability lies between these apparent outer limits of six and twelve.

Our principal (and principled) solution draws upon the dimension of "*relatedness of offending*." The concept is not new; it underpins sentencing practices such as the "single transaction" rule[8]—which states that if the offenses emerge from a single episode, they should be treated as single offense, or should attract concurrent sentences (Thomas, 1979; Ashworth, 2015). All jurisdictions, common and civil law in nature, limit the degree of punishment when an offender is convicted of crimes considered part of a single transaction (e.g., Fayet, 2016). This universal practice provides insight into the justification for the multiple-crime discount.

In light of its universality, it is odd that scholars to date, including the contributors to this volume, have not explored the justifications for the single transaction rule. It is hard to think of any near universal judicial practice which does not have some plausible theoretical foundation, even if it is seldom articulated in caselaw. It is also surprising that in light of the prevalence of this arrangement there has not been more discussion of the relationship between the offenses. After all, what dimension *other* than relatedness could justify treating several offenses as a single transaction for the purposes of sentencing?

In this essay we develop the concept, and articulate how it may be applied in a systematic and principled way. To date, much of the literature, based upon the caselaw in many jurisdictions, simply asserts the need to reduce sentence severity when the crimes are committed in temporal proximity, or are similar to each other (see, for example, Bagaric and Alexander, 2013). The single transaction rule has been too narrowly construed. Thus Thomas offers a particularly restrictive definition, noting that "the fact that the offences are committed simultaneously or close together in time *does not necessarily mean that they amount to a single transaction*" (1979, pp. 53–54, emphasis added). He then excludes from inclusion a case in which an individual breaks into a home and also assaults the homeowner.[9] Our approach would regard these offenses as comprising overlapping culpabilities, and this should be recognized in the sentence.

Justifications for Reduced Multiple-Offense Sentences

Before explaining how relatedness reduces culpability in multiple offending, we first need to address how the first-offender discount operates in multiple-offense cases. The application of this well-grounded principle should generate reduced sentences in certain multiple-offense circumstances. There are two principal justifications for treating multiple concurrent convictions differently from serial crimes.[10] First, the repeat offender has experienced penal censure and failed to respond to the message conveyed by the court; in contrast, the multiple offender has not had the benefit of this experience. Second, offenses committed during a single period or state of criminality reflect a lower level of culpability for each individual crime. In contrast, the serial offender has to generate an independent criminal intention for each crime.

The First Justification: Moral Awakening Following State Censure

The offender who commits an offense (say burglary) and who is then prosecuted, convicted, sentenced, imprisoned, and released back to the community only to burgle again is more culpable for the second offense than one who commits the same two burglaries minutes apart. The latter individual has not been sanctioned or censured, has not had the wrongfulness or harmfulness of his crime brought home to him by the criminal process. He has not had the opportunity to reflect upon his conduct in light of the censure, or to demonstrate any moral transformation. The multiple offender convicted of 10 offenses deemed sufficiently related to each other is a first offender on each count; he has yet to experience trial and punishment. Since it represents his first court appearance he can also claim first-offender mitigation; the recidivist cannot make this claim in mitigation. The argument that sentence discounts are justified when the offender has not had the opportunity to respond to censure is supported by many scholars, including contributors to this volume.[11] It represents one of the few consensual positions in the field (e.g., Bagaric and Alexander, 2013, p. 165;[12] Vibla, this volume; Frase, this volume; Manson, this volume).

First Offenders, Multiple Offenders, and Repeat Offenders

For the purposes of illustration, consider three offender profiles:[13] the single-crime first offender, the multiple-crime first offender, and the repeat (serial) offender. In the case of the multiple-crime offender, the burglaries were committed on the same evening, while the repeat offender's second conviction came a year after his sentence for his first burglary had expired. In respect of their *first* crime, all three offenders are equal, both in terms of harm and culpability. A sentencing scheme based on harm alone treats the multiple and repeat offenders equally: altogether they would receive double whatever punishment was imposed on the first offender.

Once culpability is considered, however, distinctions should be made between the offenders. The first offender is entitled to a culpability-related mitigation, for not having been ever convicted of a crime, and for not having experienced sentencing and punishment. Almost all retributive writings on criminal history endorse this distinction between the first and the repeat offenders (e.g., von Hirsch, 2010; Ashworth, 2015 and Roberts, 2010). The repeat offender is denied any such mitigation since he has experienced all these stages of the criminal process. Yet the multiple offender is also a first offender,

Table 8.1 **Hypothetical Culpability Scores, Multiple Offenders**

	Harm score (10 points per offense)	*A: Multiple Offender with 5 concurrent crimes*	*B: Serial Offender with 5 consecutive crimes, no recidivist sentencing premium*	*C: Serial Offender, with 5 consecutive crimes, with a flat rate recidivist premium*
1st crime	10	5	5	5
2nd	10	5	10	10
3rd	10	5	10	15
4th	10	5	10	20
5th	10	5	10	25
Total culpability score	**50**	**25**	**45**	**75**

entitled to mitigation for all of his crimes (if they were committed without independent prosecution and punishment). His liability for the second burglary, however, is not the full liability ascribed to the single first offender, he falls between the other two on the dimension of culpability. This may be represented by separate scores for harm and culpability. Let us imagine a scheme in which each crime attracts a harm score of 10 and a culpability score of the same magnitude.

Consider three multiple offender profiles. Each commits five offenses. Offender A commits his five in one evening, B and C's crimes are spaced, each resulting in a separate trial and sentencing. The first-offender discount is 50% so a first crime attracts a culpability score of 5, all other crimes attract a culpability score of 10. The difference between B and C is that B suffers no additional recidivist premium while C receives a flat additional 50% premium at each successive sentencing.[14] That is, each additional crime means that a further 5 points is added to the offender's total culpability score. Harm scores for the three offenders are the same: 50 (five times ten). Yet their culpability scores vary greatly, resulting in differential harm + culpability totals. A is scored 75, B = 95 and C = 125. Our claim is that these differences between offenders are retributively justified, and do not, as some aver, constitute a paradox. This is the exploding and collapsing desert which Reitz (2010) critiques but which we regard as justified within a desert-based model.

Second Justification: Diminished Culpability

Our scheme proceeds beyond the sentence reduction of multiple offenses as a result of first-offender mitigation to include the dimension of relatedness between the crimes. Crimes related to one another should be treated with less stringency than the same crimes when committed in isolation. The challenge is to determine the level of diminished culpability for the series, and hence the appropriate sentence reduction.

Earlier in this essay we argued that current sentencing practice for multiple offenses lacks principle and concrete guidance. As a result, the global sentences meted out in multiple-offense cases are susceptible to the bulk-discount critique (Reitz, 2010). At present, it remains extremely difficult for judges to arrive at a global sentence using conventional sentencing principles. As noted, the most common approach to the problem is to adopt a strictly cumulative approach at sentencing while solving the issue of an unduly harsh cumulative sentences by concurrent execution of its constituent elements. From the perspective of principled sentencing, this is unsatisfactory, because the problem evident at sentencing is solved by the judge resorting to juggling with the individual components.

It is, however, possible to arrive at a global sentence in multiple-offense cases in a predictable and principled manner without completely abandoning a unitized calculus pertaining to the individual counts. The concept of relatedness will first help to distinguish between two categories of multiple offenses: offenses that should be dealt with as a series, and offenses that should be sentenced separately. Within the first category the concept of relatedness will further play a central role in determining the global sentence. Before we explain our methodology for determining the sentence in multiple-offense cases for each category of multiple offenses in more detail, we need to explain and operationalize the concept of relatedness.[15]

Relatedness of Criminal Convictions as a Justification for Reduced Culpability

Why should an offense which was one of a series of related crimes result in less punishment than would be imposed if the crime was committed in isolation and sentenced accordingly? Whence the mitigation? As noted, it cannot be justified in terms of diminished harm. Rather, the mitigation is justified through reduced culpability.[16]

Our claim is that an offender's overall level of culpability for any particular offense is lessened when that crime is one of a constellation of related criminal acts. Why is culpability lower in these cases? There are several explanations. One is that the offender may be reacting to unanticipated circumstances, in which case he is less blameworthy for not having formed the earlier intention to commit this additional crime.

The single transaction rule is the most obvious illustration. The offender breaks into a residence, steals property, and when confronted by the homeowner, commits an assault. His culpability for the assault is not the equivalent to that of a comparable assault committed at some other time unrelated to any other criminal conduct. Similarly, the offender who commits an assault while trying to avoid arrest for a robbery is less culpable for the assault than the offender who commits an assault three months after an unrelated robbery. Without the robbery—for which the offender is fully culpable—the assault would not have occurred; his culpability for the assault is part of a more general criminal blameworthiness and to ascribe culpability for both offenses independently creates a degree of "double-counting." An offender who steals 10 CDs, one a month over a 10-month period, is more culpable than the one who enters a store and takes the same number of discs—although the loss is comparable (10 discs). In the former example the offender made 10 independent, unrelated decisions to commit a crime.

Finally, there is an argument that penalty structures for crimes such as burglary encompass multiple risks of harms. Burglars are punished for the harm of violating the privacy of a homeowner, and to a degree this also includes the potential threat to the homeowner of a hostile stranger in his house. The sentence therefore already includes some of the harm entailed in the assault of the homeowner. This should limit, partially, the additional punishment for the assault.

When sentencing multiple, related offenses, the culpability for each constituent offense is less than it would be if the offenses were completely independent. Culpability is diminished because, by virtue of the relatedness, the offenses have been committed *within a continued culpable state of mind,* or put differently, the culpabilities for the separate crimes in a related constellation of offenses *overlap.*

Dimensions of Relatedness

On one level, all criminal conduct committed within a lifetime is to some degree related; after all, the actor is common to all his actions. Yet we can distinguish degrees of interrelatedness. The concept contains three dimensions that have retributive significance. None of these alone is sufficient to establish a degree of relatedness that justifies a sentence mitigated on the ground of reduced culpability. We distinguish between *temporal contiguity, causal relatedness,* and *similarity of offending.*

Temporal Contiguity

If the crimes were committed within a short time-span, for example a single day, temporal contiguity exists. The shorter the interval between multiple offenses, the more reasonable it is to assume that these offenses were committed during a continued or overlapping state of mind not affected by a sufficient quality of deliberation. This is the most powerful dimension and *a condition sine qua non* for a culpability reduction.[17]

If the offenses are related either causally or in terms of similarity, it is safe to assume that the shorter the time frame within which these offenses were committed, the less opportunity for, and the lower the quality of, the offender's deliberation before committing the crimes.[18] This is closely related to the intent component of culpability which is already firmly embedded within the criminal law when thinking about premeditation, one of the most common and powerful factors enhancing culpability. Other factors being equal, offenders who plan their crimes are deemed more culpable than offenders who spontaneously offend.[19] Premeditation is upheld as an aggravating circumstance by appellate case law (Ashworth, 2015), is a common guidelines factor and finds support in public sentencing preferences (e.g., Roberts et al., 2009).

Temporal contiguity underpins the single transaction rule. The actor who commits a series of offenses within a short space of time, has less opportunity to reflect on the wrongfulness of his actions than the offender who has weeks or months within which to commit the same crimes. He has less opportunity for rational reflection. Although there is a vast literature on the nature of culpability, little discussion has focused on the quality of decision-making available to the defendant at the time of the crime. Culpability diminishes with the offender's opportunity to reflect upon the nature and consequences of his conduct. An individual who reacts with what seems to be excessive force in response to sudden provocation has limited time to reflect upon the appropriate level of response ("I just struck out without thinking!"). He is adjudged to be less blameworthy for his disproportionate use of force than another individual who subject to the same provocation but who then has hours to contemplate his actions in response. The offender who has the time to watch his victim slowly die is more culpable than one whose victim dies immediately. The premeditating offender has repeated and ample opportunities to reflect on his actions and their consequences. This richer reflection, based upon greater opportunity to reflect, deprives him of any claim to have acted thoughtlessly or impulsively.

Alexander, Ferzan, and Morse (2009) observe that "when an actor's decision-making is degraded, the actor is less culpable" (p. 256). We would argue that the actor's decision-making capacity is degraded on two grounds. First, as noted, he has not had the benefit of state censure following conviction and punishment.

Second, he has acted in a manner in which his opportunity for restraint following adequate reflection has been compromised. The importance of the quality of deliberation—as opposed to some simplistic aggregation of the individual harms—is also noted by Alexander (2011) when he observes that culpability "is a function of the actor's capacity to access and assess moral reasons and the quality of his deliberative circumstances" (p. 257). From the opposite perspective, "enhanced decision-making quality can aggravate culpability" (Alexander et al., 2012, p. 256). The repeat offender has ample opportunity to reach a reasoned moral decision. The point is that the offender convicted of multiple crimes within a short period of time should not be considered as culpable as the individual who commits the same offenses over a longer period.

Finally, the importance of timing of multiple offenses is borne out by intuition, and by the results of empirical research in experimental social psychology. In one of the few empirical studies to explore multiple-offense sentencing, Robinson (2013) asked subjects to sentence cases of multiple crimes committed simultaneously or separated by varying intervals of time. Consistent with earlier work (Robinson and Darley, 1995) he found that people did not simply cumulate individual sentences, but followed a discounting approach. More significantly, the timing of the offenses was important. The longer the time between offenses, the more punitive the public reaction; discounting was greatest when the offenses were temporally contiguous.[20]

Intuitively, it seems reasonable to blame the actor who transgresses repeatedly over a long period of time. The transgression is more likely to be ascribed to the actor rather than his environment. The faculty member who misses several meetings within a one-week period will be more likely to be seen as the victim of circumstances—a change in domestic arrangements, a temporary illness. The colleague who is regularly late for every faculty meeting during the entire academic year will be seen as someone who is inconsiderate of others.[21] People would ascribe the tardiness more to the actor's character rather than the environment when the behavior is dispersed over a longer period of time.[22]

However, temporal contiguity alone is not sufficient to justify a culpability reduction. Consider the example of someone who steals a phone from a shop in the morning and assaults someone in a bar during the evening of the same day. Temporal contiguity cannot justify a reduction here because there is no conceivable continued state of mind that spans these two crimes. Multiple offenses thus have to be connected in other ways as well. These other ways are causality and similarity.

Causality

If, without one particular offense, a subsequent offense would never have occurred, the offenses are causally related. Consider the burglar who tries to evade arrest and assaults a police officer in the process. As a result of the causal relation, the continued culpable state of mind is what connects the offenses further than merely temporal contiguity. The offender has not taken two autonomous, independent decisions to offend; the second decision contained a residual element of the first. Causal relatedness connects crimes that may be of a completely different nature and severity.

Similarity of Conduct

Similar crimes are substantively related. An offender who commits a domestic burglary in January and another in July has committed two similar crimes. As such these crimes are related. Without closer temporal contiguity it is hard to maintain that these offenses are committed within a continued culpable state of mind. Consider, on the other hand, the burglar who commits five burglaries in the same night. Here the similarity of the offense in combination with the temporal contiguity justify a culpability reduction: the offender's culpability for one crime overlaps with his culpability for the other.[23] The decision to enter the second house (and subsequent houses) was not independent of his decision to enter the first residence.

Importance of Judicial Discretion

Having identified the principal dimensions of relatedness, we add a caveat that courts should exercise discretion when weighing these dimensions to determine the degree of relatedness and hence the extent of the sentence reduction. Judicial discretion should also permit a court to determine whether there may be other grounds for considering the offenses related. For example, the offender has sent the same threatening letter to five members of Parliament at various points over a six-month period to convince them to vote a particular way. These offenses are temporally separated and involve separate victims. They only qualify for consideration on grounds of similarity of conduct. Yet they are motivationally related—they share the same culpable intention. Such a case may warrant additional reduction for this reason.[24]

Relatedness: Potential Outcomes

The consideration of relatedness in this particular way can have three qualitatively distinct outcomes. We argue that each of these outcomes requires a separate multiple-offense sentencing regime. We shall shortly describe the

Table 8.2 **Categories of Relatedness and Their Subsequent Sentencing Regime**

Degree of Relatedness	*Regime*	*Regime sub category*
Unrelated	Cumulative sentencing	
Modestly related	Related offenses sentencing	Modest culpability correction for relatedness
Highly related	Related offenses sentencing	Significant culpability correction for relatedness
Maximally related	Related offenses sentencing	Single incident sentencing; multiple incidents aggravating

scheme in practice. The scheme provides a retributive rationale for differential sentencing. Other contributors to this volume have provided typologies but without any underlying justification.[25]

The first possible outcome is that the multiple offenses under consideration are *independent* of one another. "Independent" means sufficiently independent not to consider the separate counts as part of a related constellation. For example, an offender is caught red-handed while committing a domestic burglary. Later he confesses to an assault in a bar, committed six months earlier. In addition, a police search of his house produces a stash of illegal drugs. These offenses would not be considered part of a related constellation.

The second possible outcome is that multiple offenses are *maximally related to each other,* so much so that they can be conceived of as the continuation of a single episode, for example, the shoplifter who steals 10 items from the same store during one particular visit. The third outcome (and the most common) is that the offenses are sufficiently related to regard them as a constellation of offenses, but insufficient to collapse them into a single episode for the purposes of sentencing. For example, consider a domestic burglar who is caught red-handed by the police but resists arrest and assaults one of the police officers. The burglar also carries a handgun.

Table 8.2 illustrates the various categories of relatedness, as well as their respective sentencing regimes. In the paragraphs that follow we discuss the proposed sentencing regimes. It should first be noted that our scale of relatedness ranges from "unrelated" to "maximally related."

The choice of sentencing regime, in our approach, thus depends on the degree of relatedness of the offenses within the constellation. Figure 8.1 represents our proposed decision-making process for sentencers confronted with multiple offenses.

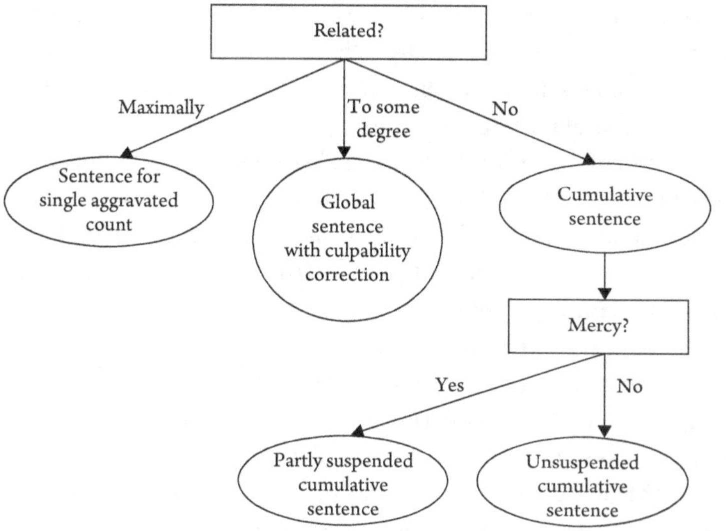

Figure 8.1 Relatedness as Key for Determining Sentence Regime for Multiple Offenses

Relatedness as Key for Determining Sentence Regime for Multiple Offenses

In the following sections we explain the distinct sentencing regimes for the different degrees of relatedness.

Sentencing Regime for Unrelated (Independent) Multiple Offenses

When the offenses are independent, there is no principled reason for any approach other than a cumulative sentence, and the sentences should not be distorted by concurrent sentencing. Since none of the individual counts is temporally, causally, or substantively related to any of the others, each offense deserves a separate sentence proportionate to harm and culpability. The sentencing judge explicitly identifies the individual sentences so that the total cumulative sentence can be understood and related to its constituent parts. We distinguish between four possible ways of dealing with such a cumulative sentence. The first three encounter practical or principled problems. The fourth one, we argue, can stand its ground.

The first and most straightforward option is the strict accumulation of the sentences into a total sentence. The execution of the sentence then consists of the consecutive execution of its constituent elements. Illustrations of these types of cumulative sentences can be observed in the United States. While such sentences may be considered in line with desert principles, from a desert point of view, one could contend that the extremely long cumulative sentences simply drown out the moral message (von Hirsch and Ashworth, 2005) that should be conveyed to the offender for the individual wrongdoings. The second objection to the execution of strictly cumulative sentences is that these are unduly harsh from a humanitarian point of view. It would result in extremely long spells of confinement for large numbers of people; from a humanitarian point of view, such a scheme is unacceptable.

The second option involves strict cumulative sentencing, but with concurrent execution of its constituent parts. We have already rejected this approach for reasons noted earlier in the essay. The third option is strict cumulative sentencing, but with considerations of mercy mitigating the severity of the sentence in the execution phase of the punishment. While this option does not generate the penal currency problem, it does imply a loss of principle in the administration of punishment. Substantive choices about the amount of punishment imposed must remain the realm of the sentencing judge. There may be grounds for modifying the sentence after the sentencing phase, but very significant reductions in the sentence would undermine the principle (utilitarian or retributive) that underlies the original sentence.

The fourth and final option incorporates the concept of mercy. The court first determines a deserved strictly cumulative sentence (the sum of the appropriate sentences for each of the individual counts). In many instances, this cumulative sentence will be unduly harsh. Consider for example a 25-year-old convicted of manslaughter, aggravated assault, burglary and theft. There is an insufficient degree of relatedness to justify considering these offenses as part of a series giving rise to a global sentence. Instead, the sentences for these multiple offenses total to 20 years imprisonment. From a humanitarian point of view, given the fact that this sentence would deprive the offender of the prime years of his life, the judge could invoke an additional consideration: mercy. In this case mercy would not be used to amend or overturn the original cumulative sentence. Rather, it would be used in its most literal translation to this particular context, that is, suspending a part of the deserved cumulative sentence. In our example, the sentence could be 20 years imprisonment, 10 of which are suspended out of mercy for the offender.[26] Why suspend rather than reduce the sentence? If the sentence is simply shortened there is a consequent loss of proportionality; this is avoided by imposing the proportionate sentence length but then making it suspended.

Sentencing Maximally Related Multiple Offenses

The relatedness analysis may produce a maximum relation between multiple offenses for which an offender stands to be sentenced. In such a case the sentencing of multiple offenses is to be reduced to sentencing a single behavior from which the original offenses are the outcome. This type of sentencing is then no different from sentencing a single offense. The multiple outcomes of the reprehensive behavior do not increase overall culpability, but rather increase the harm component in the legal evaluation of the behavior. Consider the extremely simple example of a shoplifter who steals 10 items from a store during a single visit. Since the 10 thefts are extremely related, temporally, causally, and in terms of similarity, it is reasonable to consider this a single theft with the 10 counts contributing to the aggregated harm in this case.

Sentencing Multiple Offenses with Some Degree of Relatedness

We have argued that relatedness of multiple offenses affects the culpability assessment when determining the global sentence. As a result, the global sentence should be subject to a culpability correction when sentencing related offenses. We propose a model for determining the global sentence in which this culpability correction plays a central role. The following rules guide the development of the model.

i. The model reflects a separate evaluation of the individual counts in terms of their penal value. It results in a global sentence without abandoning a unitized calculus of deserved punishment pertaining to each of the individual counts. As a result, it will always be clear how exactly the global sentence is related to its constituent deserved sentences for the individual counts. In current practice in most jurisdictions this clarity is absent. (This is important to facilitate appellate review and for transparency in sentencing more generally.)
ii. The global sentence should never drop below the level of deserved punishment for the most serious offense under consideration if this offense was to be sentenced as a single isolated offense. This constraint ensures that ordinal proportionality cannot be sacrificed during the process of arriving at a global sentence. A global sentence lower than the deserved sentence for its most serious single constituent part offends the overall rank order of crimes in terms of seriousness.

iii. To the extent that offenses within a constellation are judged to be *less* related, this should be reflected in a higher global sentence that is proportionate to the level of independence between the offenses. This means that for offenses that are more closely related, the global sentence must be lower than for the same offenses that are less related.

The proposed model therefore contains five steps and is summarized in Appendix.

Relatedness of Serial Offending

Finally, we address the application of relatedness more generally. The relevance of relatedness is not restricted to multiple contemporaneous offending. Relatedness reduces culpability and as such it is potentially relevant to all forms of offending. We do not seek to distinguish multiple from serial offending by invoking this principle. In practice, however, relatedness will be less relevant for sequential offending, for a number of reasons. First and foremost, the principal dimension of relatedness—temporal contiguity—is unlikely to benefit repeat offenders whose convictions occurred years apart. It is implausible to claim a continuous course of conduct that lasts for years. Nevertheless, there may be cases of repeat offending where the concept of relatedness has relevance, and when it does, a sentencing court should mitigate sentence severity to the appropriate degree. In such cases any recidivist sentencing premium would be milder. The fact that relatedness does not theoretically distinguish multiple from serial offending is a strength, not a weakness: it demonstrates the retributive foundation of the concept.

Summary and Conclusions

Our approach to sentencing multiple offenses can be summarized in the following propositions:

- Sentencing in multiple-offense cases is more complex, and even with greater guidance underpinned by a theoretically sound model, outcomes will inevitably be more variable than in single conviction cases.
- Attempts to structure multiple-offense sentencing based exclusively on models directly imported from single conviction sentencing are doomed to fail.
- The most common approach to sentencing multiple crimes involves the use of concurrent rather than consecutive sentences. However, this practice

creates greater variability, is obscurely related to sentencing principles, and generates additional problems, one of which is undermining public confidence in sentencing.

- We propose a separate sentencing regime for multiple-offense cases, albeit one which is guided by the same retributive concerns as the single-offense regime.
- Our analysis focuses on sentences of imprisonment, although its principled approach can be applied to noncustodial sanctions as well.
- The scheme requires a court to determine a single global sentence, the severity of which is clearly related to the individual constituent offenses.
- The key concept in determining sentence in multiple-offense cases is the degree to which the offenses for which the offender is responsible are related to each other.
- Relatedness has three dimensions: *Temporal, causal,* and *similarity of offending.* Applying these dimensions to the offender's crimes generates a "relatedness score" that ranges from completely independent to maximally related.
- The offender receives an appropriate baseline sentence for the primary (most serious) offense. To this sentence the model adds a fraction of the appropriate cumulative sentence for the remaining offenses. The fraction reflects the degree to which the crimes within the constellation are independent. The more independent, the greater the assigned punishment.
- For some cases, the resulting global sentence will still be excessive, in light of the individual characteristics of the offender. In such cases we apply mercy, but in a specific way. The court first establishes the appropriate global sentence and then suspends a part of the sentence out of mercy.

In this essay we have proposed two *principled* justifications for a different approach to sentencing in multiple-offense cases, one which is grounded in the culpability component of desert. The first invokes the application of a pre-existing and theoretically well-grounded principle of first-offender mitigation to multiple offenses. If multiple crimes are the offender's first offenses, the offender has not had the benefit of state censure and is therefore entitled to first-offender mitigation for the separate offenses. The accumulation of these separate first-offender mitigations results in a reduced sentence as compared to an offender who cannot claim such multiple mitigation.

Our second justification is specific to sentencing multiple crimes. We argue that offenses that are related both in terms of temporal and other dimensions reflect overlapping culpability: the offender's culpabilities of such related offenses are not independent. As a result, total culpability for the constellation of related offenses is less than the sum of culpabilities if these offenses were completely independent of one another.

As noted in the introduction, adjusting the sentence to reflect the fact that the crimes form a related series or constellation of crimes can only be justified in relation to the culpability branch of a proportionate sanction. The fact that a particular burglary was one of five committed within a single evening diminishes the offender's culpability for the series, but the harm remains the aggregation of the five separate harms. If sentencing were based exclusively on harm, multiple offense sentencing would conform to a simple cumulative model; there would be no basis for adjusting the severity of the penalty. We therefore reiterate that culpability and harm are separate concepts that operate independent from one another in both (desert) theory and in practice. Since our model is solely grounded on the culpability component of deservedness it cannot affect the harm component of a deserved sentence. The relative importance of both components in determining a sentence is, of course, subject to debate. That debate will determine how much work our culpability-based reduction for related multiple offenses can actually do. Whatever the outcome of that reflection, it does not undermine our principled justification advanced here.

Appendix: Applying the Model

The first four steps in the model define the necessary ingredients for the final calculation toward the global sentence in step 5.

Step 1: Determine the Appropriate Proportional Sentence for Each Individual Offense within the Constellation of Related Offenses

This should be determined for each offense as if it were committed in isolation, that is, not as one offense within a constellation of related offenses. This step is a direct consequence of rule *i*. It does, however, render determining the individual sentence a somewhat artificial step, because we have already established that as a result of relatedness, there must be some reduced culpability. Nevertheless this step is crucial for relating the total global sentence to the gravity of the individual counts within the constellation. As noted earlier, the model proceeds beyond the sentence reduction as a result of first offender mitigation. As such, the determination of the proportional sentences for each of the separate offenses within the related ensemble, may or may not be subject to a first offender discount depending on the offender's criminal history. This discount works completely independent from our culpability correction which is applied to the accumulation of those separate sentences. In a similar vein (albeit in the opposite direction), recidivism premiums could be at play for the separate offenses. Again, our culpability correction itself is not affected by such a mechanism.

Step 2: Identify the Most Serious Offense in the Constellation of Related Offenses

This step provides the baseline sentence, and is carried out using conventional single-offense sentencing approach. As a result, the most serious offense within a constellation may belong to the most serious offense category or may be the offense with the most aggravating and/or least mitigating circumstances. In any case this most serious offense will be the count carrying the highest sentence as determined in the preceding step 1.

Step 3: Calculate the Cumulative Sentence for All Counts Excluding the Most Serious Crime

Taking the appropriate sentence for the most serious count (determined in step 2) as the baseline sentence, the cumulative sentence for all remaining counts in the ensemble will be subjected to a culpability correction in the next step.

Step 4: Determine the Culpability Correction for the Ensemble of Offenses

The culpability correction is a culpability reduction used when determining the global sentence for a constellation of related offenses (in step 5). This coefficient adjusts the sentence and reflects the degree of relatedness between the offenses within the constellation. The more related the crimes are to each other, the higher the culpability correction and the lower the global sentence as compared to a strictly cumulative sentence. On the other hand, if the separate offenses are related but only to a very limited extent, the global sentence will be closer to the cumulative sentence.

Step 5: Calculate the Global Sentence

The global sentence can never drop below the baseline sentence (cf. rule ii). The added penal value as a result of the remaining counts in the constellation of related offenses must depend on the extent to which all crimes within the constellation are related; that is, the culpability correction. The more the remaining offenses are related, the less the added penal value should be. On the other hand, the more independent the remaining offenses are, the more added penal value is deserved. This added penal value can be assessed in a fair, proportional and consistent manner by weighing the cumulative sentence for the remaining offenses with the degree to which the offenses are independent. If a constellation of completely independent offenses carries a weight of 1, then the global sentence turns out as a straightforward cumulative sentence for all multiple-offense counts.

Notes

1. The authors contributed equally to this essay. Our thanks to the other participants at the Oxford seminar held in December 2015 and the following for comments on previous drafts: Andrew Ashworth, Netanel Dagan, Kimberly Ferzan, Jesper Ryberg, and Michael Tonry. We are also grateful to Gabrielle Watson and Gabriel Campos for research advice.
2. The framework of our analysis is retributive. However, it is important to acknowledge the eclectic nature of contemporary sentencing, where nonretributive factors such as plea play an important role. In our analysis we also draw upon a factor unrelated to a proportionate sentence, namely the exercise of mercy.
3. Other sentencing rationales do not necessarily confront this problem. A rehabilitationist may look at an offender with multiple, related crimes and seeing that these arose as a consequence of a common cause (e.g., drug addiction), may advocate a lenient, treatment-oriented community sentence. A disposition of this kind would reflect, not refute, a rehabilitation-oriented approach to sentencing. Retributivists, however, have the problem of accounting for each individual crime since each offense creates a specific harm and must therefore be accommodated within the retributive equation.
4. If the unit of legal punishment was a penny, and a typical crime "deserved" say a fine of 10 pence, a separate proportionate sanction could be imposed for each crime and the offender would be capable of enduring punishment for even the most prolific crime spree.
5. Another solution would entail abandoning the assignment of liability for each conviction, and adopting instead, a total sentence that would reflect the overall gravity and culpability. Thus an offender convicted of say, three burglaries, two assaults, and one robbery could be sentenced on the most serious offense (robbery) and the other offenses taken into account in aggravation. The deficiency of this approach is that it loses sight of the individual crimes comprising the offender's liability, and there will be an inevitable loss of precision in the message of penal censure conveyed.
6. Courts clearly think that concurrent sentencing makes sense to the public. In Wacker, the English Court of Appeal took the view that the public would approve an arrangement whereby the offender, convicted of 58 counts of gross negligence manslaughter, received 58 independent sentences of 14 years, only to serve them all concurrently. It seems unlikely that the public would endorse this approach, even if, as noted in this chapter, people tend to discount multiple crimes in a way that is consistent with some form of totality.
7. For example, the Sentencing Council's guidance on totality takes this approach when it recommends that in imposing consecutive sentences, "the court can consider whether all the offenses can be proportionately reduced" (Sentencing Council, 2012, p. 7).
8. The rule is too limited. Related offending is not restricted to a single "transaction" and nor should it be bounded narrowly in terms of the temporal dimension. An offender committing a series of crimes over a few days would not conform to the single transaction rule. Under the proposed model however, it would be appropriate to consider the offender's culpable state of mind as lasting longer than a few hours. In terms of multiple offenses over a sustained period of time, if the motivation is related to blameworthiness then this should trigger a related offense global sentence. For example, the drug-addicted offender who commits a robbery every week for a month, and then is apprehended and convicted should be treated under the related offense regime even though his crimes were separated by considerable temporal gaps.

9. Curiously, Thomas considers a series of assaults involving separate victims to constitute a single transaction, suggesting considerable vagueness with respect to the concept.
10. It also may be argued that the offender who commits all his crimes in one period can plausibly argue that they were a response to environmental pressures: they reflect the environment as well as the actor. The repeat offender, committing crimes over a period in which his living circumstances change, cannot make the same claim with anything like the same degree of plausibility. We do not discuss this third possible justification, as it may constitute an explanation for differential attributions rather than a penal justification for distinguishing among offenders. With respect to misconduct, the colleague who is regularly 30 minutes late for faculty meetings is more likely to be perceived as thoughtless, rather than someone who unluckily missed his bus.
11. Ashworth and Wasik (this volume) see little merit in this position "not least because there is usually no question that the multiple offenders knew they were committing offenses and were, at that stage, avoiding detection." Yet the reason speaks to mitigation and is not exculpatory in nature. An offender may know it is wrong to rob someone of a mobile phone, but a much fuller awareness of the wrongfulness of the act (and its consequences for the victim and offender) will emerge following trial, conviction and punishment.
12. Bagaric and Alexander (2013) argue that this is "the only tenable basis for conferring a sentencing discount for offenders sentenced for more than one offense" (p. 165).
13. We omit for the present discussion the additional category of offender noted in the introduction, namely those convicted of multiple crimes and with criminal histories involving multiple convictions in the past.
14. In reality of course the recidivist premium snowballs with the result that each additional conviction builds upon each prior crime. The result is that the gap between the multiple and serial offenders is even greater than suggested by these examples (see Roberts, 1997).
15. First, a caveat. Consistency is harder to achieve in some contexts. A sentencing system in which sentence severity was determined *exclusively* by retribution or by risk would result in more consistent outcomes. Multiple sentencing objectives complicate the sentencing equation and inevitably introduce more variability in outcomes. In a similar fashion, consistency across cases is greatly facilitated if all offenders are convicted of one, and only one crime. The consequence is that sentencing outcomes in multiple-offense cases will necessarily involve greater variation. This increased variability is not a collateral consequence but rather a positively desirable result.
16. Our concept of relatedness is reminiscent of Vibla's concept of connectedness (see this volume). There are important differences, however. We articulate clear dimensions of relatedness whereas Vibla's conceptualization is broader and more nebulous, including "reasons, motives, and the impetus underpinning and driving criminal behaviour."
17. It is also the most intuitively plausible, if common intuition is a consideration. Claims for mitigation that fly in the face of intuition may need to be more rigorously justified. The first-offender discount, for example, attracts widespread community support; other claims in mitigation such as social adversity are less generally accepted by laypersons.
18. See Alexander, Ferzan, and Morse (2009, pp. 255–257) on the connection between time frame and quality of deliberation.
19. Cases of premeditated mercy killing are sometimes offered as examples where premeditation does not aggravate, but this is a simplistic view. It is more accurate to see such cases as examples where planning is not relevant to culpability. Sentencing factors are not always aggravating or mitigating.
20. Thus when two assaults were committed the same day, the second assault attracted a somewhat higher punishment form subjects. When the two assaults were committed years apart the difference was greater (see Robinson, 2013, Table 7.1, p. 395).
21. As the intervals between the episodes of offending increase, it becomes less plausible to attribute the misconduct to the environment, which presumably changes over time.
22. When the behavior repeats over many different occasions, the likelihood of external or environmental causes or explanations diminishes.
23. This example is reminiscent of the pencil theft case. The person who grabs 10 pencils on a single visit is in no way equivalent to the individual who makes a separate trip once a week to

the shop, stealing a pencil each visit. Courts and community members would treat these cases very differently, even if some legal philosophers struggle to grasp the difference.

24. We are grateful to Netanel Dagan for suggesting this example.
25. For example, Manson (this volume) provides a complex, nine-cell matrix of offenses which distinguishes between similar and dissimilar crimes (and between few and many offenses), yet is silent with respect to any underlying rationale for the scheme. Drawing upon his supermarket analogy, this is akin to telling shoppers that apples cost two euros a pound, bananas three euros and Kiwi fruit ten—without offering any justification for such striking price differentials.
26. Long-term sentences of this kind should also be subject to a late-term review such as that proposed by the Model Penal Code Sentencing provisions.

References

Alexander, L. 2011. "Culpability." In J. Deigh and D. Dolinka (eds.), *The Oxford Handbook of Criminal Law*, pp. 218–238. New York: Oxford University Press.

Alexander, L., K. Ferzan, and S. Morse. 2009. *Crime and Culpability: A Theory of Criminal Law*. Cambridge: Cambridge University Press.

Ashworth, A. 1983. *Sentencing and Penal Policy*. London: Weidenfeld and Nicolson.

Ashworth, A. 2015. *Sentencing and Criminal Justice*. 6th ed. Cambridge: Cambridge University Press.

Bagaric, M., and T. Alexander. 2013. "Rehabilitating Totality in Sentencing: From Obscurity to Principle." *University of New South Wales Law Journal* 36(1): 139–167.

Fayet, N. Jr. 2016. *Do Crime Continuado*. 7th ed. Porto Alegre: Livraria do Advogado.

Jareborg, N. 2002. *Scraps of Penal Theory*. London: Coronet.

Lovegrove, A. 2004. *Sentencing the Multiple Offender: Judicial Practice and Legal Principle*. Canberra: Australian Institute of Criminology.

Reitz, K. 2010. "The Illusion of Proportionality: Desert and Repeat Offenders." In J. V. Roberts and A. von Hirsch (eds.), *Previous Convictions at Sentencing: Theoretical and Applied Perspectives*, pp. 137–159. Oxford: Hart Publishing.

Roberts, J. V. 1997. "Paying for the Past: The Role of Criminal Record in the Sentencing Process." In M. Tonry (ed.), *Crime and Justice. A Review of Research* 22: 303–362. Chicago: University of Chicago Press.

Roberts, J. V. 2010. "First Offender Sentencing Discounts: Exploring the Justifications." In J. V. Roberts and A. von Hirsch (eds.), *Previous Convictions at Sentencing: Theoretical and Applied Perspectives*, pp. 17–36. Oxford: Hart Publishing.

Roberts, J. V., M. Hough, J. Jacobson, A. Bredee, and. Moon. 2009. "Public Attitudes to the Sentencing of Offenders Convicted of Offences Involving Death by Driving." *Criminal Law Review* (July): 525–540.

Robinson, P. H., and J. M. Darley. 1995. *Justice, Liability, and Blame: Community Views and the Criminal Law*. Boulder, CO: Westview Press.

Robinson, P. 2013. *Intuitions of Justice and the Utility of Desert*. New York: Oxford University Press.

Sentencing Council for England and Wales. 2012. *Definitive Guideline on Totality and Offences Taken into Consideration*. London: Sentencing Council for England and Wales.

Thomas, D. A. 1979. *Principles of Sentencing: The Sentencing Policy of the Court of Appeal Criminal Division*. 2nd ed. London: Heinemann.

Von Hirsch, A. 2010. "Proportionality and the Progressive Loss of Mitigation: Some Further Reflections." In J. V. Roberts and A. von Hirsch (eds.), *Previous Convictions at Sentencing: Theoretical and Applied Perspectives*, pp. 1–16. Oxford: Hart Publishing.

Von Hirsch, A., and A. Ashworth. 2005. *Proportionate Sentencing: Exploring the Principles*. Oxford: Oxford University Press.

Wasik, M. 2012. "Concurrent and Consecutive Sentences Revisited." In L. Zedner and J. V. Roberts (eds.), *Principles and Values in Criminal Law and Criminal Justice: Essays in Honour of Andrew Ashworth*, pp. 285–306. Oxford: Oxford University Press.

CASE LAW

R v Wacker [2002] EWCA Crim 1944, [2003] 1 Cr App R (S) 92.

9

Toward a Theoretical and Practical Model for Multiple-Offense Sentencing

NATALIA VIBLA

Sentencing multiple-offense cases presents a challenge for desert theory. The fundamental desert principle is that of proportionality: the punishment should be commensurate with the offense committed. However, the sentencing of multiple-offense cases is seemingly at variance with that principle. In most such cases, some degree of discount is applied to the total sentence. At first glance, the very idea of a discount appears to conflict with desert. This essay attempts to untangle the conflicting positions and find some reconciliation with desert principles. It also offers some practical suggestions for implementation.

Key Pillars of Desert

Desert theory contains two major dimensions of offense seriousness: the harm caused and the culpability of the offender (von Hirsch and Ashworth, 2005). It follows that sentencing cases consisting of more than one offense should involve assessing seriousness in terms of harm and culpability. But the specifics of multiple-offense sentencing include discounting the total sentence for a case. In particular, the conventional approach to dealing with multiple-offense cases includes assessing harm and culpability for individual offenses, identifying separate proportionate sentences for those offenses, and then applying a discount either to the separate sentences or aggregating the separate sentences into one and applying a discount to the total sentence. So, can the notions of harm and culpability be accommodated to explain this discounting?

Justifying discounts on the basis of diminished harms in multiple-offending behavior is difficult: the harms remain constant. For example, if a sentence for the fifth burglary involving theft of a television is decreased to one fifth of the normal sentence, that does not mean that the harm to the victim involves the theft of one fifth of a TV. It might be possible to justify a reduction on the basis of diminished culpability.[1] It could be argued that the culpability of the offender committing multiple offenses decreases with every subsequent offense. An offender may get used to offending, and for this reason his blameworthiness decreases and that creates a basis for diminished culpability. However, there is a limit to which stretching the role of culpability as a justification for a reduction is plausible. For example, if a sentence for the tenth domestic burglary is reduced from six months of imprisonment to two weeks of imprisonment, the culpability of the offender for that particular offense would have to shrink dramatically to justify such a discount and it is difficult to see why that should be the case. Therefore, culpability as a factor in justifying a reduction in multiple-offense sentencing has limited utility.

Background Concepts

There does not appear to be a unified approach with regards to multiple-offense sentencing within the framework of desert theory. The proposals advanced by scholars vary: sentencing on the basis of the concepts of totality and a "single transaction" rule (Thomas, 1979); justifying a discount on the basis of overall proportionality (Ashworth, 2015); mercy (Bottoms, 1998); parsimony (Jareborg, 1998); humanity (Ulvang, 2005); and the principle that "each victim counts" (Lippke, 2011), to name some of the more prominent. Lovegrove, in his empirical study of multiple-offense sentencing in Australia concluded that in their decisions to discount sentences, judges rely on the idea of avoiding imposing harsh sentences, rather than on notions of proportionality. This finding echoes the English courts' attempt to avoid the sentence having a "crushing" effect on offenders (Lovegrove, 2000; 2004). Thus a single desert-based justification for a discount has yet to be articulated; the search for an ethical/philosophical basis for justifying a discounting model for multiple-offense cases continues.

A Brief Sketch of Several Sentencing Practices

Considering the lack of a unified theoretical perspective with regards to multiple-offense sentencing and in view of the frequency of such cases going through the courts (Ashworth, 2015), it is appropriate to turn to sentencing practice in an attempt to better understand the way that the discount operates. Although most jurisdictions provide for the application of discount in multiple-offense sentencing, their practices differ.

A study of sentencing decisions in Germany conducted by Albrecht reveals a diminishing incremental effect of separate sentences on the total sentence for a case (Albrecht, 1994 quoted by Jareborg, 1998). In this context, each offense is first assigned a proportionate sentence and then a total sentence is constructed in the following way: the full sentence for the most serious offense in a case is increased by a proportion for each secondary offense, in order of severity. This is done is such way that the discount for each separate sentence increases with every additional offense up to the point of disappearing fully when further offending has no further effect on the total sentence. For example, a case consisting of a robbery worth three years' custody, burglary worth one year, and a theft worth six months would warrant a sentence of three years for the robbery, five months for the burglary, and one month for the theft (three years and six months in total).

In Australia, the procedure is similar. First, each individual offense is allocated a separate sentence and those separate sentences are then arranged into a total by means of concurrency and consecutiveness. In addition, there is a third process in Australia; namely partial concurrency/partial consecutiveness, which provides flexibility as it allows for separate sentences to overlap each other. In his comprehensive study of sentencing decisions Lovegrove found that two factors determine cumulation of the secondary offenses upon the principal offense (Lovegrove, 2004). First, the more serious the principal offense, the smaller the proportion of secondary offenses cumulated, and vice versa. Second, the higher the sum of sentences for the secondary offenses, the smaller the percentage of their sentences, which is cumulated. As with Albrecht's study, Lovegrove found that cumulation of sentences for the secondary offenses occurs by way of progressively decreasing increments: as the sum of individual sentences increases, the percentage of sentences for the secondary offenses decreases.

The Swedish Penal Code contains several sections relating to multiple-offense cases. These state that the court should impose a single penalty for the whole case (Section 6, Chapter 25), that it should use a modified scale of penalties (Section 6, Chapter 25), and that the total sentence should be determined according to the overall gravity of all crimes (Section 1, Chapter 29). Further, Section 2, Chapter 26 provides upper and lower sentencing limits for multiple-offense cases. It states that imprisonment can be imposed for longer than the statutory maximum punishment for the most serious offense in a case, but should not exceed the total sum of maximum penalties for each individual offense. It also provides some specific sentencing limits for total sentences in multiple-offense cases: if the statutory maximum for the most serious offense in a case is under four years, the total sentence may be extended by one year; if it falls between four and eight years, by two years; and if it is eight years or more, it can only be extended by four years. With regards to the minimum sentence allowed, this cannot be lower than the longest minimum statutory sentence available in the case (e.g., if there are three offenses in a case with the statutory minimum sentences one, two, and three years respectively, the total sentence in that case should not be lower than the longest minimum, which is three years).

However useful in terms of providing lower and upper limits, the Swedish Penal Code provides little or no guidance on how to sentence actual multiple-offense cases, which mostly fall well below the upper limits and are close to the lower ones. The Swedish Supreme Court has issued some guidance with regards to such cases and has also provided a thorough analysis of four multiple-offense cases. Thus the starting point should be an assessment of the appropriate penalty for the most serious offense; then a gradually decreasing portion of a normal sanction for each subsequent offense should be added to the penalty for the most serious offense. Finally, a general assessment of the case must be made in order to ensure that the total sentence is not disproportionate to the crimes in the case. In addition, the gravity of individual crimes, the types and combinations of offenses involved, and the temporal relationships between the crimes have an impact on the total sentence.

With regards to the working rules of sentencing multiple-offense cases, there are two models in place. The first model is the traditional one that has been in use for a long time which suggests that 50% of the aggregated penalties of all of the sentences for the secondary offenses should be added to the 100% penalty of the sentence for the most serious offense. The second model has been designed by the Swedish Supreme Court judge Martin Borgeke on the basis of his analysis of court decisions as well as discussions held with other members of the judiciary.

Borgeke's model consists of three formulae (Borgeke, 2008), differing by the degree of punishment allocated for the most serious offense in a case. According to Borgeke's formulae, the total sentence for a multiple-offense case should consist of the full punishment for the most serious offense and decreasing proportions of punishment for the secondary offenses, in order of the offenses' relative seriousness. The proportions of punishment assigned for the secondary offenses differ in such a way that less severe punishment for the most serious offense in a case attracts higher proportions of punishment for the secondary offenses, and vice versa; more severe punishment for the most serious offense attracts higher proportions of secondary offenses punishment; hence the three formulas, rather than one. The formulae are presented in the following tables.

If the sentence for the most serious offense is less than six months, this formula should apply:

Sentence for the 1st offense	Sentence for the 2nd offense	Sentence for the 3rd offense	Sentence for the 4th offense	Sentence for the 5th offense	Sentence for the 6th offense	Sentence for the 7th offense
1/1	1/2	1/2	1/3	1/3	1/4	1/4

If the sentence for the most serious offense is more than six months but less than one year and six months, this formula should apply:

Sentence for the 1st offense	Sentence for the 2nd offense	Sentence for the 3rd offense	Sentence for the 4th offense	Sentence for the 5th offense	Sentence for the 6th offense	Sentence for the 7th offense
1/1	1/2	1/3	1/4	1/5	1/6	1/7

If the sentence for the most serious offense is more than one year and six months, this formula should apply:

Sentence for the 1st offense	Sentence for the 2nd offense	Sentence for the 3rd offense	Sentence for the 4th offense	Sentence for the 5th offense	Sentence for the 6th offense
1/1	1/3	1/6	1/9	1/12	1/15

Borgeke's model was first introduced in 2008 and is growing in popularity, especially among younger judges. Although the models yield slightly different results, they are rarely applied rigidly, and various adjustments to the final total sentences for multiple-offense cases are usually made leading to similar outcomes.

Sentencing practices from these jurisdictions suggest a common line of reasoning with regards to multiple-offense sentencing: first, the most serious offense in a case is established; then a sentence is allocated to each separate offense comprising the case; and finally the sentence for the most serious offense forms the basis of the total sentence upon which proportions of sentences for the secondary offenses are added in a way that has diminishing impact. In the absence of solid theoretical argument providing a basis for an alternative multiple-offense sentencing approach, it is assumed that an established convention should serve as a basis for constructing theory. Such a convention is found within the three jurisdictions noted earlier: Germany, Australia, and Sweden. The fundamental principle is that the total sentence for a multiple-offense case should incorporate a discount or reduction, resulting in a total sentence lower than the mere aggregation of separate sentences for the individual offenses comprising a case. A number of normative and empirically derived positions may justify this approach.

Normative Propositions

The Absence of Normative Breaks

The conventional criminal justice paradigm for dealing with crimes entails three components: charge, conviction and sentence. Each offense is separately processed through the first and second stages and, if it results in conviction, through the third stage as well. Thus the point of apprehension is an important moment in the criminal process. In particular, the difference between multiple-offense cases and repeat-offense cases, given that the offending involved is otherwise identical, is explained by apprehension and punishment in the second case and the absence of these in the first. An offender in the second case has been given an opportunity to correct his conduct and stop offending whereas in the first case an offender has had no such opportunity. It is true that any offender, apprehended or not, always has an opportunity to choose to stop offending, unless she is not capable of such decision due to certain concerns, such as mental health, age, and so on. However, here the word "opportunity" has a different meaning. It refers to the prudential dimension of punishment in von Hirsch's model of desert, namely the hard treatment (von Hirsch, 1993). Hard treatment, according to von Hirsch, by means of material deprivation provides an opportunity for the offender to learn from punishment and to avoid punishment again by desisting from crime. It follows that the offender who has not been subjected to the hard treatment dimension of punishment has been deprived of the opportunity to learn from it. Therefore, this absence of an opportunity to take lessons from punishment, in normative terms, diminishes offender's blameworthiness and provides a justification for the lower sentence.[2]

Censure is also a significant factor. Censure, according to von Hirsch's desert theory, is the state's message of blameworthiness; it is a moral condemnation that punishment is meant to convey (von Hirsch, 1993). The presence or absence of such a message is a central tenet in processing criminal cases. Censure occurs at the very end of the criminal process, namely at sentencing: it is delivered along with the judgment. A censuring message includes the state's assessment of the offense and it also provides an offender with an opportunity to modify his behavior and withdraw from offending, it introduces a *normative break* on his behavior.

An offender who commits crimes over a certain period of time but is not apprehended, convicted, and sentenced by the state after each crime, has not received a censuring message and has not been provided with an opportunity to modify his life.[3] Until he is apprehended, in normative terms he remains in the state of offending. The mechanism the law relies upon—state censure—has not been activated for such an offender: thus no normative breaks have taken place in the process. At the point of apprehension all of his offenses are being dealt with together: charging, conviction, and sentencing. The censuring message is delivered at that stage and that is when the offending behavior ends and the normative break begins. Whatever the nature and composition of a multiple-offense case and however long the time period over which the offenses were committed, in normative terms the offender remains in a continuum until he is apprehended, convicted, and sentenced and a censuring message is delivered: namely, until the normative break occurs.

Overall Proportionality Based on Living Standard Analysis

Overall proportionality, as suggested by Ashworth, refers to proportionality between categories of crimes, rather than proportionality between an offense and a sentence (Ashworth, 2015). Accordingly, the total sentence for a case should be limited by a sentence for a more severe category of crime than those comprising the case: for example, no number of burglaries should lead to a sentence corresponding to robbery. While sound in principle, it does not provide clear reasoning as to why the total sentence for a case should be limited by a sentence for more severe categories of crimes, or why a sentence for many burglaries should never exceed the sentence for a single robbery.

The answer is found in the concept of the living standard analysis. Von Hirsch and Jareborg (1991) developed a theory of criminal harm that addresses the issue of gauging the harmfulness of criminal conduct. According to their theory, harms should be assessed in comparative gravity in accordance with how much they would impair a person's standard of living. The term "standard of living" focuses on the means and capabilities for achieving a certain quality of life. These means include shelter, financial resources, and privacy (among others). Means and capabilities are standardized, so someone is considered to have a good standard of living if he or she has the resources necessary to live well.

The living standard analysis allows for comparisons between different crimes in terms of their relative harm. The authors explain why an aggravated assault is more harmful than burglary: it is because the first offense affects a person's standard of living more adversely than the second one. In addition, all offenses to some degree possess the following dimensions: (1) physical integrity; (2) material support and amenity; (3) privacy; (4) freedom from humiliation.

Each dimension is assessed in terms of an offense's impact on the victim's living standard. For example, burglary's impact upon material amenity is modest, as typically few material goods are taken but its impact upon privacy is high since entering someone's home constitutes an intrusion on an important element in people's life.

In addition, living standards can be ranked into four levels: (1) subsistence; (2) minimal well-being; (3) "adequate" well-being; (4) standard well-being. Criminal conduct can be measured against those levels of living standard with the more serious crimes affecting the first and second levels and less serious crimes affecting the third and fourth. For example, aggravated assault, a very serious crime, affects the subsistence level of the living standard.

The living standard analysis applies equally to multiple-offense cases. In order to assess the harm involved in a multiple-offense case, it is necessary to determine which level of living standard is being affected, based on the type and quality of offending involved in a case. For example, multiple wallet thefts affect the "standard" or "adequate" level of living standard; multiple wounding affects the "minimal" or "subsistence" levels. The degree of harm involved in such cases should correspond to the affected living standards and the total sentences for the case should be determined accordingly.

As an illustrative example, a case consisting of multiple thefts should yield a total sentence within the range of sentences corresponding to thefts; a case consisting of multiple wounding should result in a sentence within the range of sentences for wounding. A combination of different crimes should lead to a sentence that takes into account the most serious level of living standard affected by offending involved.

In this context, the number of offending occasions is irrelevant. Based on a living standard analysis, the harm caused by the crimes affects a certain level of living standard: that level of living standard stays the same, no matter how many crimes are involved. No number of crimes present in a case could lead to the superseding of a particular level of living standard affected by those crimes. The harms caused by separate crimes in a case do not add in any way to the level of living standard beyond which has already been determined by the type of criminality involved in the case. Thus the harm involved in a case should be assessed according to the living standard affected, and only that.

For example, the harm caused by wallet thefts affects a particular level of living standard, is most likely standard or adequate. Regardless of how many wallet thefts are committed, what counts is the particular level of living standard that is affected. Indeed, it is difficult to see how the harm caused by a multitude of wallet thefts could affect minimal or subsistence levels of living standard; those levels are usually affected by more serious crimes such as grievous bodily harm or robbery. As a result, assessing harm from this perspective should lead to placing a total sentence for a case within the range appropriate for thefts, while exceeding that range would be inappropriate.

An argument could be made here that such comparison of harms is not sustainable (this argument is discussed by Ryberg in this volume). More specifically, that it is not clear why a large number of crimes in lower category would not affect someone's life equally or even more than a single instance of crime in higher category. Consider someone who had one pound stolen from him in the course of 100 days and someone who had 100 pounds stolen all in one go. Was the first victim harmed more or less than the second victim? Another example could be a comparison of harms experienced, on one hand by a victim of three indecent assaults and, on the other hand, by a victim of single rape.

While the idea that it is possible to feel equally or even more harmed by a number of offenses of lower categories (rather than a single offense of a more serious category) is plausible, this issue belongs to the realm of personal experiences and thus should be a subject of a different study, one with an empirical component.[4] The key with regards to the living standard analysis is that, as the term suggests, it permits comparison of harms according to the established standard, as opposed to personal experiences and expectations. That standard serves as an anchoring point for comparing deviations caused by criminal acts. So, in the first example, the question is whether the living standard of a £1 theft victim has been affected more or less than the living standard of a £100 theft victim. The answer is probably not, because the harm caused to the first victim is spread out over a long period of time, so both the emotional and material shock from theft is much less severe and is not likely to affect the victim's living standard the same way as the shock of losing 100 pounds at one time would. The other example illustrates the same point: the harm caused to the victim of indecent assault, measured in terms of intrusion into privacy, applied violence, and so on is not the same as the harm caused to the victim of rape, although both victims may suffer.

Living standard analysis provides a rationale for the concept of overall proportionality, which serves as a tool for limiting the total sentence in a multiple-offense case as it calls for proportionality between categories of crimes. A sentence for a more serious crime than those involved in a case serves as a ceiling for sentence reduction in a multiple-offense cases.

A living standard analysis provides a different justification for a sentence reduction: the harm caused by the total offending behavior in a case is assessed through the lenses of living standards and thus is naturally reduced and adjusted to reflect the particular living standard being affected. The number of incidents involved plays no part in the assessment of harm. There is no particular need in this situation to search for an appropriately matching more severe crime category in order to reduce the total sentence for a multiple-offense case; living standard analysis allows for a proper assessment of harm and accordingly offense seriousness. Thus the utilization of living standard analysis ensures that the overall proportionality between categories is preserved.

Empirically Derived Propositions

In addition to these normative propositions, a further two empirically derived propositions support the concept of a discount in multiple-offense sentencing. These are derived from the research conducted with Swedish judges which identified trends in how judges perceive and sentence multiple-offense cases (Vibla, 2014). It is important to emphasize that these two propositions are not derived from desert theory: they are empirical and serve the purpose of explaining and justifying the discount as viewed and utilized in the real world. However, they have implications for desert as they allow a different understanding of the nature of multiple-offense cases.

Connectedness

The first empirical proposition is that there is a considerable degree of *connectedness* between the offenses comprising a multiple-offense case. Offenses in a multiple-offense case traditionally are viewed as separate criminal events, independent of each other. Even crimes committed in close time, type, space, or other proximity are often viewed as being independent of each other. One of the empirical patterns identified during the sentencing exercise with the Swedish judges suggests that often there are common reasons underpinning offenses comprising multiple-offense cases. For example, an offender committing multiple thefts in the course of one night might be driven by the need to get money in order to buy drugs.

This principle is extended to cover a wide spectrum of multiple-offense cases, including those where offenses are committed far apart and those consisting of different types offenses. The individual offenses comprising multiple-offense cases usually share some underlying factors: for example, they could be driven by a common impetus, motivated by the same reasons, brought about for the same purposes. Those underlying factors that are characteristic of the whole offending behavior, be it impetus, reasons, or purposes, are referred to here as connectedness. In this sense connectedness acts as a glue that connects separate criminal events into one. It allows viewing the collection of seemingly separate events belonging in a case as a single prolonged joint offending event taking place over certain period of time: short or long, small or large, including victims or being victimless.

There are various examples of connectedness: substance addiction, mental health problems, distress, anger, financial problems, greed, influence of peers; offender misperceptions (e.g., "I got away with it last time, so I can do it again, hoping to get away with it again"); along with many other examples of what would be seen as contributing factors. Connectedness is the dynamic that permeates an offender's motives, opportunities, and criminal activities.

Even in seemingly disconnected cases consisting of different types of offenses committed over a long period of time there could be a residual element of connectedness. For example, an offender supplementing his finances by specializing in late night theft might simply not have had an opportunity to steal enough goods in one night that would satisfy his needs; thus he might split his activity into many nights which would still be limited to only those days when the shops are open late at night. If the shops were only open late on Tuesdays, those would be the day when a specialist in late-night shopping theft would go to work. Thus his crimes are separated by days, perhaps by weeks and months, but they are connected by the same causes of criminality, for example, financial gain.

Offenses could be connected in various ways: one being when the reasons for committing offense A are the same as for committing offense B, regardless of whether A and B were committed in close time proximity to each other or not. For example, in order to finance his drinking habits a person regularly stole wallets from different people in public transport over the course of several months. Another way in which offenses could be connected is when one offense arises directly from another one, in a spontaneous way while only one offense was intended but the criminal activity gave rise to several events: again, proximity in time is irrelevant. For example, over the course of several weeks, a person steals a car, then forges the car documents, and finally sells the car. Whether offenses comprising a multiple-offense case are planned or occur sporadically, whether they are intended or spontaneous is of no consequence; they are still unified by the common factors of impetus, reasons, purposes, or other. The key determining factor is that a connectedness between the offenses is present.

The role of connectedness is to establish the strength of the link between different offenses. This strength of the link could be referred to as a degree of connectedness. The stronger the link or the higher the degree of connectedness, the more the offenses in a multiple-offense case could be viewed as a single criminal process or behavior and vice versa.

The idea of connectedness first appears in Lovegrove's study (Lovegrove, 2004). It is one of the findings of his research and as a result, it is included in his guidance for multiple-offense sentencing. In particular, Lovegrove refers to connectedness as a link between the principal and secondary offenses and assumes that there are different degrees of connectedness. Those degrees translate into different proportions of sentences for the secondary offenses cumulated upon the principal offense sentence: higher degrees of connectedness should result in smaller proportions of the secondary offense sentences cumulated upon the principal offense sentence. More specifically, he distinguishes between five degrees of connectedness: "full degree," which translates into 50% of punishment for the secondary offense being added to the punishment for the principal offense; "high" degree, corresponding to 70%; "moderate" degree, to 80%; "low" degree, to 90%; and "minimal degree" of connectedness, corresponding to 100% of the secondary offense sentences being added to the principal offense's sentence. Lovegrove's concept of connectedness is more limited than the one suggested here. His view of connectedness is principally determined by time and location dimensions, whereas the one suggested here is broader and less rigid: it includes offending behavior that occurs across different times and locations and is determined by common underlying reasons and motives; it also provides a basis for viewing the whole offending behavior as a continuum of criminal conduct.

Continuum of Criminal Conduct

These theoretical propositions, (connectedness and the lack of normative breaks), lead to a third: the *continuum of criminal conduct*. This third proposition suggests that individual offenses, comprising a multiple-offense case, should not be viewed in the same way as single offenses: those individual offenses need to be considered together as part of a continuum of criminal conduct. The conventional consideration of cases consisting of multiple offenses views them as a collection of separate criminal acts. For example, a case consisting of four burglaries committed over a period of six months is viewed as four separate crimes. This perspective implies the existence of breaks between the independent criminal events. The string of independent criminal events separated by breaks in offending ends when the charge is brought against the offender.

Another empirical pattern emerging from research with the Swedish judges—specifically that offenses committed closely to each other constitute one crime and the break between them becomes vague—provides the basis for developing a fresh approach thinking about the nature of multiple offending. It is plausible to view all multiple-offense cases, including those consisting of crimes committed closely to each other and those that are not, as a continuum of criminal conduct. This requires a reframing of perceptions; from viewing multiple-offense cases as consisting of a certain number of offenses toward viewing a multiple-offense case as a continuum of criminal conduct. To justify this shift and view the offenses as a continuum of criminal conduct requires disregarding the breaks between the offenses as per scheme 3, which would regard the number of offenses in a case as irrelevant. Offending behavior often involves very little rational and deliberate planning. For example, an offender may not plan to burgle six houses over the next three months, or commit four rapes against two partners, or pick the pockets of 11 people in a shop next week. Those offenses tend to develop on a more ad hoc basis, requiring an approach to sentencing that responds to such behavior.

With regards to crimes against persons (e.g., assault, rape, robbery) and crimes against the collective interest (e.g., gambling, drugs) it is easy to see that spontaneity is the major factor in many such instances. For example, a person who suffers from alcohol abuse and anger management problems gets drunk in a pub, loses his temper, and assaults people. This behavior continues for several weeks until he gets apprehended by the police and eventually is convicted and sentenced for several assaults. Two aspects are relevant to this case: (1) no planning is involved, it is spontaneous; and (2) there is strong connectedness between the offenses in a form of alcohol abuse and anger issues. Even though the criminal events had occurred over several weeks, these three aspects make it difficult to identify the break points between the offenses. It is more appropriate to see a series of such assaults as a continuum of assaulting behavior.

With regards to crimes against property (e.g., burglary, theft, arson), white collar crime (e.g., embezzlement, tax evasion), and organized crime (e.g., distribution of illegal goods or services) planning is typically involved. But the planning does not ordinarily concern the number of offending instances but rather the modus operandi of the offenses; further instances usually develop ad hoc. For example, a person who wants to supplement his income decides to rob people; he plans the modus operandi of that offense; if the first offense is successful and he does not get caught, he continues with the same activity for several months until he finally gets apprehended and is brought to court. As in the case above two aspects are relevant: (1) planning may be involved only at the stage of developing the modus operandi of the first offense, and subsequent offenses develop due to the successes of the previous criminal events; and (2) there is strong connectedness in the form of financial need to supplement an irregular income. Again, it is difficult to identify the breaks, even though the activities took place over several months. Instead of viewing the offenses as independent events separated by the break points, it is more appropriate to see them as a prolonged continuum of thefts. In this context the number of offenses is not the key factor. If the number of offenses is irrelevant, then the break points between the offenses become elusive as well.

Implications of the Four Propositions for Desert

In the conventional treatment of multiple-offense cases, the discount applied to a total sentence is not viewed as a natural element in the process of sentencing but rather as a necessary and pragmatic tool utilized for the purpose of lowering an unduly harsh sentence. The discount applied to the total sentence becomes contrived. The two concepts that are often cited in rationalizing a discount are (1) relativity to other categories of crimes, and (2) appeals to humanitarian concerns, including forgiveness and mercy. Neither of the concepts aligns well with desert theory of punishment.

A fundamental difference between the conventional approach and the approach suggested here is that instead of regarding a case as deserving a certain sentence A, which due to its length cannot be applied and therefore gets discounted to sentence B, the case is regarded as not deserving sentence A but deserving sentence B from the outset. In order to do so, the propositions of normative breaks, overall proportionality, connectedness, and continuum of criminal conduct have to be fully invoked, as all four propositions underpin the idea of deserved total sentence.

A multiple-offense case assessed through living standard analysis and scrutinized for the degree of connectedness and continuum of criminal conduct, supported by the lack of normative breaks is less serious than cumulated separate sentences for the individual offenses. An adequate way, therefore, to reflect the criminal behavior in a multiple-offense case would be by considering the quality of offending, rather than the quantity of offenses. One should consider the type of offending taking place within a case and the ways it develops, rather than counting the separate instances of that offending. The seriousness of the case judged by the quality of whole offending behavior is therefore lower than it would have been had it been derived from cumulated separate offenses. For example, a case consisting of five burglaries would be judged by the quality of the burglary offense and would be sentenced accordingly. Each of the five burglaries in a case does not deserve the same sentence as a burglary committed singly. Instead, each burglary contributes to the case qualitatively, not quantitatively, so the quality of the whole case is the centre of attention. Thus a case viewed through the lenses of the four concepts—the lack of normative breaks, overall proportionality, connectedness, and continuum of criminal conduct—naturally deserves a lower sentence than a case viewed as a cumulation of separate independent offenses.

The system of presumptive sentencing ranges is not relevant here. This was developed on the basis of single offenses, and is thus not directly applicable to offenses committed as part of a continuum of criminal conduct. The penal value of the separate offenses in multiple-offense case is different: it is lower because the whole conduct must be evaluated as a whole. This provides a response to Wells's question regarding the dissonance between proportionate separate sentences leading to a disproportionate total in a multiple-offense case (Wells, 1992). The argument is that the individual sentences, if calculated on the basis of offenses committed singly, would not be proportionate but rather inflated.

Such inflated sentences naturally lead to a disproportionate total. If, on the other hand, the notions of connectedness and continuum of criminal conduct are incorporated into the calculation of separate sentences, those separate sentences can be viewed as one joint offending event, the sentence for which can be lower in comparison to sentences calculated on the basis of singly committed offenses. Such a reduced sentence is actually a proportionate one in relation to multiple offense viewed a single offending event. This explains why separate, seemingly proportionate sentences for multiple offenses need to be reduced in order to reach the proportionate total. So, to address Wells's challenge, it is not that the proportionate separate sentences lead to disproportional total; it is that those "proportionate" sentences are actually inflated and thus cannot result in a proportionate total. In order to reach the proportionate total, separate sentences need to be reduced in order to reflect the joint offending behavior.

Thus the main reasons behind including the empirical concepts of connectedness and continuum of criminal conduct into the model is that they allow viewing multiple-offense cases differently than they have been traditionally: instead of being perceived as a collection of seemingly independent offending events, those offenses are viewed as a single joint offending event. In this respect a useful tool is a "helicopter perspective":[5] that is, looking at the multiple offenses from afar. Such a perspective leads to viewing the multitude of offenses as a continuum, and also pays attention to the quality of offending involved, rather than the quantity of separate offenses. Assessing multiple-offense case seriousness is thus conducted with respect to the quality and type of offending involved, rather than offense quantity.

Connectedness itself does not directly influence desert: the type of motives, impetus, or reasons do not regulate desert-based sentencing, just as there is no claim made that connectedness itself reduces culpability. However, connectedness provides a basis for viewing multiple offending differently. This alternative perspective allows a different perception of a case: on the basis of harm and culpability but also taking living standard analysis into consideration. To illustrate, consider two offenders, both having committed two identical thefts but in the first case the crimes were motivated by offender's need for food whereas in the second case the first crime was motivated by offender's hunger and the second one by her thirst. The main question here would be to establish whether crimes in both cases could be viewed as a continuum of criminal conduct, and the degree of connectedness should be established. The first case is quite clear since the motives behind offending behavior are identical, so it should be viewed as a continuum of criminal conduct and the degree of connectedness is high. The motives behind offending in the second case are slightly different yet they are very similar in nature, so the case should also be viewed as a continuum of criminal conduct and the degree of connectedness would be high as well. The assessment of case seriousness should then be carried out taking into consideration the living standard analysis. If, on the other hand, a theft was motivated by hunger and then, six months later, another theft motivated by the desire to have fun, then the continuum of criminal conduct is looser and degree of connectedness: the assessment of case seriousness should incorporate the fact that offenses perhaps do not form a tight continuum.

Finally, the main strength of both connectedness and continuum of criminal conduct is in their link to the real world. This is how judges view multiple-offense cases and this knowledge should not be alien to the consideration of principles. Penal theory should not attempt to justify existing practice, but nor should it be blind to such information. After all, sentencing principles are designed to help sentencers; a link to the real world should facilitate, not impede, the development of principles.

Limitations of the Model

Principles of Connectedness

The concept of connectedness in this essay is defined as the reasons and motives underpinning crimes. This definition requires further refinement if it is to become fully operational. The following issues, just to mention a few, need to be defined further: similarities and differences between the offenses; the extent to which the common causality and temporal continuity should affect the total sentence; rules on aggregation of offenses comprising a multiple-offenses case; and other. A related issue that needs to be thought through is whether it would be useful to develop different types of connectedness for different types of cases, such as cases consisting of offenses of the same type and offenses of mixed types; cases consisting of offenses of different gravity; cases with long gaps between offending; and other types.

Continuum of Criminal Conduct: Low Visibility Cases

Cases in which the continuum of criminal conduct was less than obvious were referred to earlier as "low-visibility" cases. Sometimes, however, the visibility is so low that the continuum is practically invisible. Three types of cases are immediately identifiable: firstly, cases consisting of crimes of different types and gravity; secondly, cases with particularly long time gaps between them such as year; thirdly, cases in which the underpinning motives result in different kinds of offenses.

If continuum of criminal conduct is not immediately obvious it does not mean that it is nonexistent. Perhaps the possibility of a continuum should not be eliminated until the analysis of a case proves it inexistence; deconstructing a case allows discovering weak or opportunistic continuum. Generally, the solution to the challenge of both connectedness and continuum of criminal conduct could possibly be found in an extensive study and analysis of real-world cases.

Aligning Multiple Offenders with Repeat Offenders

The difference in sentencing outcomes for multiple and repeat offenders, namely discounted punishment for multiple offenders and inflated punishment for repeat offenders, has been viewed by some scholars as being incompatible with desert (Reitz, 2010). One successful attempt to justify the difference has been suggested by Bennett and related to desert in nonlegal settings (Bennett, 2012).

This essay has explained the difference in sentencing outcomes between multiple offenders and repeat offenders by the presence of normative breaks in the latter. Censure is viewed as a powerful message from the state to an offender which gives him a chance to rethink his behavior. The normative model proposed here fully conforms with the idea of a censuring message and the role it plays in the difference between an overall cumulative sentence for a repeat offender and a discounted sentence for a multiple offender. The role of censure makes the divergent rules on sentencing those who are multiple and repeat offenders fair.

Beyond this, while the levels of sentence in multiple and repeat offenders could be regarded as fair, the level of apprehension is likely to be less so. It is a matter of luck that a multiple offender was not apprehended while the repeat offender was arrested. The end result is that two offenders committing exactly same offenses with the only difference that one is unfortunate and gets caught every time and the other one is fortunate and does not get caught, receive two very different overall sentences. Fairness here is a matter for a discussion other than that of sentencing.

Toward a Guiding Model

The guidance suggested here is based upon two assumptions. First that that there should be single total sentence for a multiple-offense case. Viewed from the perspective of such notions as the lack of normative breaks between the offenses and continuum of criminal conduct, it is easy to see why a multiple-offense case warrants a single total sentence, rather than a combination of sentences. Second, that a discount should be applied to the total sentence for multiple-offense cases. Again, viewed in the light of the propositions suggested in this paper, namely the lack of normative breaks between the offenses, overall proportionality based on living standard analysis, connectedness between the offenses and a single continuum of criminal conduct, the discount or rather the reduction of the total sentence becomes a natural step.

This an approach may present a challenge for a common-law jurisdiction operating under the rules of concurrency and consecutiveness. Wasik discusses several options available for judges when applying the totality principle in England and Wales (Wasik, 2012). The preferred option in such cases would be using the rules of concurrency in order to arrive at the correct total sentence, rather than reducing each individual sentence. The solution suggested here would be to introduce the concept of partial concurrency/consecutiveness to the system. Such solution is already offered by the sentencing system in Australia (Lovegrove, 2004). Although partial concurrency/consecutiveness still breaks the total sentences into several separate sentences for the individual offenses, it is a step closer to a single total sentence arrangement. This single total sentence, however, does not preclude the allocation of separate sentences for the individual offenses. The purpose of those separate sentence would be to act as building blocks in the construction of the total, thus their role is nominal rather than real.

Then the initial formula for arranging separate sentences into a total sentence should be designed. An example of such a method is Borgeke's set of three formulae that operate in Sweden. Each jurisdiction, however, should design its own formulae based on their legal traditions and established conventions. Any formula has the potential for misplaced precision, therefore it is not advocated here as the only step in the process of sentencing multiple-offense cases. Rather it is the first step, the starting point upon which the rest of the process is built.

Once the formula is established, a set of operational principles can be developed. Among such operational principles could be connectedness itself: analyzing offending patterns may lead to identification of the underlying reasons, motives, or impetus behind offending behavior. If a sentence arrangement in which the total sentence for a case consists of a full sentence for the most serious offense and proportions of sentences for the secondary offenses, connectedness should guide the adjustment of those proportions. As such, the higher the degree of connectedness between the offenses, the smaller the proportion of separate sentences which should be added to the total. In some cases, where the degree of connectedness is very weak, it could lead to full separate sentences (as opposed to their proportions) constituting the total sentence. Other principles of connectedness could relate to the gravity of offenses involved, the combination of offenses in a multiple-offense case, the number of victims involved and so forth. The main emphasis here is that establishing solid operational principles would firstly, help judges and, most importantly, discourage discretionary sentences.

Finally, this approach allows for the total sentence to be viewed as having a deserved rather than discounted basis for the whole criminality involved. A total sentence for a multiple-offense case is naturally reduced and thus is viewed as being deserved in light of the circumstances involved in the case and based on the four principles advanced in this paper: the lack of normative breaks, overall proportionality, connectedness, and continuum of criminal conduct. Although still open to challenge, this model allows for the dominant view of multiple-offense sentencing, namely that emphasizing discounts and their dissonance with desert theory, to be put aside.

Notes

1. Roberts and de Keijser's chapter in this volume focuses on culpability as a justification for a different approach to sentencing multiple crimes.
2. In some ways, though not entirely, it echoes with von Hirsch and Ashworth's concept of a lapse when first-time offenders (sometimes also second- and third-time offenders) should be given a reduced sentence.
3. This does not imply that offender does not have the opportunity to modify his criminal conduct in general. Being a rational human being he has such opportunity every time.
4. In fact, victims of different crimes may have very different experiences. For example, a common assault may cause more emotional harm to one person than grievous bodily harm or wounding would to another.
5. This term was often referred to by the Swedish judges during the sentencing exercise conducted by the author.

References

Ashworth, A. 2015. *Sentencing and Criminal Justice*. 6th ed. Cambridge: Cambridge University Press.

Bennett, C. 2012. "Do Multiple and Repeat Offenders Pose a Problem for Retributive Sentencing Theory?" In C. Tamburini and J. Ryberg (eds.), *Recidivist Punishments: The Philosopher's View*, pp. 137–156. Lanham, MD: Lexington Books.

Borgeke, M. 2008. *Att bestämma påföljid för brott*. Stockholm: Norstedts Juridik.

Bottoms, A. 1998. "Five Puzzles in von Hirsch's Theory of Punishment." In A. Ashworth and M. Wasik (eds.), *Fundamentals of Sentencing Theory: Essays in Honour of Andrew von Hirsch*, pp. 53–100. Oxford: Clarendon Press.

Jareborg, N. 1998. "Why Bulk Discount in Sentencing?" In A. Ashworth and M. Wasik (eds.), *Fundamentals of Sentencing Theory: Essays in Honour of Andrew von Hirsch*, pp. 129–140. Oxford: Clarendon Press.

Lippke, R. L. 2011. "Retributive Sentencing, Multiple Offenders, and Bulk Discounts." In M. D. White (ed.), *Retributivism: Essays on Theory and Policy*, pp. 212–231. New York: Oxford University Press.

Lovegrove, A. 2000. "Proportionality, Sentencing and the Multiple Offender: Towards a Numerical Framework." *Punishment & Society* 2(4): 453–469.

Lovegrove, A. 2004. *Sentencing the Multiple Offender: Judicial Practice and Legal Principle*. Canberra: Australian Institute of Criminology.

Reitz, K. 2010. "The Illusion of Proportionality: Desert and Repeat Offenders." In J. V. Roberts and A. von Hirsch (eds.), *Previous Convictions at Sentencing: Theoretical and Applied Perspectives*, pp. 137–160. Oxford: Hart Publishing.

Thomas, D. A. 1979. *Principles of Sentencing: The Sentencing Policy of the Court of Appeal Criminal Division*. 2nd ed. London: Heinemann.

Ulvang, M. 2005. *Påföljdskonkurrens—problem och principer*. Uppsala: Justus Förlag.

Vibla, N. 2014. "Sentencing for Multiple Offences: Towards a Conceptual Model within a Retributive Framework." Unpublished PhD thesis, University of Cambridge.

Von Hirsch, A., and N. Jareborg. 1991. "Gauging Criminal Harm: A Living Standard Analysis." *Oxford Journal of Legal Studies* 11(1): 1–38.

Von Hirsch, A. 1993. *Censure and Sanctions*. Oxford: Oxford University Press.

Von Hirsch, A., and A. Ashworth (2005). *Proportionate Sentencing: Exploring the Principles*. Oxford: Oxford University Press.

Wasik, M. 2012. "Concurrent and Consecutive Sentences Revisited." In L. Zedner and J. V. Roberts (eds.), *Principles and Values in Criminal Law and Criminal Justice: Essays in Honour of Andrew Ashworth*, pp. 285–305. Oxford: Oxford University Press.

Wells, M. 1992. *Sentencing for Multiple Offences in Western Australia*. University of Western Australia: Crime Research Centre.

10

Multiple-Offense Sentencing

Some Additional Thoughts

ANDREAS VON HIRSCH

The present discussion is based on Natalia Vibla's article in this volume.[1] It sets forth additional comments on the present subject of multiple-offense sentencing.

The Recalcitrance of the Issue of Multiple Offenses

When the contributors to the earlier volume on sentencing and previous criminal convictions addressed that issue,[2] we found it conceptually difficult but were able to make some progress. Various authors were able to generate desert-based accounts of why and how sentences should be adjusted on account of offenders' prior criminal convictions.[3] The present topic—concerning the sentencing of offenders convicted of multiple offenses—seems more recalcitrant. There exists greater difficulty in devising any systematic desert-based account at all. This makes it worth considering, at the outset, the source of this apparent difficulty.

The problem brings to mind an influential 1977 article by the philosopher John Taurek,[4] titled "Should the Numbers Count?" His thesis was the intrinsically problematic character of making aggregative judgments of harm across multiple victims. The question "How much worse is it when *A, B* and *C* are made to suffer than when only *A* must suffer?," he argues, has no determinate answer. He offers no full justification for his indeterminacy thesis, but provides interesting illustrations in its support. Taurek's thesis has generated much debate among philosophers, but the outcome of that debate remains uncertain.[5]

In multiple-count cases, the indeterminacy thesis has some degree of plausibility. Let me sketch why. With a single criminal offense, the conduct's harmfulness can be assessed with the aid of the "living standard" theory of criminal harm.[6] According to that theory, the seriousness of an offense may be gauged according to how much the conduct typically affects a victim's personal resources (noneconomic as well as economic). With multiple offenses, however, there can be no such standard individual whose personal resources may thus be deemed affected. Multiple victims are affected instead: Smith, Jones, and Robinson. Each individual's living standard is not affected by the fact of the others' victimization. And there can be no compound person, Smith-Jones-Robinson, whose hierarchy of interests may be utilized as the touchstone for gauging of the criminal conduct's aggregate injuriousness.[7]

We nevertheless have an intuitive sense that with a given type of crime, it is worse if several persons must suffer such conduct than if only one does. And notwithstanding the uncertainties, it seems appropriate for the criminal law to reflect that sense, by providing for an adjustment of the sentence in multiple-offense cases. But that requires us to decide: *what* adjustment?

Multiple Offenses: Any Desert-Based Limiting Principles?

Are there any desert-based limiting principles applicable to multiple-offense situations? There are two, referred to in Vibla's analysis: *normative breaks* and *overall proportionality*.[8]

The normative-breaks principle serves to distinguish multiple-offense cases from prior-conviction ones. In an article in the earlier volume on previous convictions in sentencing, Kevin Reitz has pointed out a seeming anomaly.[9] It is that an additional offense tends to add more to the total sentence when the offender has previously been convicted than when the offense is one of a series of criminal acts in a multiple-offense situation.

The normative-breaks principle provides reason for this differing treatment. In the previous-conviction situation, the offender has already been confronted by the criminal law's formal disapprobation through the judgment of conviction and through the sentence he has been made to serve for his earlier misconduct. This disapprobation should provide him with special reason for desistance from further offending. In the multiple-offense situation, however, no such intervening censure and punishment has been provided—which seemingly makes continuing to offend somewhat less reprehensible.[10]

The overall proportionality principle holds that in a multiple-offense situation involving a series of criminal acts, sentences for the lesser offenses in the series should not exceed in aggregate the highest permissible penalty for the most serious offense in the series. For example, no number of burglaries (being of medium seriousness) should yield a sanction exceeding that imposed for an armed robbery (which is much more serious). The basis for this norm is that the interest protected by the robbery norm (of personal safety) is of substantially greater importance than those protected by the burglary norm (viz., protection of property and privacy). Thus the penalties for the lesser offenses in the series need to be "discounted" in determining the aggregate sentence.

What Next? Heuristic Models and the Borgeke Formula

The forgoing two principles, standing alone, provide a modest degree of guidance—but would not suffice to yield a consistent standard for dealing with multiple-offense cases. But how can a more detailed standard be devised, given the previously mentioned difficulty in aggregating judgments of criminal harm across several offenses? What comes to mind is the possibility of utilizing a heuristic model—an example being Martin Borgeke's scheme for scaling multiple offenses.[11]

Martin Borgeke is an influential Swedish Supreme Court Justice, who has written extensively on sentencing policy in Sweden in recent years. His suggested scheme, sketched in Vibla's essay,[12] involves diminishing additions to the sentence, depending on the number of the crimes involved. For more serious crimes, his proposed progression is as follows:

Sentence for the 1st offense	Sentence for the 2nd offense	Sentence for the 3rd offense	Sentence for the 4th offense	Sentence for the 5th offense	Sentence for the 6th offense
1/1	1/3	1/6	1/9	1/12	1/15

He does not attempt to derive his model from broader desert principles. Rather, he asserts that the scheme reflects his own analysis of court decisions, as well as discussions with other judicial colleagues.[13]

Borgeke's scheme may be viewed as a *heuristic model.* It constitutes *a* way of reflecting applicable desert principles—including those of normative breaks and overall proportionality. Those principles, however, would not suffice to account for the details of his proposed scheme—which under his approach represent simply a convention.

Notwithstanding its character as a convention, Borgeke's model has certain advantages. First, it provides greater guidance. It adds considerably more specificity about what adjustments to the sentence should be made. Such specificity is preferable to leaving the matter to individual judges' discretion, with the potential for disparity that could involve. Second, it provides an additional degree of proportionality among its constituent elements. For example, it provides that the fifth offense should receive about one-half the amount of the third.

Relying on heuristic models in this fashion may seem a disappointing result. Why not develop a scheme with full normative justification? But desert theory, helpful as I certainly believe it is, has limitations which we should recognize. It may not be able to assist us all the way in formulating sentencing doctrine. Sometimes, additional expedients will be needed, and heuristic models such as Borgeke's will be useful.

Notes

1. See Vibla, this volume.
2. Roberts and von Hirsch (eds.), 2010.
3. See, e.g., the Roberts, Lee, and von Hirsch essays in that volume.
4. Taurek, 1977.
5. For an analysis of the numerous philosophical discussions in this area, see, e.g., Lawlor, 2006.
6. See von Hirsch and Jareborg (1991), and more recently von Hirsch, 2017, ch. 6. For utilizing the theory in the context of English sentencing law, see Ashworth, 2015, ch. 4.
7. It might be objected that this prejudices the argument, by assuming than an individual's economy of interests should be decisive. Due to the separability of persons, however, such interests cannot meaningfully be fused across a multiplicity of persons. That, I think, is the gravamen of Taurek's argument.
8. See Vibla, this volume.
9. Reitz, in von Hirsch and Roberts (2010), ch. 8.
10. See also Vibla, this volume.
11. Borgeke, 2008.
12. Vibla, this volume.
13. Ibid.

References

Ashworth, A. 2015. *Sentencing and Criminal Justice*, 6th ed. Cambridge: Cambridge University Press.

Borgeke, M. 2008. *Att bestämma påföljd för brott*. Stockholm. Norstedts Juridik.

Lawlor, R. 2006. "Taurek, Numbers and Probabilities." *Ethical Theory and Moral Practice* 9(2): 149–166.

Lee, Y. 2010. "Repeat Offenders and the Question of Desert." In J. V. Roberts and A. von Hirsch (eds.), *Previous Convictions at Sentencing: Theoretical and Applied Perspectives*, pp. 49–72. Oxford: Hart Publishing.

Roberts, J. V. 2010. "Re-Examining First Offender Discounts at Sentencing." In J. V. Roberts and A. von Hirsch (eds.), *Previous Convictions at Sentencing: Theoretical and Applied Perspectives*, pp. 17–37. Oxford: Hart Publishing.

Roberts, J. V., and von Hirsch, A. (eds.) 2010. *Previous Convictions at Sentencing: Theoretical and Applied Perspectives*. Oxford: Hart Publishing.

Taurek, J. M. 1977. "Should the Numbers Count?" *Philosophy and Public Affairs* 6(4): 293–316.

Von Hirsch, A. 2010. "Proportionality and the Progressive Loss of Mitigation: Some Further Reflections." In J. V. Roberts and A. von Hirsch (eds.), *Previous Convictions at Sentencing: Theoretical and Applied Perspectives*, pp. 1–17. Oxford: Hart Publishing.

Von Hirsch, A. 2017. *Deserved Criminal Sentences: An Overview*. Oxford: Hart Publishing.

Von Hirsch, A., and N. Jareborg. 1991. "Gauging Criminal Harm: A Living-Standard Analysis." *Oxford Journal of Legal Studies* 11(1): 1–38.

11

Principles and Procedures for Sentencing of Multiple Current Offenses

RICHARD S. FRASE

Introduction

This paper seeks to resolve a seeming paradox—when multiple crimes are sentenced at one time or close together in time (hereinafter: *simultaneous* offenses) they are often sentenced much less harshly than when the same crimes are sentenced over a longer period of time (hereinafter: *sequential* offenses). For example: three burglaries committed over a period of six weeks and sentenced in a single hearing will receive a lower total sentence than the same three burglaries committed over a period of several years and sentenced separately. The reduced severity of simultaneous sentencing—often referred to as the granting of a bulk discount for multiple crimes—operates on two distinct levels, one involving the extent to which multiple current offenses receive cumulative penalties, and the other involving the imposition of sentencing premiums for prior convictions. Thus:

- Sequential offenses almost always receive penalties that are, in effect, fully cumulative (because all earlier sentences have already been entirely served). And at each successive sentencing event the previously sentenced offenses are treated as prior convictions which enhance the severity of the current sentence (hereinafter: the prior record enhancement, or PRE).
- Simultaneous offenses typically receive less than fully cumulative penalties. In the United States, judges most often impose fully concurrent sentences (the longest of which is the controlling sentence), although judges typically have unfettered discretion to sentence consecutively and sometimes do so.

> In other common-law countries less than fully cumulative punishment is achieved by application of a vague totality principle (Ashworth, 2015). As for PRE, in most US and other common-law systems simultaneous offenses are rarely treated as sentence-enhancing prior convictions even if some of them occurred or were sentenced prior to one or more other simultaneous offenses.

In this essay, I show why these different treatments of simultaneous and sequential offenses are frequently justified, and I offer a set of rules to guide judges in deciding when and to what extent simultaneous offenses should receive less severe punishment. Unlike many writers who have addressed these issues, I strongly challenge the assumption that simultaneous and sequential offenses are directly comparable, or that there should be at least a presumption of equally severe punishment in both contexts. As I will show, simultaneous and sequential offenses are typically quite different in ways that often merit less severe punishment of the former.

Because the approaches of US and other common-law systems are so different, the remainder of this paper will only address these problems in the US context. As noted earlier, US judges focus on the choice between concurrent and consecutive sentencing of multiple current offenses, while also applying various rules (discussed later) permitting "concurrent-plus" sentencing. Judges in many other common-law countries first invoke the totality principle to decide the most severe appropriate total sentence for all of the current offenses, and then use concurrent sentencing and other tools to achieve that sentence.

Here is an overview of how I propose to resolve these problems, with a brief summary of my reasoning. The first proposal is meant to clarify the scope of the problem, and probably reflects existing law and practice in most US states. The second and third proposals could actually increase the average severity difference between simultaneous and sequential sentencing, but they will make these differences more principled and more consistent. The fourth and fifth proposals should reduce simultaneous versus sequential disparities. But again: I am arguing that simultaneous penalties are properly less severe in most cases, and should remain so.

I propose:

1. A conclusive presumption of fully concurrent sentencing of multiple current offenses that are really only "one crime" because, for example, they reflect different legal theories of liability for the same acts, or one crime is a lesser included offense of another.
2. A rebuttable presumption in favor of concurrent sentences when multiple, legally distinct crimes (those not falling within the first proposal) are

sentenced simultaneously. My reasons are as follows: some sort of presumptive rule is needed, to give judges a starting point; general principles of parsimony and benefit-of-the-doubt weigh in favor of a presumption of lesser rather than greater severity; and, as will be shown, simultaneous offenses are often different from sequential offenses in ways that further support presumptive leniency. In a few cases the opposite presumption—in favor of consecutive sentencing—is appropriate; but in most multiple-current-offense cases consecutive sentencing should require a finding of atypical, aggravating circumstances and a statement of reasons showing why consecutive sentencing is justified.

3. For the same reasons that justify presumptive concurrent sentencing, when consecutive sentences are imposed the total sentence should be subject to presumptive upper limits on the severity of the total sentence. Specifically: the aggregate severity of consecutive sentences should only rarely exceed twice the sentence the judge would impose if sentencing only the most serious current offense. As with the presumption stated in (2), this doubling limit may be overcome by a finding of atypical aggravating facts and a statement of reasons.
4. Where legally distinct simultaneous offenses are sentenced concurrently it is usually appropriate to increase the severity of the longest concurrent sentence (i.e., the controlling sentence) to take account of the multiplicity of current convictions. Doing this will acknowledge all victim and public harms caused or threatened and avoid "free" crimes, while also reducing the magnitude of disparity between concurrent and consecutive sentencing of simultaneous cases, and between simultaneous and sequential sentencing. US guidelines systems have employed at least four kinds of rules to enhance concurrent sentences. I will note the advantages and disadvantages of each of these concurrent-plus options, and the circumstances under which each can and should be employed.
5. Because the magnitude of sentencing enhancements based on criminal history (PRE) is often excessive in American jurisdictions, and also contributes to the wide disparity between simultaneous and sequential sentence severity, PRE magnitude should be reduced. Drawing on previous work, I will briefly summarize a number of ways in which this can and should be done.

Before launching into the body of the chapter a few additional preliminary comments are in order regarding my normative, structural, and tactical assumptions. As to the former: all sentencing rules and standards must be justified by reference to one or more purposes of punishment. My proposals assume a limiting retributive (LR) model under which considerations of desert and retributive proportionality define a range of permissible sanction severity within which consequentialist (crime control) purposes and constraints are applied. My preferred LR model is asymmetric: desert sets firm upper limits on sanction severity, while the lower limits are determined by consequentialist goals (Frase, 2013). Other writers, most notably Norval Morris (1974), have advocated a more symmetric but imprecise LR model in which desert sets both upper and lower limits on penalty severity, producing a range of "not-undeserved" penalties within which consequentialist goals may be pursued.[1] But either of these LR models (indeed, perhaps, any hybrid or mixed theory, see Hoskins, this volume) greatly simplifies the task of justifying more lenient simultaneous sentencing. Desert will sometimes lower the maximum allowed severity of simultaneous penalties, but further leniency can be based on consequentialist goals (because the state is permitted but not required to fully impose the offender's deserved punishment).

However, since my preferred asymmetric LR model incorporates both retributive and consequentialist/crime control purposes, I'll be addressing all major punishment purposes. To that extent, my proposals and their underlying rationales will have applicability even in jurisdictions and for writers adopting a purely retributive or purely consequentialist model, or a more symmetric LR model. With respect to crime control goals, I will focus on those related to the offender's elevated risk of committing further crimes, justifying more intensive supervision and rehabilitative programming efforts and, where shown to be necessary and cost-effective, physical restraint by incarceration. I will disregard specific and general deterrence because there is insufficient empirical evidence to support using these rationales to justify enhanced penalties (Doob and Webster, 2003; Durlauf and Nagin, 2011), particularly on a case-specific basis.

As for my procedural framework, I strongly favor and generally assume a guidelines system in which judges' decisions are structured in two ways: 1) with presumptive starting points, consisting of recommended sentences that are deemed to be correct for typical cases of that type; and 2) with rules and standards that guide judges in deciding whether a case is sufficiently atypical to justify departure from the starting-point presumption, and that also guide judges in deciding on the magnitude of departure. But my proposals can also have application in nonguidelines systems in the United States, since judges in such a system may choose or be required to apply a similar two-step process when sentencing simultaneous offenses.

Finally, I think it important to emphasize that the goals of this paper are fairly modest. I am proposing rules, standards, and procedures to guide judges in sentencing multiple offenses, and to promote incremental development of policy in this area. I am not seeking to identify a set of detailed, a priori rules that specify when simultaneous offenses should be treated differently from similar sequential crimes. This is because, as will be shown, multiple offending patterns are very diverse, and I don't think we currently know enough about this phenomenon to craft more detailed rules.

Overview

The remainder of this paper is organized as follows. First, I identify the diverse forms that multiple offending and the resulting criminal charges can take. I next note several consistent differences between simultaneous and sequential offenses that justify presumptions in favor of more lenient treatment of simultaneous offenses cases. The next section presents and defends my five proposals to make sentencing of multiple offenses more principled and consistent, and I then offer some concluding remarks.

Varieties of Multiple Offending and Multiple-Offense Processing

In order to have a clear picture of the problems we are seeking to resolve, it is necessary to recognize the varieties of multiple offending and the ways in which such offenses are processed and appear for sentencing.

Varieties of Simultaneous Offenses

Multiple offenses may be very closely related to each other in time and place, loosely related, unrelated, similar or dissimilar, and these variations may have relevance to how severely the crimes should be punished (Roberts and de Keijser, this volume). At one end of this continuum are legally distinct crimes committed in a single incident that victimize more than one person; involve more than one criminal objective (for example, rape and robbery of the same victim); or otherwise constitute more than one crime. Further along on this continuum are crimes that, while not committed in a single incident or even at the same location, are related in that one crime was committed solely to facilitate the other crime (for example, stealing a car shortly after escaping from prison). Finally, unrelated crimes committed in separate incidents (but sentenced simultaneously) may all be the same or similar types of crimes, such as a series of burglaries, or they may be completely different kinds of crime (for example, when a search of a house for drugs also turns up stolen property, illegal weapons, or child pornography).

Simultaneous offenses also vary in their underlying circumstances and motivations. Any given crime or group of crimes might reflect, for example: the need to raise funds to support a drug habit; the offender's desperate efforts to support himself and his dependents due to lack of employment opportunity; alcoholism or mental illness; gang or other criminal associates; or simply the offender's preference to make a living through crime. A particular circumstance or motivation might explain all of an offender's crimes or only some, and a given crime could reflect more than one such factor.

Simultaneous offenders display further variation in their offending pattern over time—did the offender have an active criminal career before the earliest of the simultaneous offense, or is he (officially at least) a first offender? If he had prior convictions, were those crimes less serious or more serious? Were they of a type similar to the current offenses, or dissimilar?

Other important simultaneous offense variations and sentencing difficulties relate to problematic law enforcement practices and sentencing laws. A high number of current drug offenses may be the result of police decisions to target particular neighborhoods or individuals; indeed the police can often produce a large number of separate incidents by simply continuing to buy drugs from the same offender. Severe statutory or guideline penalty provisions can also substantially raise the stakes in multiple-offense sentencing. For example, some child pornography laws define each image as a separate offense, even though offenders often download a large number of images at one time. Both drug and child pornography laws often carry severe penalties per offense, and may mandate consecutive sentencing.

Functionally Simultaneous Sentencing

As defined in this paper, the simultaneous offense category includes not only (1) offenses being sentenced in a single sentencing hearing; but also (2) offenses being sentenced at the same time but in different courts; and (3) offenses that were previously sentenced (even by the same court) for which the sentence has not yet been fully discharged (for example, the offender is still in prison on earlier charges). The second and third categories raise some of the same issues as the first category. Judges in category 2 and 3 cases must likewise decide whether to make the new sentences consecutive to or concurrent with the prior, undischarged sentences. Moreover, in most category 2 cases and many category 3 cases there will have been no conviction for any of the crimes prior to commission of the other crimes (this is almost always true in category 1 cases). As will be discussed, the absence of any intervening conviction and sentence has implications for both retributive and crime-control sentencing purposes.

Multiple Offenses Sentenced Concurrently via Prosecutorial Charging Leniency

Prosecutors, in effect, make sentencing decisions when they decide whether to dismiss or never file certain charges. When such charges are sufficiently provable that they could have resulted in conviction, the decision to drop them amounts to a form of "concurrent sentencing" (and also limits the offender's future criminal history scores); conversely, retaining more charges through conviction by trial or plea permits (but usually does not require) partial or fully consecutive sentencing, and also adds to the offender's future criminal history score. In short—the dropping of provable charges amounts to another form of bulk discount; what judges do is only the most visible form of discounting. Moreover, as further discussed below, what prosecutors do in simultaneous offense cases may help to explain and justify judicial decisions to apply concurrent sentencing.

Why Simultaneous Offenses Often Merit Less Total Punishment Than Comparable Sequential Offenses

The variety of multiple-crime offending and charging patterns described earlier casts doubt on whether any simple rule or theory can apply to all cases where multiple crimes are to be sentenced at one time (or a prior sentence has not been fully discharged). But simultaneous offense cases have several common features that often justify or allow less severe total (aggregate) punishment, in comparison to the total punishment that is merited for similar crimes when they are sentenced sequentially and not close in time to other sequential offenses. In light of those common features, I will argue that it is appropriate to adopt several presumptions tending to favor less severe punishment for simultaneous offenses, along with standards for overcoming each presumption and other rules limiting the degree of reduced simultaneous offense severity.

Five typical features of simultaneous offense cases provide grounds for reduced punishment severity. The first three factors relate to traditional punishment goals. The fourth and fifth factors (and to a lesser extent, the third) relate not to the crimes themselves but to their procedural context: in several important respects, simultaneous offense cases are not comparable to sequential offense cases. When we eliminate the false equivalence between simultaneous and sequential offenses, we give judges more leeway to sentence simultaneous offenses moderately, because there is less appearance of undue leniency.

Lack of an Intervening Conviction Between Simultaneous Offenses

As many writers have recognized (see, e.g., Lippke, 2011), simultaneous offense cases typically lack an important element found in most sequential offense cases—a previous conviction for one of the offenses. The paradigmatic sequential offender is sentenced for each new crime after previously being censured and punished for one or more prior crimes; such an offender is arguably more culpable for disregarding his prior censure, and also seems to pose an elevated risk of further crime in light of his failure to desist despite the prior censure and any crime-reducing treatments or other interventions he received.

In contrast, simultaneous offense offenders (including both those with multiple current convictions and almost all of those with current plus undischarged prior sentences) have not committed any of their current crimes after having been convicted and sentenced for one of the other crimes. The simultaneous offender has thus not disregarded recent censure (or, if he lacks earlier convictions, any censure), nor has he failed to respond to recent treatments or other interventions. Lacking such censure and interventions, he has had no recent opportunity to respond and mend his ways. Of course, he has also had no opportunity to disregard recent censure and intervention, and thereby show how defiant and risky he is. When we compare the simultaneous offender, lacking such a two-edged opportunity, to the sequential offender who receives it and fails to respond, we face an insoluble uncertainty—what would the simultaneous offender have done, if he had been given the same censure and intervention? Faced with such uncertainty, and consistent with the reasonable doubt and other pro-defendant criminal procedure rules, I believe we must give the simultaneous offender the benefit of the doubt and not simply assume that he would have committed exactly the same later crime if he had received censure and intervention for the earlier ones. However, I am only arguing for a general presumption of greater leniency in the simultaneous offense context; as will be further discussed, there may be clear grounds to overcome the presumption in some cases.

Likelihood That Simultaneous Offenses Reflect Situational or Other Temporary Circumstances

Simultaneous offense cases typically involve a series of crimes committed over a short period of time. Such crime sprees often reflect situational pressures and other circumstances that tend to reduce the offender's culpability, and that may also (if temporary or subject to intervention and change) indicate a lower risk of future crime than the sheer number of the crimes would suggest. Spree-inducing situational pressures might include a period of acute economic stress, new or worsening chemical dependency, the bad influence of particular associates, and panicky reactions to and attempted escape or concealment of the initial crime. In contrast, sequential offense cases tend to involve offending over an extended period of time, suggesting a more persistent pattern of offending, and more deliberate choices to commit each additional crime.

Of course, the opposite may also be true—simultaneous offenses can be highly deliberate, and sequential offenses may reflect persistent excusing pressures. Moreover, the pattern of closely spaced offending that characterizes simultaneous offense cases may suggest an elevated recidivism risk: because such crimes are all likely to have been committed recently they will tend to reflect the offender's current living situation, companions, mental state, and other risk factors indicative of an active criminal career; and if the recent crimes are numerous, this is suggestive of a "high-rate" offender.

But again, all I am trying to show is that a substantial proportion of simultaneous offenses merit less total punishment than sequential offenders committing the same crimes. If that is the case, any presumption of consecutive simultaneous offense punishment would risk overpunishing many offenders; we should therefore choose to err on the side of leniency and adopt a rebuttable presumption of concurrent sentencing for most simultaneous offense cases.

Problems of High-Magnitude, All-at-Once Consecutive Simultaneous Sentences

The very nature of simultaneous sentencing raises several problems that can be ignored (or at least, are less problematic) in sequential sentencing. Consecutive simultaneous sentences impose a large total sentence all at once, whereas in sequential offense cases the same crime-specific penalties are spread out, usually over a number of years. Thus, even if the total punishment in prison years or another severity measure is the same, the simultaneous total is perceived as greater, and in some respects it *is* greater or less cost-effective. One problem relates to the expressive function of criminal sentences—the severity of a sentence sends an important message about how serious society considers this crime. Such messages serve to reinforce norms of acceptable conduct and habits of law-abiding behavior; such norms and habits, in turn, encourage would-be offenders to abstain, or at least to choose a less serious crime, even when the risk of detection and punishment is small (which it often is). Consecutive simultaneous sentences can easily add up to a sentence more severe than would normally be imposed on offenders committing much more serious crimes; a multicount simultaneous offenses thief may be punished more severely than a single-count armed robber, which sends confusing messages about the relative severity of these crimes. Even if the sum of sequential offense sentences for a series of minor crimes can likewise be greater than the normal penalty for a much more serious crime, the public is less likely to notice this cumulative effect.

Problems of all-at-once consecutive simultaneous penalties are particularly acute when the number of current offenses is large, the per-crime penalty is severe, and/or the offender is no longer young. If five simultaneous offense burglaries, each worthy of a four-years-to-serve prison term, are given consecutive sentences, a 45-year-old offender will be held in prison until he is 65; the 20-year total sentence will have consumed most of his expected remaining life (or all of it, with earlier death or additional counts). Moreover, his risk of further crime, and especially violent crime, is likely to have substantially declined long before his release, while the costs of incarcerating him, especially medical costs, will have risen rapidly. If the same five prison terms were imposed sequentially, with the final sentence likewise imposed at age 45, the offender would only be held until he is 49.

Of course, the force of this comparison depends on the precise ages when these hypothetical simultaneous and sequential burglars are sentenced. On the other hand, it is difficult if not impossible for an offender to be sequentially punished for more than a handful of serious crimes—he would not have enough years free on the street, in between prison terms, to commit a larger number of crimes. This shows that at least in the inflated-penalty-scale context of American systems, hypotheticals involving dozens of serious crimes sentenced sequentially are unrealistic, and there is no real-world sequential counterpart for comparison to simultaneous versions of such crimes.

Lack of a Concurrent Sentencing Option for Sequential Offenses

In sequential sentencing, the judge separately sentencing each crime will quite reasonably feel the need to give the offender a new sentence at least as severe as the offender received in his previous sentencing, for reasons of deterrence, risk-management, and the need to hold the offender accountable for his latest offense. In such a context, if the prior sentence has already been fully served it would seem very odd to say that the sentence for the latest crime is deemed to have already been served concurrently with the previous sentence. Concurrent sentencing makes more sense (or at least, is more palatable) in the simultaneous context because the offender is being newly punished and held accountable, albeit not as fully as he would be if sentenced consecutively. In short: sequential and simultaneous sentencing is fundamentally noncomparable with respect to the option of concurrent sentencing—the latter does not and cannot exist in the sequential context.

Differing Roles of Charging and Bargaining in Simultaneous and Sequential Cases

As noted earlier, the power that prosecutors have to decline or dismiss provable, legally distinct crimes allows these officials to effectively grant bulk discounts in the simultaneous context—something that prosecutors are very unlikely to do across a series of sequential offenses. If, instead, the prosecutor files and refuses to dismiss additional provable simultaneous charges, these decisions preserve the option of consecutive sentencing. But even in that scenario, where some or all multiple charges are retained through conviction, charging and bargaining practices can give judges at least two reasons to sentence concurrently. First, there may be a plea-bargain agreement calling for at least partially concurrent sentencing; again, in the sequential context there is rarely if ever an occasion for a negotiated bulk discount across all of the offenses. Second, even if there is no such plea agreement, judges may choose to sentence simultaneous offenses concurrently in light of typical prosecutorial practices in that jurisdiction—if an offender faces three counts at conviction, while other similar offenders are typically charged with or allowed to plead guilty to a single count, the judge may consider it unfair and inconsistent to punish this offender more for his two additional counts. In sum, differences in charging and bargaining make simultaneous and sequential cases noncomparable.

Five Proposals to Improve Multiple-Offense Sentencing

Here are my proposals to reduce sentencing severity in simultaneous cases, limit the degree of these reductions, and make differences between simultaneous and sequential sentencing more principled and more consistent.

Fully Concurrent Sentencing of Simultaneous Offenses That Are Essentially a Single Crime

In some simultaneous cases the multiple convictions clearly reflect only one crime, and thus should always be sentenced concurrently. Sometimes the multiple convictions simply embody different legal theories of liability for the same act or acts. For example, in most US states a serious homicide can be charged as intentional murder, felony murder, or extreme-recklessness murder, but even if the jury finds that more than one theory has been proved this is still only "one crime." Similarly, multiple convictions may be duplicative where the charges formally or effectively constitute greater and lesser-included offenses, for example: armed robbery and unarmed robbery; possession with intent to sell and simple possession. In all such cases (alternate theories; greater/lesser) the defendant should only be sentenced for the most serious of the crimes.[2] And because there is only one crime, there will rarely if ever be a need to consider using one the concurrent-plus options discussed later in the chapter.

Presumptive Concurrent Sentencing (But Occasionally Presumptive Consecutive)

I propose the adoption of a general presumption in favor of concurrent sentences when multiple, legally distinct crimes are sentenced simultaneously or there is an undischarged prior sentence or sentences. In selected cases the opposite presumption—in favor of consecutive sentencing—is appropriate, but in most cases consecutive sentencing should require a finding of atypical, aggravating circumstances, and a statement of reasons showing that consecutive sentencing is justified. Presumptive rules are standard features of sentencing guidelines systems, but they can also be applied in a nonguidelines system. In systems permitting appellate review of sentences, consecutive sentences contrary to the presumption would properly attract increased scrutiny on appeal.

Presumptions in favor of concurrent sentencing have been adopted in several guidelines states,[3] and such a presumption is also recommended in the revised Model Penal Code (American Law Institute, 2017, Sec. 6B.08(2)). Some foreign systems have gone even further, applying a flat requirement of concurrent sentencing (see Frase, 1990, pp. 618–619, discussing the French rule). In several guidelines states there are also a few crimes subject to presumptive consecutive sentencing (Frase, 2015, Table 10.2).

Rationales for the General Presumption of Concurrent Sentencing

The concurrent-sentencing presumption recognizes that consecutive sentencing is sometimes justified. Some simultaneous offenders are as culpable as they would be if their crimes had arisen and been processed in a sequential-sentencing context. Moreover, consecutive sentencing may be necessary and cost-effective from a crime control perspective in at least some of these cases. However, some sort of presumption is needed, so that all judges have the same starting point and the same standards to guide them when deciding whether to depart from the presumption; it is unacceptable to leave such a momentous decision to the unfettered discretion of each judge.

Judges could, of course, be given the opposite general presumption, one favoring consecutive sentencing. But the more lenient starting point is a better choice, for several reasons. First, it is likely that the proper punishment for simultaneous offenses is often far less than would be produced by fully consecutive sentencing, and may typically be closer to the fully concurrent end of this spectrum. As was discussed earlier, there are several principled and practical reasons to impose less punishment on simultaneous offenses than on sequential offenses. Thus, even if consecutive sentencing is the de facto norm for sequential penalties, it should not be the norm for simultaneous offenses.

A second reason to prefer a presumption of concurrent sentencing is the principle of parsimony. This principle is very important when courts are applying crime-control and other consequentialist sentencing purposes—a central tenet of consequentialist and utilitarian philosophy, particularly as applied to intrusive government measures, is that such measures should be no more severe than necessary to achieve their purposes (Sullivan and Frase, 2009). This principle, which is sometimes referred to as the principle of necessity or the requirement of narrow-tailoring or least restrictive means, operates in an asymmetric fashion—there is no counterpart principle of such widespread application specifying that government measures should be *no less severe* than necessary to achieve their purposes. Underlying the asymmetric parsimony principle are two more fundamental beliefs. One is the recognition that assessments of government needs can easily err in both directions—the proposed government measure can be too severe, or too lenient. The other underlying assumption is that, as a normative matter, it is better to respond to the inherent risk of government error by choosing to err more often on the side of too little rather than too much, particularly where such harsh measures as criminal punishment are concerned. The parsimony principle therefore requires a presumption of concurrent sentencing; a general presumption in favor of consecutive sentencing poses an unacceptable risk that penalties will often exceed valid crime control purposes.

Some have argued that the parsimony principle has no application to punishments justified by retributive goals (Lippke, this volume). However, I believe that retributivists should also favor an asymmetric, parsimony-type principle—preferring to err on the side of imposing too little rather than too much punishment. As with consequentialist assessments, retributivists must recognize the inherent risks of error in making judgments of desert, even relative (ordinal) judgments. Given those risks, a retributivist might—and I believe, *should*—further conclude that penalties exceeding desert are normatively a worse outcome than penalties less than desert. Similar premises underlie the requirement of proof beyond reasonable doubt (it is worse to convict an innocent person than to acquit a guilty person), and the rule of strict construction of criminal statutes (it is better to have too few convictions than too many). Such an asymmetric weighting of the two kinds of error supports the choice of a presumption in favor of concurrent sentencing rather than a presumption in favor of consecutive sentencing.

Regardless of one's rationale for punishment, erring on the side of less punishment seems particularly appropriate in the current US context, given the widely condemned phenomena of extreme sentence severity, mass incarceration, and disproportionate confinement of minority offenders. Although the public and political mood may be shifting in the United States, I expect we will continue to see frequent pressures to impose excessively severe sentences; thus wherever possible, we should craft rules that point judges in the opposite direction, placing the burdens of proof and persuasion on those who favor severity, rather than on those who favor leniency.

A final set of reasons for the concurrent-sentencing presumption is to lessen the disparities caused by prosecutorial discretion—as noted previously, many offenders receive what amounts to partial or completely concurrent sentencing as a result of the prosecutor's decision to not file additional new charges, or to dismiss those additional charges in plea bargaining. Presumptive concurrent sentencing gives additional offenders the benefit of that treatment and lessens sentence disparities caused by charging and bargaining variations, while also lessening the potential for racial bias and disparate impact that is always present when officials exercise unfettered discretion.

Standards for Overcoming the Concurrent-Sentencing Presumption

The presumption in favor of concurrent sentencing can be overcome in exceptional cases, to permit partially or even fully consecutive sentences. The court must find, stating reasons: 1) that the proposed degree of consecutive sentencing is needed and cost-effective to achieve crime control goals which cannot be adequately met by applying the available concurrent-plus options to be discussed; and 2) that the proposed degree of consecutive sentencing will not exceed the offender's deserved punishment.

The question then arises: what kinds of facts might justify such findings and permit consecutive sentencing? Since these matters have traditionally been left to judicial discretion in the United States there is little guidance to be found in reported case law; indeed, there is relatively little law even in the US systems that restrict consecutive sentencing.[4] But if more US systems adopt the proposed concurrent-sentencing presumption, then more and better law will emerge.

To provide a more concrete sense of how I think this law should develop, and to encourage further discussion, here are some sample fact scenarios and my proposed dispositions.

- Consecutive sentencing should rarely be allowed in the cases of diminished culpability and risk suggested earlier—multiple current offenses reflecting highly situational or short-term factors such as a period of economic stress, dominance by bad associates, or worsening chemical dependency. I also strongly favor concurrent sentencing in drug cases where the police have continued to buy small amounts from one person, or have insisted that the offender increase the amounts each time (see, e.g., *State v. Steadman*, 827 So.2d 1022 (Fla. App. 2002)). Particularly if the defendant had no criminal record before the first of his multiple current offenses, judges should presume that he would have desisted after that offense if he had been promptly convicted or had not been subject to police inducements (benefit-of-the-doubt rationale). Police often justify such practices by the need to identify suppliers and other more serious actors, but that does not justify consecutive sentencing.

- Conversely, consecutive sentencing seems appropriate on both desert and crime control grounds if it is clear that the offender would have continued to commit further offenses independent of the police inducement, or even after being caught and sanctioned for the earlier crimes—for example, if the offender already had a lengthy record of this kind of crime, and had no treatable condition or other circumstance likely to have caused him to desist. But it may be necessary to limit consecutive sentencing on these grounds to violent or other very serious offenses, to ensure the availability of adequate correctional resources for those offenders.
- Consecutive sentencing should rarely be allowed when multiple current offenses arise out of a single behavioral incident in which the number of separate conviction offenses depends on circumstances beyond the offender's control, and is not even arguably within his intention, for example: a drunk-driving vehicular homicide case with multiple victims. In such a case the defendant is not three times more culpable or more dangerous because there happened to have been three persons in the other vehicle and not one person. Some have argued for consecutive sentencing under the principle that "every victim counts" (Lippke, 2011). But such considerations can be given adequate scope under the concurrent-plus options discussed below.
- Conversely, consecutive sentencing will often be both deserved and justified on crime control grounds when multiple violent crimes have been committed intentionally or in separate incidents (e.g., a series of rapes). Notwithstanding the absence of an intervening conviction, there seems less reason to give such offenders the benefit of the doubt as to their culpability and danger to public safety. Some multiple intentional nonviolent crimes might also be sufficiently aggravated to justify consecutive sentencing, for example, multiple serious frauds against elderly victims.
- After conviction by trial, multiple current offenses that were offered to be dismissed in return for a guilty plea (or that are customarily dismissed) should not be sentenced consecutively.

Exceptional Presumptions in Favor of Consecutive Sentencing

In some categories of cases the need for consecutive sentencing may be so likely to be present that this choice should be deemed the norm (subject to mitigating departure in atypical cases). The Minnesota guidelines apply such a presumption to escapes and other crimes by prisoners (MSGC 2015, Sec. 2.F.1). Particularly in the case of escape, there is a strong need for deterrence, and also a likelihood of achieving it if inmates are frequently reminded of the added penalty for escape and the high probability of being intercepted or recaptured.

Presumptive Doubling Limit on Total Consecutive-Sentence Severity

When consecutive sentences are imposed, the total duration or quantum of the sentence should rarely be more than twice as severe as the sentence that would be imposed for the most serious of the crimes being sentenced. A similar doubling limit is found in some state sentencing guidelines,[5] and is also recommended in the revised Model Penal Code (American Law Institute, 2017, Sec. 6B.08(7)). With or without guidelines, the base on which the doubling rule operates is the sentence the court would impose for the most serious current offense if that were the only crime being sentenced.

A presumptive upper limit on the total severity of consecutive sentences is justified by the same reasons that support the presumption in favor of concurrent sentencing, discussed earlier. Judges need to be given a common starting point which, given the diversity of simultaneous cases described earlier, would probably have to be stated either with reference to a presumptive low figure that can be raised, or a presumptive high figure that can be reduced. The same reasons of parsimony and inherent risks of excessive punishment and disparities, discussed earlier, justify preferring the lower (severity-minimizing) start point, rather the higher (severity-maximizing) alternative.

Standards for Overcoming the Presumptive Doubling Limit

To overcome the presumptive doubling limit, the sentencing court should be required to find that the chosen, more-than-double sentence is *both* deserved and also necessary to achieve valid crime-control purposes. Again, however, there is little guidance to be found in existing guidelines or case law. As a practical matter, the doubling limit is only likely to come into play when there are more than two current offenses and the court wants to impose a sentence more severe than is merited for the most aggravated of the crimes. If double the latter sentence already yields a severe penalty, a very strong showing should be required to move the sentence still higher.

Encouraged Use of Concurrent-Plus Sentencing Options

Concurrent sentences should normally be more severe than the sentence that would be appropriate for the most serious of those crimes—concurrent-plus sentencing. It is important for the combined sentence to acknowledge all victim and public harms caused or threatened by the offender's conduct, and avoid giving the impression that additional crimes are "free." Concurrent-plus sentencing (especially when combined with the PRE reforms proposed in the next section) also serves to reduce the magnitude of disparity between concurrent and consecutive sentencing of simultaneous cases, and between simultaneous and sequential sentencing. US guidelines systems employ at least four kinds of concurrent-plus rules. Here is a summary of those rules, and some suggestions as to the pros and cons of each.

Option 1: Multiple Current Offenses Are Treated as a Single (Greater) Offense

When multiple current offenses involve quantifiable amounts of harm (e.g., dollar amounts of theft or fraud; quantity of drugs or other contraband), statutes and guidelines sometimes permit the harms of the offenses to be added together (at least if not too widely separated in time) and treated as a single, more serious crime (see, e.g., Minn. Stat. Sec. 609.52 subd. 3(5) (2016); US Sentencing Commission 2015, Sec. 3D1.2(d)). Such treatment can sometimes yield a sentencing range lower than would be produced by sequential or consecutive sentencing —another bulk discount—if the rate of sentence enhancement declines as dollar or drug amounts rise.[6]

This option makes sense if one views a series of small crimes as equivalent to one large crime—either because the crimes may be part of a single scheme, or simply because aggregate harm is the best single measure of the total seriousness of these crimes. On the other hand, this approach cannot be the sole concurrent-plus option, since aggregation is not possible for many crimes. More fundamentally, unless a single scheme is proven, parsimony and benefit-of-the-doubt principles dictate that we treat the defendant as a repeat minor offender, not someone who has chosen to commit a single, major crime.

Option 2: Treat Multiple Current Offenses as Aggravating Factors

Even if multiple offenses cannot be viewed as one big crime, the additional crimes sentenced concurrently may be closely enough connected to the crime with the longest concurrent sentence to be viewed as aggravating circumstances for that crime (for example, property damage caused upon entry to commit burglary).

But this option, like the first, is not suitable as the sole concurrent-plus option since some multiple offenses are not closely enough related to the controlling-sentence crime. And even when they are, any system based on individualized assessment of crime aggravation will, unless combined with further guidelines or formulas, tend to produce disparity between judges sentencing similar cases.

Option 3: Treat Multiple Current Offenses as Prior Convictions

Under some sentencing guidelines multiple current offenses can be added to the offender's criminal history score *during* the sentencing process, increasing the offender's criminal history when other current offenses are sentenced (Frase, 2015). These rules appear to reflect less formal, preguidelines sentencing practices, and are based on practical considerations, not desert (Parent, 1988)—if such offenses are not added to current criminal history they will never be counted unless the offender has future sentencings.

Under the Minnesota guidelines multiple current offenses are sentenced in the order the crimes were committed and, if sentenced concurrently, the offender's criminal history score grows with each additional crime sentenced (MSGC 2015, sec. II.B). The result is a controlling concurrent sentence longer than if current offenses did not add to criminal history, but usually shorter than consecutive sentencing. Washington applies a more severe version of this approach—all current offenses are counted in the criminal history of all other current offenses (Wash. Rev. Code Sec. 9.94A.589); moreover, upward departure is permitted when multiple current offenses produce a criminal history score greater than required for the highest criminal history category (*id.*, Sec. 9.94A.535(2)(c)).

This concurrent-plus option could be a good choice if it is combined with limits on the magnitude of criminal history enhancements, as proposed in the next section. Of the two versions of this option described, the Minnesota variant is more parsimonious (less severe), and thus also limits the magnitude of disparity that can result from charging decisions.

Option 4: Multiple Offenses Increase Sentence Severity According to Other Formulas

Five sentencing guidelines systems permit or require that multiple current convictions enhance sentence severity under a formula that can yield a penalty less severe than fully consecutive sentencing (another bulk discount) but more severe than fully concurrent sentencing. For example, the federal guidelines (US Sentencing Commission, 2015, sec. 3D1.4) provide that the most serious offense determines a starting point and is assigned a value of one unit; additional offenses are assigned one or one-half unit, and the total number of units raises the offender's offense severity level by from one to five severity levels.[7]

Four state guidelines take different approaches (Frase, 2015). In Utah, when multiple crimes are sentenced concurrently each additional crime increases sentence severity by 10 percent. In three states (Alabama, Florida, and Virginia) that use a point system rather than a grid to derive recommended sentences, multiple current offenses add to the total number of points, which then determines disposition (prison versus nonprison) and the duration of custody.

Any version of this fourth option could, depending on the formula, yield similar results as under the third option (adding to current criminal history). But at least in a system that already has criminal history enhancement rules, choosing the fourth option requires devising, justifying, and applying a second enhancement scheme.

All Options

Whichever concurrent-plus option is chosen, policymakers will need to consider not just enhancement of the quantum of punishment (e.g., prison duration), but also its form, that is: whether, and when, multiple current offenses should cause an offender to be sent to prison who would not have been prison-eligible for any one of his crimes.

Reduced Magnitude of Prior Record Enhancement (PRE)

One of the reasons why sequential sentencing yields more severe aggregate penalties than simultaneous sentencing of the same crimes is that PRE has a greater impact in the sequential context—PRE is routinely applied, and grows in magnitude with each successive sentencing. In contrast, when multiple offenses are sentenced simultaneously those crimes generally are not added to the offender's criminal history for current PRE purposes, or are not added fully. One of the concurrent-plus sentencing options discussed in the previous section—adding multiple current offenses to the offender's criminal history score—tends to partially reduce this difference, but would not eliminate it: that option assumes concurrent sentencing, so the enhanced PRE only applies to one of the charges (whereas, in sequential sentencing, the PRE applies to each charge, and grows over time). And of course, a jurisdiction might choose to employ different concurrent-plus options, not involving additions to criminal history, or might choose to make no change at all in simultaneous sentencing. It therefore seems likely that PRE will continue to have a greater effect in sequential cases, helping to maintain the much higher levels of severity imposed on those crimes. It was argued earlier that simultaneous cases often merit less severe penalties than sequential cases. But if policymakers are troubled by these differences, they may need to find additional ways to reduce them. One way to do that would be to decrease the aggregate severity of sentencing in sequential cases by reducing the magnitude of PREs (since the latter have, and will continue to have, a greater enhancing effect in sequential sentencing).

In other writings (Frase, 2010, 2013; Frase et al., 2015), I have argued that PREs are often excessive as a retributive matter, and have a number of other undesirable consequences—they yield recommended and imposed sentences that are disproportionately severe relative to the offender's current offense; undercut the goal of reserving prison beds for very serious or violent crimes; increase the numbers of aging, low-risk but high-expense inmates held in prison; and contribute to the problem of racially disproportionate prison populations. Thus, reducing PRE magnitude is already a desirable goal; but it can also help to reduce the difference between sentence severity in simultaneous and sequential cases.

There are many ways to reduce the magnitude of PREs (see generally, Roberts and Frase, 2017). To cite but four examples:

- Limit the dispositional (in/out) magnitude of PRE by lowering the proportion of cases in which an elevated criminal history score turns a recommended-probation sentence into a recommended-prison term.
- Limit the custody-duration magnitude of PRE and the frequency of offense-disproportionate sentences by, for example, specifying that recommended terms for the highest-history offenders at a given offense severity level cannot be more than two times higher than recommended terms for lowest-history offenders. This particular limit can be justified on the grounds that prior convictions should never count more (add more to the sentence) than the current offense itself, which a more-than-doubling PRE would.
- Cut back or eliminate many of the problematic components typically found in criminal history formulas, including: juvenile court adjudications; misdemeanors; in-custody status at the time of the offense; and heavy weighting of prior felonies based solely on their severity ranking.
- Shorten the "look-back" period, to more often exclude older convictions (in many guidelines systems, current rules specify no look-back limit at all for some or all prior convictions).

Conclusion

In this essay I defend the common practice of punishing simultaneously sentenced offenses (simultaneous offenses) less severely than when the same crimes are sentenced sequentially (sequential offenses). My approach rejects the assumption that simultaneous and sequential offenses are comparable if they involve the same crimes. On the contrary, I argue, these two sentencing contexts are substantively, procedurally, and practically noncomparable. The principal substantive punishment goals, retribution and crime control, often justify reduced punishment of simultaneous offenses. Procedurally, the dispositional options are not the same—in the sequential context there is no counterpart of either concurrent sentencing or prosecutorial bulk discounting. Practically, the problem of very high magnitude cumulative simultaneous-offense punishment finds few sequential-offense counterparts in highly punitive US systems because criminal careers end before offenders can sequentially serve a large number of lengthy prison terms.

In short, judges can and should reject the false equivalency of simultaneous and sequential offenses, and should continue to sentence simultaneous offenses less harshly, applying the presumptive rules and limiting principles I have proposed. Judges should also make use of the concurrent-plus options I discuss. Policymakers can further limit simultaneous–sequential sentencing differentials by reducing the magnitude of prior record enhancements. All of these proposals, if adopted, should make sentencing of multiple crimes more principled and consistent.

Notes

1. My most recent work (Frase, 2013) defends a more precise but asymmetric conception of desert, and contrasts it to the Norval Morris model that I advocated in earlier works (Frase, 1997; 2004). My recent work also gives increased attention to the expressive goals of punishment, and I will make reference to the latter at several points in this paper.
2. Many US states have statutes preventing cumulative punishment of greater and lesser-included offenses (see, e.g., Minn. Stat. Sec. 609.04 (2016)). Some states also bar cumulative punishment of alternate-theory charges, under statutes requiring merger of convictions arising out of a single act or behavioral incident (see, e.g., *id.* Sec. 609.035; Calif. Penal Code Sec. 654 (2016)).
3. See Frase, 2015, Table 10.2 (presumptions in favor of concurrent sentencing for at least some types of crimes are found in the District of Columbia, Minnesota, Oregon, and Washington; presumptive rules that effectively reject fully consecutive sentencing are found in Alabama, the federal system, and Utah).
4. Some state guidelines treat consecutive-sentencing departures as a species of durational departure, invoking the standards applicable to upward durational departures in single-crime cases; the latter, in turn, tend to focus on factors showing elevated harm and/or culpability in commission of that offense. See, e.g., *State v. Kirsch* 338 N.W.2d 45 (Minn. 1983) and *State v. Heywood*, 338 N.W.2d 243 (Minn. 1983). But my proposal goes further—courts would need to find that consecutive sentencing is both deserved and necessary for crime control purposes.
5. See Frase, 2015, Table 10.2 (doubling limits in Kansas and Oregon guidelines provisions); *State v. Kirsch, supra* (court-imposed presumptive doubling limit on consecutive sentences).
6. For example, under the federal guidelines for drug-trafficking crimes, aggregation of marijuana amounts yields a much lower total penalty, especially at higher drug amounts, than if the crimes were sentenced sequentially (US Sentencing Commission, 2015, secs. 2D1.1 and 3D1.1).

7. On much of the federal grid a five-level increase raises the duration of recommended prison terms by about 70%; percentage changes in duration are less at the top of the grid (low offense severity), greater at the bottom.

References

American Law Institute. 2017. *Model Penal Code: Sentencing, Proposed Final Draft* (April 10, 2017) (Approved May 24, 2017). Philadelphia: American Law Institute.

Ashworth, A. 2015. *Sentencing and Criminal Justice*. 6th ed. Cambridge: Cambridge University Press.

Doob, A., and C. Webster. 2003. "Sentence Severity and Crime: Accepting the Null Hypothesis." In M. Tonry (ed.), *Crime and Justice: A Review of Research* 30: 143–195. Chicago: University of Chicago Press.

Durlauf, S. N., and D. S. Nagin. 2011. "Imprisonment and Crime: Can Both Be Reduced?" *Criminology & Public Policy* 10(1): 13–54.

Frase, R. 1990. "Comparative Criminal Justice as a Guide to American Law Reform: How Do the French Do It, How Can We Find Out, and Why Should We Care?" *California Law Review* 78(3): 539–683.

Frase, R. 1997. "Sentencing Principles in Theory and Practice." In M. Tonry (ed.), *Crime & Justice: A Review of Research* 22: 363–433. Chicago: University of Chicago Press.

Frase, R. 2004. "Limiting Retributivism." In M. Tonry (ed.), *The Future of Imprisonment*, pp. 83–120. New York: Oxford University Press.

Frase, R. 2010. "Prior-Conviction Sentencing Enhancements: Rationales and Limits Based on Retributive and Utilitarian Proportionality Principles and Social Equality Goals." In J. V. Roberts and A. von Hirsch (eds.), *Previous Convictions at Sentencing: Theoretical and Applied Perspectives*, pp. 117–136. Oxford: Hart Publishing.

Frase, R. 2013. *Just Sentencing: Principles and Procedures for a Workable System*. New York: Oxford University Press.

Frase, R. S. 2015. "The Treatment of Multiple Current Offenses." In R. S. Frase, J. V. Roberts, R. Hester, and K. L. Mitchell, *Criminal History Enhancements Sourcebook*, pp. 91–96. Minneapolis: Robina Institute of Criminal Law and Criminal Justice.

Frase, R. S., J. V. Roberts, K. Mitchell, and R. Hester. 2015. *Criminal History Enhancements Sourcebook*. Minneapolis: Robina Institute of Criminal Law and Criminal Justice.

Lippke, R. 2011. "Retributive Sentencing, Multiple Offenders, and Bulk Discounts." In M. D. White (ed.), *Retributivism: Essays on Theory and Policy*, pp. 212–231. New York: Oxford University Press.

Minnesota Sentencing Guidelines Commission [MSGC]. 2015. *Minnesota Sentencing Guidelines and Commentary, August 1, 2015*. St. Paul, MN: MSGC.

Morris, N. 1974. *The Future of Imprisonment*. Chicago: University of Chicago Press.

Parent, D. 1988. *Structuring Criminal Sentences: The Evolution of Minnesota's Sentencing Guidelines*. Stoneham, MA: Butterworth Legal Publishers.

Roberts, J., and R. Frase. 2017, forthcoming. *Risk and Retribution: Exploring Prior Record Sentencing Enhancements*. New York: Oxford University Press.

Sullivan, T., and R. Frase 2009. *Proportionality Principles in American Law: Controlling Excessive Government Actions*. New York: Oxford University Press.

US Sentencing Commission. 2015. *Federal Sentencing Guidelines Manual*. Washington, DC: US Sentencing Commission.

12

Sentencing the Multiple Offender

In Search of a "Just and Proportionate" Total Sentence

ANDREW ASHWORTH AND MARTIN WASIK

The multiple offender will receive a shorter (perhaps much shorter) sentence if she or he is dealt with for several offenses on a single sentencing occasion than if sentenced for those same offenses on two or more separate sentencing occasions. This is the "discount for bulk offending," a practice which is widely adopted in different sentencing systems but which is hard to justify theoretically, either in retributive or deterrent terms. In this chapter we focus on custodial sentences, where the issues are at their most stark.

In England, the jurisdiction with which we are mainly concerned in this chapter, the tools for determining custodial sentences in the case of multiple offenders are threefold: concurrent sentences, consecutive sentences, and the totality principle. Custodial sentences imposed on the same sentencing occasion in England cannot overlap. This means that the total sentence must always be arrived at through a combination of concurrent and/or consecutive sentences.

We begin the chapter by attempting to identify the rationale of the totality principle, examining how it operates and seeking a justification for the principle. We then turn to scrutinize the component parts of the totality principle, examining six problematic issues. We then develop our argument that totality should be regarded as the determining principle when sentencing for multiple offenses, discussing the approach of some other jurisdictions before formulating what we regard as necessary changes in the sentencing guidelines for England and Wales.

Identifying the Rationale of the Totality Principle

The totality principle applies to all multiple-offense cases, whatever combination of concurrent or consecutive sentences a particular judge adopts. Whether sentences are imposed concurrently, or consecutively, or in a mix, the total sentence should, in principle, be unaffected. The practical operation of this principle can clearly be seen in many English appellate decisions. If the Court of Appeal finds that the judge has achieved totality in his or her sentence then only rarely will the Court quibble about the particular combination of concurrent and / or consecutive sentences which were employed by the judge to reach that result. The overriding requirement when sentencing multiple offenders is that the judge has reflected totality—an appropriate overall custodial sentence.

Three questions need to be addressed in connection with the central concept of totality. First, how does the totality principle operate? Secondly, what is the rationale for the principle? And thirdly, what are its component elements?

First, the operation of the totality principle (in outline). Everyone agrees that in the case of a multiple offender the total sentence should be greater than the proportionate sentence for any one of the offenses. This is true whether the judge employs consecutive or concurrent sentences, or a mixture of both, to achieve the final outcome. The totality principle, however, operates to restrict the sentence that might otherwise result from adding together the single sentences for each of the offenses. This restrictive principle applies so as to reduce the sentence for someone who has committed several offenses, whether these were committed close together in time or over a considerable period.

This prompts the question (posed forcefully by Reitz, 2010, p. 138) of why the multiple offender's sentence is restricted when the repeat offender who is caught and sentenced on each separate occasion receives enhanced sentences (not restricted sentences) on account of the persistence of the offending. Before confronting that question, two preliminary points must be noted. First, one should beware of exaggerating the difference between those two sentencing approaches. Desert theory does allow modest increases in sentence for persistent offenders, subject to a "ceiling" reached after three or four offenses, after which there should be no further increases (an approach clearly reflected in Crown Court sentencing practice; see Roberts and Pina-Sanchez, 2014). Multiple offenders do receive an incremental increase for each subsequent offense, although the size of the increment diminishes as the number of offenses rises. Empirical evidence is lacking here, but the rarity with which Crown Court judges exceed the "offense range" set out in sentencing guidelines strongly suggests that sentences passed for multiple offenses do generally fall within the same broad parameters as sentences passed for a single offense. However, that said, the difference in approach remains considerable, and the responses to both multiple offenders (sentenced "simultaneously," as Frase 2013, ch. 4, puts it) and persistent offenders (sentenced "sequentially") ideally ought to be incorporated into a single and consistent matrix.

Justifying the Principle

The second preliminary point is that the presence of multiple offenses and the presence of previous offenses on the offender's record are each taken into account at two stages of reasoning. At the first stage the presence of the other offenses requires that the total sentence imposed on the present occasion is always higher than it otherwise would be. A serious prior criminal record, the presence of other offenses for which the offender is being sentenced at the same time (and "offenses taken into consideration," for that matter),[1] all serve to increase the seriousness of the case. At the second stage, however, the total sentence is scaled back so as to set a limit upon the effect which the presence of multiple offenses or offenses on the offender's record would otherwise have. We argue that the previous convictions of the offender with a serious record, and the "non-lead offenses" of a multiple offender, simply provide part of the context within which the assessment of offense seriousness can fairly be made.

How can the rationale for the totality principle be explained? Three possible explanations can be considered. First, it might be argued that the multiple offender who is sentenced on one occasion for several offenses differs from other persistent offenders because the latter have had authoritative warnings (in the shape of convictions and sentences) which the multiple offender has not received, and indeed may have served sentences that have a criminogenic (rather than a rehabilitative) effect. This is certainly a distinction between the two classes of offender, but it is not clear that the difference is weighty enough to justify the different approaches to sentencing, not least because there is usually no question that the multiple offenders knew they were committing offenses and were, at that stage, avoiding detection.

Secondly, it is sometimes argued that the basis for the restrictive effect of the totality principle lies in the direction of mercy, the principle of parsimony or restraint, or even the right to human dignity. These are indeed important principles, but it is not clear why they should apply to multiple offenders rather than to any offender who is likely to receive a substantial custodial sentence. All such sentences are hard, and are likely to have a "crushing effect" on many of those subjected to them. However, it is fair to note that one of the problems of consecutive sentencing (especially if it operates in an unbridled way) is that it may result in a total punishment of years amounting to much of the offender's remaining life-time or even (illogically) running well beyond that period. Consecutive sentences rapidly become nonsensical, particularly with elderly offenders being sentenced for multiple historic offenses. In principle—and this is supported by the right to human dignity—the total sentence imposed on an offender should always be one which is capable of being served within the offender's lifetime (subject to the whole-life minimum term issue, considered in *Vinter v. UK* [2013] and *Hutchinson v. UK* [2015]).

Thirdly, and notwithstanding the fact that the two arguments seem less than compelling, it appears that a majority of members of the public support some kind of totality principle (see Robinson and Darley, 1995, p. 193; Roberts, 2008, pp. 180–182), and that intuitively interoffense proportionality is the dominant consideration. In other words, several lesser offenses should not combine to produce a sentence above that which is appropriate for a significantly more serious offense. Thus, while part of the thrust of this rationale is that it is based on public opinion, its deeper roots lie in the intuitive attraction of a version of proportionality theory that privileges interoffense proportionality above intraoffense proportionality. In other words, the primary determinant of proportionality here is the most serious of the offenses for which sentence is being passed, rather than the sheer number of lesser offenses. There is some philosophical support for the "strong intuitive basis" for the reduction in multiple-offense sentencing (see Bennett, 2012, p. 138). We would concede that there may be combinations of facts that challenge the intuitive attraction of interoffense proportionality (see Reitz, 2010, p. 146), but in many cases the primacy of interoffense proportionality is a reasonable starting-point.

What Are the Component Parts of the Totality Principle?

Without concluding our tentative discussion of rationales, it is now appropriate to examine the component elements of the totality principle. A major element is the proposition that it is inappropriate to sentence the multiple offender simply by doing the arithmetic and adding together the sentences for the individual offenses. The Sentencing Council moves from this proposition to the repeated assertion that the sentence must be "just and proportionate," without further elaboration (Sentencing Council, 2012, criticized by Ashworth, 2015, pp. 282–286). This formulation should be rejected on the ground that it ducks the issues and leaves relatively unbridled judicial discretion. While (as we elaborate in the next section) a major purpose of multiple-offense sentencing should be to achieve proper presentation and communication, the notion of totality is dependent on the resolution of some tough normative questions.

What goes into judgments of totality? For example, is there not a significant difference between three or four offenses arising out of the same incident, and three or four offenses committed over a period of time? In calculating totality there must surely be a difference between these two types of core case; although it is true that (a) there are some contestable cases where the idea of a single incident is stretched as a concept (for examples, see Wasik, 2012, pp. 294–297) and (b) there is at least a presentational argument for a different approach where, for example, different legal prohibitions have been violated in the incident. This is not about consecutive or concurrent sentences; it is about the elements that go to make up totality, ensuring that there is no undercounting or double-counting. Similarly, when calculating totality, should it matter whether several offenses were committed against the same victim or against different victims?

These are among the questions we need to answer, in order to unpack the notion of a just and proportionate overall sentence. In the following section we set out six possible aspects of the relationship between the offenses to be sentenced, that may affect the quantum of the total sentence—factors that tend to move the total sentence upward or downward:

1) The genuine single incident (the nonproblematic cases); such as the robbery with a carried weapon or the burglary with a weapon. In principle, if there are two charges (robbery, carrying an offensive weapon) the sentence should be the same as it would be if only robbery were charged and the carrying of the weapon were treated as a factor aggravating the robbery. It can fairly be regarded as a single incident or single transaction. Thus, if a person were charged with a robbery last week and carrying an offensive weapon this week, these two offenses cannot be seen as a single incident and one might therefore expect the total sentence to be higher than in the "single incident/transaction" case. However, as one of us has argued before (Wasik, 2012), the boundaries are often blurred and so there are limits to the usefulness of the "single incident" concept. Thus, consider a case where D commits a house burglary to take the car keys, steals the high performance car belonging to the householder, and then drives it dangerously, ultimately resulting in a police chase and D's arrest. These three offenses are certainly linked together (in time and context), but it is not very helpful to ask whether this is one incident or two or three. In order to achieve totality one would expect there to be some aggregation of the sentences for the burglary, the theft and the dangerous driving.
2) Where there is a series of similar offenses over a period of time, the best approach is to aggregate the offenses and to sentence as if it is a composite offense. This is straightforward where there is a series of benefit frauds, or thefts from an employer, where it is possible to aggregate the loss/gain into a single total. Where there is a series of similar sexual or physical abuse cases over time, this aggregative approach may still be adopted in principle, but the detailed approach is likely to be different. Several offenses of assault occasioning bodily harm could be cumulated by adding the sentences together, and the same for a series of sexual offenses; but whereas the approach to repeated

property offenses is to produce a figure for total gain/loss, the approach to other offenses is to aggregate the individual *sentences*. This would clearly engage the restrictive element of the totality principle; but should not the aggregation of gain/loss in property offenses also engage the totality principle?

3) Where the series of offenses is committed against the same victim, is this more or less serious than the same offenses against different victims? The Sentencing Council seems to say different things, by suggesting that repetitive thefts from the same person should usually attract concurrent sentences whereas repetitive offenses of domestic violence or sexual offense against the same person should attract consecutive sentences (Sentencing Council, 2012, pp. 6–7). Admittedly these remarks do not relate to the totality principle directly, but there is a strong implication in the Council's discussion that the totality principle may exert a more restrictive effect when property offenses are committed against the same person than when sexual offenses or domestic abuse are committed. There seems to be no good reason to distinguish between repeated victimization of the same person and of different persons, unless there is evidence that a vulnerable person was targeted—an independent aggravating factor.
4) If one or more of the offenses are committed while on bail for another offense being sentenced on the same occasion, this should raise the total sentence by a significant amount.[2] Two reasons for this are that (a) the new offense is clearly separated in time from the original offense, and (b) offending on bail violates a separate interest, in the sense that an important element of trust is breached by the commission of offenses while awaiting a court hearing on other charges.
5) If one or more of the offenses involve assault on the police, for example to try to escape arrest in relation to another offense being sentenced on the same occasion, this should raise the sentence by a significant amount. Two reasons for this are that (a) the new offense is likely to violate a separate interest (unless the original offense was also an attack on the police), and (b) this separate interest is one that requires extra protection, since police officers are required to place themselves in vulnerable positions in order to carry out their public duties.
6) If one of the offenses is an offense against the administration of justice committed in relation to another offense being sentenced, this should raise the sentence by a significant amount. This is along similar lines to point (4), but it relates to offenses such as perverting the course of justice, as by trying to conceal evidence or to claim that the offense was committed by another or to bribe a witness to keep quiet. The main rationales for this would, again, be that the offense violates a separate and socially important interest.

These six factors are relevant to determining whether the total sentence should be adjusted upward or downward, and therefore to the principle that the sentence of the multiple offender should attempt to reflect the offending behavior as a whole. Where should the court start in its assessment of totality? Other jurisdictions have tackled this problem by developing formulae to guide sentencers in arriving at totality in multiple-offense cases. In Germany, for example, the traditional model has been to give full penal weight to the most serious offense to be sentenced and then to add to that figure roughly half of the total penal weight attaching to the sum of all the other offenses. An account of this is provided by Jareborg (1998, pp. 135–137), describing the work of Hans-Jorg Albrecht and Joachim Bohnert. A more elaborate model has been developed in Sweden, whereby full penal weight is given to the most serious offense, to which is added half of the penal weight for the second most serious offense, one third of the penal weight for the third most serious offense, and so on. The model, as developed by Borgeke, a Swedish Appeal Court judge, is considered in more detail by Vibla (2013, pp. 86–88). In Vibla's interviews with Swedish judges (pp. 89–104) she found a broad acceptance of Borgeke's approach as a way to achieve greater consistency in multiple-offense cases, provided that the formula was applied flexibly. This approach certainly has something to recommend it, but the relationship between the mathematical models and the six factors identified earlier needs to be more clearly elaborated. The discussion suggests that interoffense proportionality is the key guide, taking the lead offense as a pointer but adding incrementally to reflect the other offenses.

From this discussion of the factors that may determine the assessment of the total sentence, we now move on to the presentational issue of concurrent/consecutive sentences. There would be some difficulty in accommodating the German/Swedish approach to multiple-offense sentencing within the English tradition of concurrent/consecutive sentencing. In English sentencing practice the position is that all the offenses in a multiple-offense case must receive their proportionate sentence, but that some or all of those sentences will be ordered to run concurrently rather than consecutively, to comply with totality. The sentence imposed for each offense will appear on the offender's criminal record. In the German–Swedish model the sentences for all individual offenses other than the lead offense are artificially shortened to achieve totality. It is simply the global sentence which then appears on the offender's record.

Presentation, Communication, and the Totality Principle

We take the view that totality is the determining principle when sentencing multiple offenders, rather than just a limiting principle (as Thomas, 1979, pp. 56–61 argued, and as reflected in Sentencing Council guidelines). If we are right that totality is the determining principle, then, if a judge chooses to deal with one of the offenses by way of a consecutive sentence, there must be some adjustment to sentences for other offenses in order to retain totality. The selection of concurrent and consecutive sentences within totality is, for the most part, a matter of presentation of the total sentence (to the defendant, the victim, and the wider public). There is no proportionality issue in the choice between concurrent and consecutive sentences. Of course presentation is important for communicative reasons, and can be particularly so in sensitive cases, such as those involving multiple deaths (see the examples in Wasik, 2012, pp. 299–301). While it is possible to imagine the English sentencing system operating without consecutive sentences at all, the importance of presentation in some cases means that there is value in their occasional use. There should, however, be a clear presumption in favor of concurrent sentences.

The most straightforward case, perhaps, is one where there is a clear lead offense in terms of seriousness, and then one or more lesser offenses. The principle is to pass a somewhat enhanced sentence for the lead offense (enhanced by treating the other offenses as aggravating the lead offense) and then to use concurrent sentences for the rest. This principle certainly applies both at the lower end of the custodial sentencing scale (for example, dangerous driving, plus no tax, no insurance) and at the higher end. For example, in *Pinnell* (2011) the Court of Appeal said that where an extended sentence is to be imposed on a multiple offender all the offenses should be looked at in the round before imposing the extended sentence for the most serious matter and passing concurrent sentences for the rest. Then there is the case of several offenses (say, assault) committed against the same victim, or against different victims. Generally, this is better dealt with by concurrent rather than consecutive sentences because (especially if there are more than two offenses) using consecutive terms means that some or all of the assaults have to be undersentenced to keep within totality. Concurrent sentences allow the judge to pass a proportionate sentence for each assault.

The most difficult case is where the offender falls to be sentenced for two entirely unrelated matters (burglary committed on one occasion and assault on another). Some would prefer consecutive sentences here, but that approach requires each sentence to be shorter than it would be if standing alone. Concurrence allows the judge to pass appropriate sentences for each matter, and thereby to impose a proportionate overall sentence. If, as sometimes happens, the defendant faces charges on two separate but unrelated indictments, the best approach may be to select the lead offenses from each of the two indictments, pass consecutive sentences for those and concurrent sentences for all the rest.

In the context of the sentencing guidelines for England and Wales, our arguments in this chapter point to the need for two major changes—the first relating to the standard contents of the offense guidelines, and the second relating to the generic guideline for sentencing multiple offenders.

Offense Guidelines

On the first point, we think that the totality principle should be more clearly incorporated into offense guidelines, which have hitherto focused on single offenses and have largely ignored the complexities of multiple offending. Given the frequency with which multiple offenses are sentenced, and the determining role of totality, it is not appropriate to relegate totality to step 6 of the Sentencing Council's guidelines, as it currently is.[3] In addition to step 6 (which we think should be retained as a useful check), more detailed guidance should be given earlier, at step 2 (starting point and category range). Guidelines at step 2 set out a table of "factors increasing seriousness" and "factors reducing seriousness or reflecting personal mitigation," and typically contain the following wording (e.g., guideline on *Assault*, 2011):

> The table . . . contains a non-exhaustive list of additional factual elements providing the context of the offence and factors relating to the offender. Identify whether any combination of these, or other relevant factors, should result in an upward or downward adjustment from the starting point. In some cases, having considered these factors, it may be appropriate to move outside the identified category range.

The table does not cater for multiple offenses, and indeed there is no mention of the issue at all. In something of a change of direction, a recently published offense guideline (on *Theft Offences*, 2016) contains the following additional statement at step 2:

> The table . . . refers to single offences. Where there are multiple offences consecutive sentences may be appropriate: please refer to the Offences Taken into Consideration and Totality guideline.

This wording appears in relation to *some* of the particular offenses covered (general theft, theft from a shop, handling stolen goods, and going equipped for theft), but not others (abstracting electricity and making off without payment). It seems clear from the context that the reference in the guideline to multiple offenses is meant to be limited to multiple instances of the same particular offense, and not to sentencing multiple offenses more generally.[4]

We think that more assistance should be provided, and suggest that the following should be incorporated at step 2 of each offense guideline:

> If sentencing the offender for more than one offence:
>
> (i) There is a presumption in favor of passing concurrent sentences for all offences being dealt with, but in some cases consecutive sentences may

be appropriate: please refer to the Offences Taken into Consideration and Totality guideline.

(ii) It will normally be appropriate to pass a total sentence which is within the category range appropriate to the most serious of the offences, although the presence of one or more other offences (whether similar to or different from the most serious offence) will normally require the adoption of a higher starting point than would be appropriate for a single offence. In some cases, having considered these factors it may be appropriate to move outside the identified category range.

And, in the table column "Factors Increasing Seriousness: Other Aggravating Factors Include" the following additional wording should appear:

> Offender being sentenced for more than one offence.

English Guideline on Totality

Moving to the second major change that is necessary, we would recommend reconsideration of the Sentencing Council's guideline on *Offences taken into Consideration and Totality* (2012), so as to make it clear that the totality principle is a determining principle that should form an important part of the court's reasoning from step 2 onward in all multiple-offense cases, rather than simply a late-stage check at step 6 to see whether the sentence intuitively seems too high. There are some features of the totality guideline with which we agree. We agree that when sentencing a multiple offender the court "should pass a total sentence which reflects all the offending behaviour . . . whether the sentences are constructed as concurrent or consecutive," and that "there is no inflexible rule governing whether sentences should be . . . concurrent or consecutive."

We disagree, however, with the Sentencing Council's general approach that the court should "consider the sentence for each individual offence," then "determine whether the case calls for concurrent or consecutive sentences," and then "test the overall sentence(s) against the requirement that they be just and proportionate." At present the guideline usefully summarizes the earlier case-law on the use of concurrent and consecutive sentences, but actually says nothing about the proper role of the totality principle, and gives no clues as to how the court should assess totality in any particular case. What appears at step 6 in the offense guidelines under totality principle is:

> If sentencing an offender for more than one offence . . . consider whether the total sentence is just and proportionate to the offending behaviour.

Neither this statement, nor the totality guideline as a whole, assists a judge in selecting the just and proportionate sentence for all the offending behavior. So, what additional ground should a revised totality guideline cover?

We said earlier that the most straightforward multiple offense case is one where there is a clear lead offense in terms of seriousness, and then one or more lesser offenses. We think that the advice should be for the judge to move at step 1 to the category range appropriate for the lead offense. The judge should always explain his or her conclusion on step 1 before moving to step 2, as required by the decision in *Attorney-General's References (Nos 15, 16 and 17 of 2012)* (2013). Almost inevitably, the presence of multiple offenses will justify a move upward within the category range. There will be some cases where the presence of multiple offenses (taken together with all other factors) will require the court to move up from one category range to the next. Moving from one category range to another is not a departure from the offense guideline, but it was said in *Datsun* (2014) that it was always desirable for the judge to explain why this has occurred. Very occasionally the presence of multiple offenses (taken together with all other factors) may justify a provisional sentence at the end of step 2 (prior to any reduction for a guilty plea, etc.) which is above the top of the offense range. To arrive at a sentence above the top of the offense range is a *departure* from the offense guideline and would require the judge to explain that to pass a sentence within the offense range would be contrary to the interests of justice (Coroners and Justice Act, 2009, s.125(1)).

Pausing there, it is worth noting in more detail the empirical evidence which shows that in practice in the Crown Court upward departures from offense guidelines are very rare (Sentencing Council, 2014). In 2014 they occurred in 2% of cases involving assault occasioning actual bodily harm, 3% of cases of domestic burglary, and 0.5% of cases of cultivation of cannabis. These figures strongly suggest that in the great majority of cases the upper category range in the offense guidelines is perfectly adequate to deal with the worst multiple-offense cases. Ordinarily in the offense guidelines there is a significant gap between the top of the offense range and the maximum penalty for the offense to cater for cases where the court does need to depart from the guideline. For assault occasioning actual bodily harm the top of the offense range is three years but the maximum is five years. For domestic burglary the top of the offense range is six years but the maximum is 14 years. For cultivation of cannabis the top of the offense range is 10 years but the maximum is 14 years. In very rare cases aggravating factors, including the presence of multiple offenses, may justify the passing of a final sentence which is higher than the maximum penalty for any one of the offenses being sentenced. Sentencing in excess of the maximum can only be achieved by the use of consecutive sentences. The recent offense guideline on general theft

(theft carries a maximum penalty of seven years) recognizes that, and contains the following statement at step 2:

> Where multiple offences are committed in circumstances which justify consecutive sentences and the total amount stolen is in excess of £1 million, then an aggregate sentence in excess of seven years may be appropriate.

This is the first time that such a statement has appeared in an offense guideline,[5] and there is no explanation given in the text for singling out the offense of theft in this way. It could be taken as confirmation that the Crown Court should not normally use consecutive sentences to exceed the maximum. As we have seen, the maximum for assault occasioning actual bodily harm is five years, so the inference is that no matter how many instances of that offense are being sentenced on the same occasion the sentence should never exceed five years before adjustment for guilty plea and any other matters. Relatively technical these issues may be, but they ought to be resolved if the sentencing guidelines system is to cater properly for the sentencing of multiple offenses.

Conclusion

In this chapter we have sought to confront some of the difficult practical issues that arise in multiple-offense sentencing, and to place them in the context of the strongest justification for the totality principle. Our argument is that totality should be regarded as the determining principle when sentencing multiple offenders, rather than simply as a limiting principle. We also argue that the choice between concurrent and consecutive sentencing should be seen as a presentational and communicative issue, and we make concrete proposals about ways in which the totality principle should be reformulated in the generic guidelines on totality, and more clearly incorporated into the various offense guidelines issued by the Sentencing Council for England and Wales.

Notes

1. The English practice of taking offenses into consideration means that an offender who is about to be sentenced can ask the court to take account of other offenses that he admits to committing but with which he has not been charged. In practice, this usually happens in relation to offenses similar to the type for which he is already being sentenced, and the effect will be to increase the overall sentence (see further Ashworth, 2015, p. 275).
2. One cannot prescribe what the incremental increase would be, but it should be a just noticeable difference in order to signify the violation of this separate interest.

3. Some explanation is necessary for those unfamiliar with the structure of the English sentencing guidelines. Each guideline relates to one offense or one group of offenses. The court is usually required to go through 8 or 9 steps in order to impose the appropriate sentence and orders. In brief, step 1 sets out the harm and culpability factors on the basis of which the court should determine which offense category the offense falls. Step 2 sets out a number of aggravating and mitigating factors that the court may use in order to determine whether to move upward or downward from the starting point in the appropriate offense category. Step 3 concerns further reductions for assistance to the prosecution; step 4 requires the court to reduce sentence to reflect a plea of guilty; step 5 (where applicable) requires the court to have regard to the criteria for sentencing dangerous offenders; step 6 is the totality principle; step 7 requires the court to consider ancillary orders; step 8 requires the court to formulate its reasons; and step 9 requires the court to adjust the sentence accordingly if the defendant was subject to a qualifying curfew while remanded on bail.
4. The new wording does not appear in relation to abstracting electricity. It is perhaps unlikely that a defendant would fall to be sentenced for multiple instances of that offense, but abstracting electricity is commonly encountered as an offense associated with other offenses, especially production of cannabis.
5. Nor does it appear in relation to the other offenses covered in the *Theft Offences* guideline, such as theft from a shop or handling stolen goods.

References

Ashworth, A. 2015. *Sentencing and Criminal Justice*. 6th ed. Cambridge: Cambridge University Press.

Bennett, C. 2012. "Do Multiple and Repeat Offenders Pose a Problem for Retributive Sentencing Theory?" In C. Tamburrini and J. Ryberg (eds.), *Recidivist Punishments: The Philosopher's View*, pp. 137–156. Lanham, MD: Lexington Books.

Frase, R. S. 2013. *Just Sentencing: Principles and Procedures for a Workable System*. New York: Oxford University Press.

Jareborg, N. 1998. "Why Bulk Discounts in Multiple Offence Sentencing?" In A. Ashworth and M. Wasik (eds.), *Fundamentals of Sentencing Theory: Essays in Honour of Andrew von Hirsch*, pp. 129–140. Oxford: Clarendon Press.

Reitz, K. 2010. "The Illusion of Proportionality: Desert and Repeat Offenders." In J. V. Roberts and A. von Hirsch (eds.), *Previous Convictions at Sentencing: Theoretical and Applied Perspectives*, pp. 137–160. Oxford: Hart Publishing.

Roberts, J. V. 2008. *Punishing Persistent Offenders: Exploring Community and Offender Perspectives*. Oxford: Oxford University Press.

Roberts, J. V., and J. Pina-Sanchez. 2014. "Previous Convictions at Sentencing: Exploring Empirical Trends in the Crown Court." *Criminal Law Review*: 575–588.

Robinson, P., and J. Darley. 1995. *Justice, Liability and Blame: Community Views and the Criminal Law*. Boulder, CO: Westview Press.

Sentencing Council for England and Wales. 2011. *Definitive Guideline: Assault*. London: Sentencing Council for England and Wales.

Sentencing Council for England and Wales. 2012. *Offences Taken into Consideration and Totality: Definitive Guideline*. London: Sentencing Council for England and Wales.

Sentencing Council for England and Wales. 2014. *Crown Court Sentencing Survey Annual Publication* (January to December 2014). London: Sentencing Council for England and Wales.

Sentencing Council for England and Wales. 2016. *Definitive Guideline: Theft Offences*. London: Sentencing Council for England and Wales.

Thomas, D. A. 1979. *Principles of Sentencing: The Sentencing Policy of the Court of Appeal Criminal Division*. 2nd ed. London: Heinemann.

Vibla, N. 2013. "Sentencing for Multiple Offences: Towards a Conceptual Model within a Retributive Framework." Unpublished PhD thesis, University of Cambridge.

Wasik, M. 2012. "Concurrent and Consecutive Sentences Revisited." In L. Zedner and J.V. Roberts (eds.), *Principles and Values in Criminal Law and Criminal Justice: Essays in Honour of Andrew Ashworth*, pp. 285–306. Oxford: Oxford University Press.

CASE LAW

Attorney-General's References (Nos 15, 16 and 17 of 2012) [2013] 1 Cr App R (S) 52
Datsun [2014] 1 Cr App R (S) 25
Hutchinson v. United Kingdom (2015) 61 EHRR 393
Pinnell [2011] 2 Cr App R (S) 168
Vinter v. United Kingdom [2013] ECHR 645

LEGISLATION

Coroners and Justice Act 2009, UK

13

Multiple-Offense Sentencing

Looking for Pragmatism, Not a Unifying Principle

ALLAN MANSON

For decades, sentencing scholars and punishment philosophers have been searching for a general unifying principle or theoretical justification that explains the totality approach to multiple-offense sentencing which can conform with proportionality (e.g., Bottoms, 1998; Jareborg, 1998; Reitz, 2010). During this period, two things about this problem became clear. First, some conception of totality exists in virtually every jurisdiction regardless of the relevant sentencing scheme. Second, no one has cracked the problem. When I put my mind to it, I started by looking at one group of offenses: those which attracted high-end sentences (Manson, 2013). While this represented a small part of the problem, I derived some common factors and attempted to offer a kind of practicable methodology. More importantly, I reached the conclusion that there may be too many distinct situations of multiple-offense sentencing to find a general unifying principle that can tie them together in a way that would provide some helpful guidance to sentencing judges.

As you will discern from the chapters in this book, there are at least two streams of contemporary thinking about multiple-offense sentencing. One is the laudable continuing search for a theoretical justification or single unifying theme that can apply to all multiple-offense situations. In contrast, the second is the pragmatic recognition that multiple-offense sentencing is a part of all sentencing systems and we need to get on with the task of developing a methodology or methodologies to deal with them (see contributions from Ashworth and Wasik, and the chapter by Bottoms). The purpose of this paper is to explain, first, how the myriad instances of multiple-offense sentencing are sufficiently different that the pursuit of a single theory or theme will not satisfactorily provide a basis for dealing with the array of situations that necessarily will occur. For this, I use a conceptual typology of multiple-offense situations. The conceptual typology attempts to capture important distinctions that, I will argue, cannot all be addressed by a single theory. These distinctions encompass a variety of issues: the number of offenses, low-order and high-order offenses, differences in gravity across the set of offenses, where the most serious offense sits on a scale of ordinal proportionality, and the "culpability space" between the most serious offense and the next offense up on the scale of ordinal proportionality.

Secondly, if one accepts that there cannot be a single unifying theory, or at least that the search for it has proven unduly onerous and elusive, this should lead to the conclusion that a sentencing system needs to develop a few different methodologies to address different multiple-offense situations. Sentencing is an instrumental exercise. A system needs to be capable of generating answers in concrete cases that offer some degree of uniformity. The developed typology will permit me to consider different justifications and potential methodologies.

Throughout this chapter, I will refer to a small selection of Canadian cases. Mostly, this is because of my familiarity with that source. However, it is also appropriate for two reasons. Canadian sentencing jurisprudence and the Criminal Code accept proportionality as the fundamental principle of sentencing. Also, Canada has no formal scheme of sentencing guidance with the possible exception of guidance offered sporadically by appellate courts. While totality has attracted some judicial attention, the interpretations have not moved beyond skeletal expressions. I will discuss briefly (for discussion of the various approaches to multiple-offense sentencing in the United States, see Frase, 2013). But first we need to consider some of the underlying issues, myths and obstacles which have prevented the development of a coherent approach to multiple-offense sentencing. These include the controversy over concurrent and consecutive sentences, bulk-discount criticism, and the need to find overall or total proportionality.[1]

Underlying Issues

We all recognize that a group or series of offenses means greater culpability than a single offense from that set. Beyond that, we have observed a number of issues which appear and reappear in judicial and academic discussions of multiple-offense sentencing. Some of these have distracted attention from more acute scrutiny but they permit some conclusions that can serve the evolution of this question either as points of consistent application or as markers in the pursuit of totality.

Concurrent and Consecutive Sentences

The basic Canadian approach to totality derives from the statements of Lamer, CJC in *R. v. C.A.M.* where he said:

> In the context of consecutive sentences, this general principle of proportionality expresses itself through the more particular form of the totality principle. The totality principle, in short, requires a sentencing judge who orders an offender to serve consecutive sentences for multiple offences to ensure that *the cumulative sentence rendered does not exceed the overall culpability of the offender.*[2] (emphasis added)

This brings into focus the notion of overall culpability, but, regrettably, subsequent cases have not developed the point. Lamer, CJC also adopted the interpretation of Clayton Ruby that a cumulative sentence "may offend the totality principle if the aggregate sentence is substantially above the normal level of a sentence for the most serious of the individual offenses involved, or if its effect is to impose on the offender "a crushing sentence" not in keeping with his record and prospects."[3] The "unduly harsh" test has utility when age and future prospects can be easily evaluated, for example long multiple sentences imposed on youthful offenders or most multiple sentences imposed on elderly offenders. However, these do not address the question of overall culpability that ought to apply in other situations.

In practice, consecutive and concurrent sentences are just tools used by sentencing judges as the mechanics for meeting the totality principle challenge. The intrinsic difficulty has been expressed in a recent Quebec Court of Appeal decision:

> In the case at bar, the numerous offences raised the issue of consecutive sentences. While the exercise is anything but an exact science, and is a "profoundly subjective process," it must not become arbitrary. Despite apparent and relative flexibility, the approach to adopt when faced with multiple offences, especially where there is no agreement between the parties and that the offences arise from separate events, is to establish the sentences for each of the offences; decide whether they should be served concurrently or consecutively; and, finally, decide whether they infringe the principles of totality and proportionality. Adjustments are thus allowed in order to mete out a fit sentence.[4]

This was an unusual case involving 30 offenses including assaults, offenses against police officers and various bail breaches all occurring within 12 months in the larger context of domestic violence. But the facts, the array of offenses, and the courts view of the law capture the difficulties in multiple-offense sentencing.

Most Canadian judges and scholars agree that it is important to prescribe appropriate sentences for each offense before making any totality adjustment. This has two advantages. First, it properly expresses the individual sentences for the benefit of both denunciation and addressing the perspectives of each victim. Secondly, it easily accommodates a successful conviction appeal against one of the component sentences. The alternative is to set the total and work backward. This may seem attractive to those who want to look for overall or total culpability. However, it not only negatives the two benefits but also leads back to the essential puzzle: how does one determine overall culpability?

Another point needs mention and that is the expression of the sentence which is often referred to as the "presentational" issue. Sometimes, the consecutive/concurrent question is more about how a total sentence should best be communicated to accommodate the interests of the offenders, the victims, and the public, and official documentation needed for subsequent processes. This is not a trivial matter but it does distract attention from the substantive dimensions of totality.

One substantive aspect of the concurrent/consecutive debate which is accepted in Canada and also by the Sentencing Council for England and Wales (see discussion in Ashworth, 2015) is that separate sentences arising from one criminal transaction ought usually to be served concurrently. As put recently by a Saskatchewan Court of Appeal Judge:

> The judge did not give any consideration to whether the two offences were distinct or whether they formed a single criminal adventure, although he was alive to the principle of totality.[5]

In such cases, the gravest offense provides both the gauge for culpability and also the limit on the sentence since internal elements that may constitute other offenses will be treated as aggravating. Some scholars have criticized this rule because of apparent difficulties in defining a single transaction (see Wasik, 2012). For criminal procedure purposes, although there are occasionally some subtle distinctions to be made, Canadian courts have managed to work these out. In *R. v. Kienapple*,[6] the Supreme Court held that there cannot be multiple convictions for a single delict. In practise, this means that "the requirement of sufficient proximity between offenses will only be satisfied if there is no additional and distinguishing element that goes to guilt contained in the offense for which a conviction is sought to be precluded by the *Kienapple* principle."[7] A corollary is that where "the offences are of unequal gravity, *Kienapple* may bar a conviction for a lesser offence, notwithstanding that there are additional elements in the greater offence for which a conviction has been registered, provided that there are no distinct additional elements in the lesser offence."[8] In the early years after these rulings controversies arose but judges worked them out. There is no reason why this approach to when multiple convictions may be barred can also be applied to the sentencing context. Even though some of the results may arguably seem fuzzy, they are soluble by judges. The single transaction rule serves a useful totality purpose and should be preserved. It puts the focus on overall culpability; a robbery is not the same as a robbery with a weapon. It should be maintained and used when applicable.

However, the single transaction tool has led to an unfortunate flip side in Canadian law. It seems to have entrenched the proposition that, for sentences arising from distinct offenses, a judge should start with consecutive sentences subject to the elusive notion of totality. This makes consecutive sentences the default position subject to some assessment of undue harshness. On its face, this may seem logical but it tends to avoid any consideration of what a "just and appropriate" sentence ought to be and ignores the question of overall culpability. Perhaps this is why Canadian courts have made little progress on this question.

Bulk Discount

This is a common but, in my view, a facile and misleading characterization. Because of its pejorative connotation, it has hampered efforts to develop an approach which addresses overall culpability. Certainly, it is true that a person convicted on one occasion of 10 separate offenses will likely receive a lesser total sentence than someone who, over a period of years, was convicted individually of the same offenses. However, the culpability comparison is inapt. While it might appear that there is a discount for multiple offenses, this ignores a basic difference between the two situations. It is like saying that two weightlifters who each lifted 300 kilos are equally strong without noting that one did it in a single lift and the other lifted 30 kilos 10 times. The real question is about strength not total poundage. In sentencing, the comparison requires a similar assertion of equality. That is, the real question is about culpability. This should take into account the fact that one expects the process of arrest, charge, prosecution, conviction, and sentencing to have some remedial effect on the offender. The absence of an earlier process is a factor that legitimately bears on the culpability calculus. This is similar to the recognized first-offender discount; the culpability of the first offender is viewed differently. Offenses committed individually and sentenced over time should be viewed differently from the multiple-offense situation. Indeed, in many systems the cumulative effect of offenses committed over time is considered, to some extent, aggravating.

The point here is a simple one. In most situations, the question of totality cannot be determined by a simple arithmetic sum. This should not be viewed as some form of discount but rather a recognition that overall culpability is a more nuanced calculation.

Proportionality and Overall or Total Culpability

This is both the key to the answer about multiple-offense sentencing and the heart of the problem. As Ashworth has explained, it highlights a different strain of proportionality:

> Implicit in the principle is a rather different sense of proportionality than that commonly used. The point is not whether one type of offence is *ceteris paribus* more heinous than another; it is a question of how a series of offences sometimes all of the same kind and sometimes of different kinds, can be brought into a conceptual scheme which relates principally to single offences.[9]

Yes, an assessment of total or overall culpability would provide a route to a proportionate total sentence but how does one go about this task given the myriad situations that can, and do, occur? There are some markers that assist but they cannot do the whole job. For example, the gravest offense committed can establish an important marker in determining overall culpability but it is only a starting point. A scheme needs the capacity to add to it in an explicable way to reach overall culpability.

Culpability Cap

A useful idea discussed by various scholars is the suggestion that one can look higher up the ordinal proportionality scale and find the gravest offense in the same category to provide a notional limit. Then, one applies some fraction to determine totality. The actual fraction is not as important as the concept which may be viewed as an application of "fair labeling" to sentencing theory. For example, no matter how many assaults are before the court, the court ought not to impose a sentence that gets too close to the culpability and fit sentence for an attempted murder: an assaulter is never an attempted murderer, and ought not to be treated like one. In this paper, I shall refer to this model and its variations as the "culpability cap" and use the term "fractional adjustment" to refer to additional sentences added to reach it.

The culpability cap seems attractive because it is practical and promotes fair labeling fair, but the difficulty lies in the amount of sentencing space between the higher culpability offense and the lower culpability one. For example, in Canada the category of assault offenses not resulting in death would include assault, assault causing bodily harm, aggravated assault and attempted murder. There is sufficient space between an assault and an attempted murder to use the culpability cap but it does not work for multiple offenses of aggravated assault. Here, there is not sufficient sentencing space to provide a fractional relationship. Moreover, if the number of aggravated assaults exceeds two, even the full sentence for attempted murder may not provide a useful cap on total culpability. Then, there are categories of offenses in which, from bottom to top, there is not enough sentencing space, for example sentencing for "administration of justice offences" in Canada. These represent a large number of convictions in Canada and, while there may be aggravated examples, there is no real ordinal hierarchy within the category.

There are two additional difficulties with the utility of a culpability cap. One arises when the package of offenses involves multiple offenses within different categories of offenses. What is the higher culpability offense? Here, perhaps one can look to the gravest offense committed and use the higher culpability offense in that category. Depending on the array offenses, this may often work, but not always. Another solution might be to use the gravest category but this only works where it is clear which category is of graver. This is reminiscent to one of the criticisms of ordinal proportionality itself: how does one compare gravity across categories? How does one compare the gravity of a sexual assault with a massive fraud on vulnerable victims?

A second difficulty is a methodological obstacle which lies in the number of offenses. Even assuming that we can use the gravest offense as a starting point marker and can find a culpability cap for overall culpability, how does a sentencing judge get there? The number of offenses might be sufficiently great that the culpability cap will be quickly reached. One response might be for the judge to use smaller and smaller fractional adjustments. Unfortunately, this has the result of diminishing or perhaps even trivializing the gravity of the additional sentences. Alternatively, the judge can resort to some use of concurrent offenses. These methodological problems are not insurmountable but they suggest the need for some flexibility and some residual judicial discretion.

Low-Order and High-Order Offenses

Canadian courts, as is common in most Western jurisdictions, consistently emphasize that sentencing is an individualized process. Regardless of how fervently a jurisdiction embraces individualization, there will always be some scope for distinctions based on some set of relevant mitigating and aggravating factors, some relating to the offense and some to the offender. The sentencing matrix can be long and broad. How does one look at totality through a lens that incorporates myriad factors? This sounds daunting but we can start with one distinction that provides some help: the need for differential treatment of low order and high-order offenses.

By low order offenses I mean those offenses that individually would warrant a noncustodial sentence or a period of incarceration of six months or less. Granted, there are some scholars and some jurisdictions which argue with some legitimacy for the elimination of short periods of incarceration. However, I am addressing those jurisdictions like Canada which commonly impose many short sentences for low order offenses. As high-order offenses, I mean those which ordinarily warrant a sentence of five years or more imprisonment.

The reason for making a distinction between low and high-order offenses is that there are good pragmatic and conceptual reasons for different methodologies. Because sentencing happens along a spectrum of gravity, and because my goal in this paper is to encourage methodological pragmatism, I need not address middle order offenses. If a system can sort out low and high-order offenses, middle order ones will be accommodated easily between these methodologies.

A Limited Compounding of Sentences

Here, I need to examine the potential role, in limited circumstances, of being able to simply add two or three sentences to reach an acceptable level of overall culpability. As you will see, this flows from the distinction I make between low and high-order offenses. Because the scheme outlined involves some degree of compounding, I need to consider its legitimacy and efficacy.

Low-order offenses with their consequential short custodial sentences or even noncustodial sentences, may readily permit some compounding to find overall culpability when the number of offenses is small. They will likely fall within similar degrees of gravity. For example, assume two unsophisticated daytime break-ins of an empty garage resulting in the theft of a vehicle. Assume each offense would warrant a three month sentence. A compound sentence of six months conforms to the simplest view of proportionality while not terribly offending a notion of totality. This is because the total sentence is sufficiently low that we do not encounter concerns about undue harshness. Compounding can produce total culpability without the need to consider totality for some of these offenses. However, most multiples of high-order offenses will likely produce a totality issue involving distinct questions relating to age, life expectancy and even the length of any gaps between offenses. Accordingly, I argue that any approach to multiple-offense sentencing could benefit from a threshold separation of low-order from high-order offenses.

Separating low-order and high-order offenses is a pragmatic point of departure. Of course, this is not the whole story. One could argue that any simple compounding ignores the normative question and indeed ignores what I have referred to as the central issue, overall culpability. However, I am assuming that any application of overall culpability will be, to some extent, arbitrary. If the approach involves fractional adjustments, they need to be predetermined and there is no magic to the reducing fractions other than the need for internal coherence. The levels will be difficult for the public and victims to understand in terms of responsibility and accountability. For example, a pure decremental scheme as one sees in Sweden involves the addition of diminishing fractional adjustments until the end of the set of offenses is reached. This has the advantage of easy implementation by judges but, aside from pure arbitrariness, it does not recognize situations where some of the additional offenses are of equal gravity. The obvious point is that some multiple of low-order offenses will involve such small numbers that the additional sentences become a meaningless array of days with limited consequences in terms of sentencing outcomes.

Returning to proportionality, there is an intuitive, albeit facile, appeal to simply aggregate sentences for distinct offenses. Indeed, this has become the starting point for Canadian sentencing judges: can an aggregate of consecutive sentences be justified without violating totality? At least for a small set of low-order offenses, compounding avoids this question and seems to promote proportionality. Certainly, it avoids the issue of explaining the reason for a total sentence. Moreover, the total will be sufficiently small that any notion of undue harshness does not arise. Accordingly, in the scheme, there will be some use of compounding.

Developing A Typology of Multiple-Offense Sentencing

I offer two scales for a typology of multiple-offense sentencing, one based on the number of offenses and the other on the type of offense. I am assuming that we maintain the single criminal transaction rule so that concurrent sentences will apply. Moreover, I am assuming that each cell could be subdivided to account for low-order and high-order offenses but this is not necessary to make my point: the multiplicity of multiple-offense sentencing situations defies a unifying principle and requires more pragmatic methodologies.

Here is the typology:

A. Number of Offenses	*B. Types of Offenses*
1. Two Offenses	1. Same Offense
2. More than Two Offenses (3 to 5)	2. Same Category of Offense
3. Many Offenses (more than 5)	3. Different Categories of Offense

Table 13.1 **The Typology of Offenses**

	Same Offenses	*Same category of Offense*	*Different categories of Offenses*
Two Offenses	Group One	Group Two	Group Three
Three to Five Offenses	Group Four	Group Five	Group Six
More than Five Offenses	Group Seven	Group Eight	Group Nine

This produces nine permutations (see Table 13.1) with different characteristics and different sentencing challenges.

Is there a theory of totality that will underpin a methodology that can be applied fairly and consistently to all nine? I will argue that this cannot be achieved. While a theory may appear workable, in practical terms it will not satisfy the methodological requirements. I am not suggesting that a theory needs to explain all instances. But a useful theory must be capable of offering reasons that explain most cases. We need to understand the different requirements and adopt practical methodologies that answer the variety of situations which regularly occur. A general theory of totality would have to be bent, pulled and reshaped for each situation. This will not be satisfactory.

Analyzing the Groups

Same Offenses (Groups 1, 4, and 7)

For these groups, we assume that the offenses before the court are the same. This makes a gravity comparison easier, requiring only a consideration of aggravating and mitigating factors that might relate to a specific offense. Here, the gravest sentence, if any, can be the marker. Moreover, one can look for graver offenses in the same category to see if a culpability cap is available.

At this point, we can go directly to the impact of the number of offenses. If we call the offense "x" and start with group 1, we can call the total of applicable sentences "2x." For low-order offenses calling for short dispositions, we can simply compound the sentences producing a total sentence of "2x." Whether it is possible to compound for high-order offenses depends on two things: (i) is there an applicable culpability cap, and (ii) does the total length of the sentences on the table bring undue harshness into question taking into account the age of the offender? In both situations, a consecutive sentence with some fractional adjustment to the second sentence would be the preferable.

For group 4, we have total offenses from "3x" to "5x." Here, I would argue that some low-order offenses with short dispositions could still be handled by compounding. For example, a series of three or four separate cases of offense "x" each warranting a 30 day sentence would result in a 90 or 120 sentence (3x and 4x). This leaves a residual question for guidance whether these totals are acceptable in terms of overall culpability. That is, does this offend the relevant conception of totality? Is 4x too harsh? Perhaps. However, high-order offenses in this group will always require some totality adjustment. In these cases, the methodology ought to start with looking for a culpability cap. If it can be found higher up the gravity scale, then this can answer totality. Otherwise, it will be necessary to start with the longest sentence and then add the fractional adjustments.

Group 7 will start at "7x." It is unlikely that any compounding will be available. Therefore, an assessment of total culpability will be required. This takes us back to the same questions addressed earlier: look for a culpability cap, or start with the longest sentence and then add the predetermined fractional adjustments.

Same Category of Offense (Groups 2, 5, and 8)

Here, there is no issue of comparing gravity; the internal scale of the category answers that. The first question is whether a culpability cap is available which depends on the sentencing space between the offenses and the availability of a higher mark within the category. If there is a potential culpability cap, this provides the overall culpability measure and the methodological issue becomes how to measure and apply the fractional adjustments. For low-order offenses in group 2, compounding to some extent may be legitimate but is less likely, possible for part of group 5, but certainly not for group 8. When there is no easily identifiable culpability cap, likely the case with higher order offenses, one needs to find a substitute to determine overall culpability. To be consistent with the discussion above, the answer should be to start with the longest sentence and then add the predetermined fractional adjustments.

Different Categories of Offenses (Groups 3, 6, and 9)

These always present a need for guidance to (1) assess gravity between categories; and (2) determine overall culpability. The first question is the same issue that has been discussed in some of the critiques of the von Hirsch–Ashworth conception of ordinal proportionality. Those sentencing scholars argue that it is not an insurmountable problem. However, it is exacerbated in the situation of multiple-offense sentencing. While a sentencing judge can start by trying to identify the most serious conviction (or convictions) this will only go a small way depending on the number of convictions and the different nature of the offenses. Accordingly, finding total culpability and determining totality will rarely be an easy task. These offenses will require a methodology determined through guidance to answer these questions. The sentencing system will need to decide and stipulate assessments of relative gravity. There will always need to be adjustments to avoid offending totality. For the sentencing judge, these adjustments need to be predetermined; otherwise, we are back to the beginning: how should totality be assessed?

The Implications of the Typology

In the chart in Table 13.2, I have tried to summarize the different considerations and implications across the nine groups. I am not suggesting that there need be nine different methodologies to address these nine groups. I am merely arguing that pragmatism will require methodologies that can deal with these differences. Building on this discussion, the analysis of the typology follows these premises:

1. All offenses should be individually determined before looking to totality.
2. Offenses encompassed within a single transaction ought to be sentenced concurrently.
3. A small set of offenses, especially low-order offenses, can be treated by compounding sentences.
4. If a culpability cap is available, totality is reached by imposing fractional adjustments to additional sentences. Where the cap is quickly reached, concurrent sentences need to be imposed.
5. Where there is no available culpability cap, some assessment of overall culpability must be determined judicially with guidance.

Table 13.2 **Assessing the Typology**

	Same Offenses	*Same category of Offense; Different Gravity*	*Different categories of Offenses*
Two Offenses	Group One: – For low-order offenses, can compound to find overall culpability – For long sentences, may need to adjust for totality	Group Two: – Use gravest as starting point and culpability marker – Look for culpability cap – Need some consecutive sentences with fractional adjustments to reach totality	Group Three: – Need to assess gravity across categories to assess culpability – Need to adjust for totality – Need some consecutive with fractional adjustments to reach totality
Three to Five Offenses	Group Four: – Possible to compound culpability but only for some low-order offenses – For high-order offenses, need to adjust for totality in all cases – Look for culpability cap – Need some consecutive sentences with fractional adjustments to reach totality	Group Five: – Can use gravest as culpability marker – Will need to adjust for totality – Look for culpability cap – Some concurrent sentencing potential but otherwise will need some consecutive sentences with fractional adjustments to reach totality	Group Six: – Need to assess gravity across categories to find gravest offense and any culpability cap – Will need to adjust for totality – Consecutive sentencing with fractional adjustments
More than Five Offenses	Group Seven: – Compounding possible only to limited extent and may not be available – Need to adjust for totality by looking for culpability cap – Some potential to group some offenses and use concurrent sentences	Group Eight: – Can use gravest as culpability marker – Will need to adjust for totality – Look for culpability cap – Need some consecutive sentences with fractional adjustments to reach totality	Group Nine: – Need to assess gravity across categories to find culpability – Will need to adjust for totality – Look for culpability cap – Need some consecutive sentences with fractional adjustments to reach totality

Conclusion

I would suggest that the typology shows that there must be at least three methodologies for multiple-offense sentencing that distinguish between (1) same offenses; (2) same category of offense but different gravity; and (3) different category of offenses. Inherent in my assessment of the typology are three potentially controversial assumptions:

- the general distinction between low-order and high-order offenses;
- the utility of compounding sentences when possible; and
- the availability of a culpability cap.

But these controversies are simply matters that need to be considered when constructing pragmatic methodologies. A sentencing system will need to decide whether these assumptions are acceptable, but these decisions will not undermine the basic observation that different methodologies are required. Fearful of being repetitive, I need to emphasize that developing these methodologies is a pragmatic problem because judges require yardsticks that will promote consistency, not disparity. The solution requires decisions that will need to be nuanced. Ultimately, they may appear to be arbitrary but that is intrinsic to the problem of totality. Given the multidimensional nature of the problem and the number of elements that need to be predetermined to produce useful methodologies, hard decisions will need to be made. The relevant considerations need to be on the table and then viewed through the lens of overall culpability. Once decisions are made about acceptable assumptions, the path to resolving the problem may be statutory or through official guidance. This will depend on the nature of the sentencing system in question and which source of authority can provide the degree of reflection needed to produce useful, authoritative and comprehensive answers to multiple-offense sentencing problems. What should be clear is that the search for an overarching theoretical justification is less important than getting on with the job.

This brings us back full circle to the question of proportionality.[10] While the analysis suggests the need for different methodologies, the ultimate goal is still proportionality. My point is not that multiple-offense sentencing involves a different conception of proportionality but rather that one needs to identify proportionality through the lens of overall or total culpability. For a single offense, proportionality is rooted in an assessment of offense seriousness. This assessment is derived from the facts of the offense as interpreted by the relevant gravity scale which, of course, is based primarily on culpability. Then, this is adjusted, to whatever extent the system allows, for individualized circumstances. For multiple offenses, the goal is the same but different types of calculus are required to reach it because of the number of offenses and the various ways in which they can combine.

As an example, we can move from sentencing and proportionality to the more mundane context of the supermarket where the goal is to determine the grocery bill. One shopping cart filled with bananas may cost $50 while another cart filled with apples costs $100 and a third one filled with pears and peaches may cost $200. The cost of the first and the second is the simple calculation of weight times cost per kilogram of bananas and apples respectively. The cost of the third cart involves multiple elements and even different arithmetic, especially if there is a discount because a few of the peaches are bruised. All shoppers still get a bill which shows the cost and an explanation of how it has been calculated. By the same token, all offenders ought to receive a proportionate sentence and ought to know how it was calculated. For multiple-offense sentencing, this requires different methodologies with predetermined elements that require assumptions and approximations. But all methodologies will have the same objective: to find the sentence which reflects, in the individual circumstances, overall proportionality. This is how a system can produce a just sentence in accordance with both the rule of law and proportionality.

Notes

1. The notion of total or overall culpability is discussed in a number of chapters in this book. It is rejected in the chapter by Jesper Ryberg.
2. [1996] 1 S.C.R. 500, at para. 42.
3. Ibid.
4. *R. v. Guerrero Silva* 2015 QCCA 1334, (Que.CA), from English version of headnote.
5. *R. v. Mooswa* 2015 SKCA 3
6. [1975] 1 S.C.R. 729
7. See *R. v. Prince* [1986] 2 S.C.R. 480, at para. 32
8. Ibid., at para. 33
9. Supra, note vi, at 278.
10. I want to thank my colleague Professor D. Sorvatzioti of the University of Nicosia for pointing out the importance of returning to proportionality before concluding this chapter.

References

Ashworth, A. 2015. *Sentencing and Criminal Justice*. 6th ed. Cambridge: Cambridge University Press.

Bottoms, A. (1998). "Five Puzzles in Von Hirsch's Theory of Punishment." In A. Ashworth and M. Wasik (eds.), *Fundamentals of Sentencing Theory: Essays in Honour of Andrew von Hirsch*, pp. 53–100, Oxford: Clarendon Press.

Frase, R. S. 2013. *Just Sentencing: Principles and Procedures for a Workable System*. New York: Oxford University Press.

Jareborg, N. 1998. "Why Bulk Discount in Multiple Offence Sentencing?" In A. Ashworth and M. Wasik, *Fundamentals of Sentencing Theory: Essays in Honour of Andrew von Hirsch*, pp. 129–140. Oxford: Clarendon Press.

Manson, A. 2013. "Some Thoughts on Multiple Sentences and the Totality Principle: Can We Get It Right?" *Canadian Journal of Criminology and Criminal Justice*. 55(4): 481–495.

Reitz, K. 2010. "The Illusion of Proportionality: Desert and Repeat Offenders." In J. V. Roberts and A. von Hirsch (eds.), *Previous Convictions at Sentencing: Theoretical and Applied Perspectives*, pp. 137–159. Oxford: Hart Publishing.

Wasik, M. 2012. "Concurrent and Consecutive Sentences Revisited." In L. Zedner and J. V. Roberts (eds.) *Principles and Values in Criminal Law and Criminal Justice: Essays in Honour of Andrew Ashworth*, pp. 285–297. Oxford: Oxford University Press.

14

Solving the Multiple-Offense Paradox

MICHAEL TONRY

The multiple-conviction paradox is that punishments of people convicted of multiple offenses are often discounted if sentences are imposed at one time but enhanced if imposed at different times. A bulk discount characterizes sentencing for concurrent convictions. A "recidivist premium" attaches to successive convictions (Reitz, 2010).

This distinction on its face is perverse. Ten specific instances of wrongdoing imply the same objective blameworthiness and victim harm whether tried and sentenced simultaneously or successively. The mens rea, actus reus, and offense circumstances are identical. A prosecutor presented with credible evidence of 10 drug sales, burglaries, or assaults committed over six weeks could file all simultaneously, thereby triggering the offender-friendly discount, or file them separately, thereby precipitating the premium. Ethical prosecutors presumably try to avoid arbitrariness when such choices arise. However, those gross potential differences testify to the power of inconsistent intuitions that punitive punches should be pulled when people are sentenced for multiple offenses but swung harder when people have previous convictions.

Most writing on punishment mistakenly treats the subject in theoretical isolation, ignoring the reality, as Isaiah Berlin showed, that difficult problems almost always implicate competing normative principles. The way forward becomes clearer when we recognize that punishment implicates not only blameworthiness and crime prevention but also fairness, equality, and human dignity.[1]

A just punishment system would in Dworkin's (1978) terms treat offenders as equals, with concern and respect, allowing each to be assessed according to appropriate criteria in his or her individual circumstances and situation.[2] It would in Rawls's (1958) terms be fair, using procedures and standards that are transparent, consistent, and even-handed. It would in Whitman's (2004; 2016) and Snacken's (2015) terms be respectful of human dignity, taking account of the likely effects of punishments on offenders and their prospects for later living satisfying lives. Usually in this article I collapse equality and fairness into the construct of "individualized moral responsibility."

David Luban has observed that "subjectivity" lies at the heart of human dignity and that "having human dignity means having a story of one's own." Subjectivity is essential, he writes: "Human beings have ontological heft because each of us is an "I", and I have ontological heft. For others to treat me as though I have none fundamentally denigrates my status in the world. It amounts to a form of humiliation that violates my human dignity" (2007, pp. 70–72).

William James in *The Varieties of Religious Experience* (1902) offers a similar, more general observation:

> Any object that is infinitely important to us and awakens our devotion feels to us also as if it must be *sui generis* and unique. Probably a crab would be filled with a sense of outrage if it could hear us classify it without ado or apology as a crustacean, and thus dispose of it. "I am no such thing," it would say; "I am MYSELF, MYSELF alone." (1902, p. 3)

Plutarch quotes Bion of Borysthenes (325–250 B.C.), who observed of boys playing by a stream on a summer day, "Though boys throw stones at frogs in sport, yet the frogs do not die in sport but in earnest" (Plutarch, 1957, p. 355). The frog's perspective, Luban's "I's" perspective, cannot justly be ignored. A just sentencing system must harness the tension between the requirement of fairness that there be general standards that apply to all and the requirement of justice that all ethically important grounds for distinguishing between individuals be taken into account when decisions about their lives are made.

By those criteria, most influential sets of punishment theories provide inadequate guidance. Positive retributivist theories prescribe proportionate punishments scaled to offense seriousness, leaving no room for other considerations (e.g., von Hirsch, 1976; Moore, 1993). Classic consequentialist approaches would sometimes ignore blameworthiness, however calculated. Enrico Ferri's (1921) positivist and Sheldon Glueck's (1928) consequentialist approaches called for lifetime confinement of minor offenders believed to be especially dangerous.

Some hybrid theories provide more encompassing frameworks but largely ignore multiple current and prior convictions. Negative retributivist theories, such as those of Norval Morris (1974) and H. L. A. Hart (1968), acknowledge upper limits linked to blameworthiness, but otherwise allow other considerations to be taken into account. John Braithwaite's restorative justice theory likewise respects retributive upper limits but allows unfettered individualization (2002; Braithwaite and Pettit, 2001).

Building upon hybrid theories, at the end of this essay I propose a framework for addressing the multiple-offense paradox within just sentencing systems. It includes tight statutory limits on sentence severity generally, retributive upper limits in particular cases keyed to the most serious current offense, prohibition or radical limitation of the recidivist premium, and strong presumptions in favor of parsimonious and human-capital-enhancing punishments.

The first section of this essay uses empirical data to show that the multiple-conviction paradox is the central issue that normative accounts of punishment must adequately address. The paradigm case is not the first-time offender convicted of a single offense but the repeat offender convicted of multiple offenses. The second discusses efforts by theorists—in my view unpersuasive—to justify the bulk discount and somewhat more successful efforts, particularly by judges and lawyers, to explain it. I've elsewhere discussed efforts to justify the recidivist premium so only touch on them here (Tonry, 2010). The third section sets out a framework for just sentencing systems, incorporating principled considerations in addition to blameworthiness and crime prevention.

Multiple Convictions, Past and Present

Contemporary theoretical writing about punishment treats the first offender convicted of a single offense as the paradigm case. This is odd. Such offenders constitute less than half of people convicted of crimes, probably many less.[3] Tables 14.1 and 14.2 illustrate this. They present 2009 US data, the most recent available, on multiple current charges and prior convictions of felony defendants in state courts in the 75 most populous counties. Fifty-five percent of all felony defendants' cases involved multiple charges, including 61 to 68% of violent crimes and 53% of property crimes.

Table 14.2 presents data on prior convictions and arrests. Overall, 60% of felony defendants had at least one prior conviction; 43% had prior felony convictions. Thirty percent had two or more. For specific offenses, 48% of murder defendants had prior convictions as did 53% of violent crime defendants, 56% of property crime defendants, and 66% of drug defendants.

Those data do not indicate how many defendants charged with multiple current offenses had prior convictions. The last column in Table 14.2 comes closest. Seventy-five percent of all felony defendants had previously been arrested, ranging from two-thirds for murder and rape to nearly 80% for motor vehicle theft, burglary, and drugs. The first-time defendant with a clean record is neither the modal nor the typical case.

The salience of the multiple-offense paradox varies widely between countries. In the United States, prior convictions can increase sentences under state

Table 14.1 **Multiple Charges, by Most Serious Felony, 75 Largest US Counties, 2009**

Most Serious Charge	*No Other Charge*	*Other Charges*
All felonies	**45%**	**55%**
Violence	**37%**	**63%**
Murder	39%	61%
Rape	32%	68%
Robbery	39%	61%
Property	**47%**	**53%**
MV Theft	48%	52%
Burglary	33%	67%
Drugs	**46%**	**54%**

Source: Reaves 2013, Table 2.

Table 14.2 **Prior Convictions and Arrests, by Most Serious Felony, 75 Largest US Counties, 2009**

Most Serious Charge	*No Prior Convictions*	*Misdemeanor Convictions Only*	*One Felony Only*	*Two to Four Felonies*	*Four-plus Felonies*	*Prior Arrests*
All felonies	**40%**	**17%**	**13%**	**19%**	**11%**	**75%**
Violence	**47%**	**16%**	**13%**	**16%**	**8%**	**69%**
Murder	52%	9%	13%	14%	13%	66%
Rape	49%	15%	14%	12%	10%	66%
Robbery	48%	13%	13%	17%	9%	70%
Property	**44%**	**16%**	**11%**	**16%**	**13%**	**72%**
MV Theft	38%	14%	11%	20%	17%	78%
Burglary	39%	17%	13%	18%	13%	77%
Drugs	**34%**	**16%**	**13%**	**22%**	**15%**	**80%**

Source: Reaves 2013, Tables 7 and 10.

guideline systems from 1.7 times in the District of Columbia up to 14.4 times in Kansas (Frase et al., 2015, Table 2.2). Some states impose a recidivist premium even on people without prior convictions when they are convicted of multiple current offenses, counting the most serious as the first offense and treating the others as if they were recidivist events (Frase, this volume). States without guidelines presumably are comparably diverse: no national data are available. Career criminal and three-strikes laws based on the number but not necessarily the seriousness of convictions result in decades-long sentences up to life without possibility of parole.

In other English-speaking countries, where a totality principle typically governs cases involving multiple current offenses, the stakes are lower; the recidivist premium however often attaches to successive offenses. In Scandinavian and other continental European countries where prison sentences are comparatively rare, terms are usually short, one-third remission is automatic or nearly so, criminal history is given comparatively little weight, and maximum sentences for individual and multiple offenses top out at 12 to 20 years (most are much shorter), the scope for the recidivist premium is necessarily much smaller. Common-law countries, by contrast, typically have much longer maximums—the United States as in most such things is the outlier—so the potential scope of a recidivist premium is much greater. Partly for that reason, in the rest of this essay I mostly refer to common-law countries.

Those differences are not the result of fundamental differences in crime patterns or rates. The international literature on criminal careers suggests that the prevalence of offending, the likelihood of reoffending, age-crime curves, patterns of desistance, and career lengths are similar in all developed countries (Jolliffe, Farrington, and Piquero, 2015; Rocque, 2015). The consequences of the multiple-offense paradox are most extreme and ornate in the United States, but the empirical data on the prevalence of multiple convictions is broadly similar everywhere.

Multiple Offenses in Theory

Most writers on punishment theory bow to the widely shared intuitions that prior convictions somehow aggravate a crime's seriousness or an offender's blameworthiness, and to the evidence, at least in English-speaking countries, that almost everyone believes prior convictions justify additional punishment for new crimes (Roberts, 2008; 2011). Those intuitions shape every Western country's sentencing practices though to greater and lesser extents. Prior convictions are hugely important in the United States as Table 14.2, the plethora of career criminal and three strikes laws, and every competent statistical analysis of sentencing patterns attest. In Scandinavian countries governed by statutory sentencing principles, the role of prior convictions is limited and specified, but exists (Asp, 2010; Hinkkanen and Lappi-Seppälä, 2011). English law authorizes increases for prior offenses that are recent and relevant (Roberts and

Pina-Sanchez, 2014). Other English-speaking countries allow increases subject to loose, subjective case law limits (Manson et al., 2008; Freiberg, 2014).

Theoretical explanations vary. Consequentialists have little difficulty explaining the recidivist premium. Although philosophers tend too quickly to discount deterrent and incapacitative effects of punishment (e.g., Lippke, this volume; Ryberg, this volume), there are some, and no one challenges the robust finding that past offending is the best predictor of future offending.[4] Proponents of retributive theories have a harder time though unpersuasive efforts have been made based on ordinary-life intuitions and imputations (Bennett, 2010) and special duties of convicted persons to desist from crime (Lee, 2010).

Multiple current convictions trigger a different and inconsistent widely shared intuition supporting the bulk discount. There is no question it exists as data from Germany, Australia, Finland, and Sweden demonstrate (Albrecht, 1994; Lovegrove, 1997; Hinkkanen and Lappi-Seppälä, 2011; Vibla, 2015; this volume). Australian and Canadian appellate case law (Bottoms, this volume), English case law and guidelines (Ashworth and Wasik, this volume), and American sentencing guidelines (Frase, this volume) offer similar demonstration.

Australian, Canadian, and English courts apply a "totality" doctrine that sentencing for multiple offenses should be limited to, typically, the most severe punishment that could have been imposed for the most serious offense or in any case should not exceed the normal sentence for a qualitatively more serious kind of crime (Thomas, 1979; Manson, this volume; Ashworth, 2015; Ashworth and Wasik, this volume). These doctrines depend not on application of detailed rules and policies but ultimately, as appellate case law shows, on idiosyncratic decisions by trial and appellate judges (Bottoms, this volume). In the United States, the original *Model Penal Code* did not mention a totality principle but effectively observed one. It delegated to judges the decision whether to impose consecutive or concurrent sentences for multiple offenses but hugely reduced the practical significance of consecutive sentences (American Law Institute, 1962).[5] Various rationales have been offered for the bulk discount. Somewhat artificially I separately discuss policy arguments offered usually by lawyers and philosophical arguments.

Policy Arguments

There are four main arguments.[6] Judges should act empathetically toward some people whose multiple offenses were influenced by circumstantial emotions. No matter how many crimes were committed, justice requires limits on aggregate punishments. Judges should be merciful. Conviction and sentencing are blaming exercises and, no matter what the number of offenses, punishments should not imply equal or greater blame than do sentences imposed for palpably more serious offenses.

Morbid Psychology

Multiple offenses may be manifestations of a troubled, ongoing state of mind and in such cases, some argue, should be merged and thereby benefit from the discount (Ashworth, 2015; Roberts and de Keijser, this volume). Examples include offenses arising from a single incident, such as a burglary in which property was taken, an assault occurred, and an auto was stolen in escaping, or a series of offenses—six burglaries in a week or two—that may all be the product of a troubled mental state. The rationale is presumably a psychological one which, for lack of a better term, I call "morbid psychology." People involved in a crime gone wrong panic and do things they otherwise would not. People under circumstantial stress—a lost job, a loved one's death, a financial meltdown, an existential crisis, a mental health problem—may commit a series of offenses that then seem to them to make sense but normally would not. "There but for the grace of God go I," one might say. Everyone has experienced stressful or emotionally charged times when things were said or done that were later regretted.

Several difficulties arise. One is to reconcile the morbid psychology argument with the argument for reduced sentences for first, and possibly second and third, offenses on the rationale that the behavior may have been out of character. The absence of prior offenses is the evidence that the conduct may be less blameworthy than a typical offender's. The morbid psychology argument treats the presence of multiple offenses as equivalent evidence of reduced blameworthiness. Explanations are required for that seeming contradiction.

Another challenge is to reconcile the morbid psychology argument with criminal law doctrine which generally makes background mental considerations irrelevant. Mens rea analyses disregard motive (the mercy killing), stressful circumstances (Jean Valjean), environmental conditions (social disadvantage), and heightened emotion (domestic or political violence), asking only whether the proscribed act and the required intention, recklessness, or negligence have been shown. If so, end of story. Likewise, criminal law doctrine disregards mental states except concerning insanity, incompetence to stand trial, and diminished capacity. The morbid psychology argument by contrast calls for mitigation of sentences for mentally competent offenders for whom the required mens rea is shown, posing the question why motives, most mental conditions, and other extenuating circumstances are irrelevant in the criminal law but dispositive at sentencing. One response might be that sentencing is inherently discretionary and judges may properly be more compassionate at that stage. That is plausible, but it must then be shown why that latitude is appropriate only in some kinds of multiple-offense cases but not in others or for that matter in all cases.

Perverse incentives pose another difficulty. A traditional maxim insists that the criminal law should speak its loudest when temptation is greatest. Bentham's

(1970) classic utilitarian prescription calls for use of incremental punishments that provide marginal disincentives. Attempts should be punished less severely than completed offenses to provide incentives to desist. Punishments should be scaled to offense seriousness to provide incentives to commit less serious crimes. That logic applied to the burglary gone wrong or the short-term crime spree calls for increased penalties for successive crimes. The morbid psychology argument calls for decreased penalties.

Even if those issues can be satisfactorily addressed, the morbid psychology argument arises only in some multiple-offense situations. It neglects the commonplace generalist charged with multiple offenses who commits diverse offenses over an extended period.

Crushing Sentences

Nils Jareborg (1998) argued that human lives are short and no punishment should deprive individuals of a large fraction of what remains. Such sentences are often referred to as "crushing." *R v M* (CA), (1996) 1 SCR 530, a leading Canadian case, establishes that a multiple-offense sentence is "unduly harsh" when "the effect of the 'aggregate sentence is . . . to impose on the offender a crushing sentence not in keeping with his record and prospects.'" The term recurs in the sentencing jurisprudence of English-speaking Commonwealth countries (e.g., Bottoms, this volume).

An equivalent principle is implicit in statutory limits in some European countries on maximum aggregate sentences for individual and multiple offenses. The Norwegian mass murderer Anders Breivik, for example, received the maximum term of 21 years because nothing longer was possible. Most European countries prevent crushing sentences through a combination of absolute limits (often 12 to 21 years) on any nonlife sentence, short maximums, and near automatic one-third remission.[7] The *Model Penal Code* achieved that by authorizing judges to impose consecutive sentences, but subject to the maximums and minimums for the most serious offense.[8]

I found no literature that offers criteria for knowing when a sentence should be considered crushing. Retributive ordinal proportionality offers guidance for sentencing single offenses, but provides no obvious answers for multiples. Consequentialists could justify a general crushing offense doctrine. Lengthy sentences cannot be justified on the basis of evidence about deterrent or incapacitative effects, except possibly for a tiny number of chronic dangerous offenders. There is compelling evidence that longer sentences have no greater deterrent benefit than shorter ones and that incapacitative effects are small to nonexistent. Natural desistance from crime, even among chronic offenders, occurs early in most lives, making long sentences ineffective in preventive terms. "Residual career lengths" are short; few criminal careers extend beyond the early thirties and most end much sooner (Travis, Western, and Redburn, 2014, ch. 5). Traditional ideas about parsimony and use of the least restrictive alternative posit that no punishment is justifiable that exceeds its expected benefits (Tonry, 1994). However, most modern punishment theory involves retributivist premises, so consequentialist analyses do not signify.

Canadian and Australian cases refer to crushing sentences but offer no useful law-like generalizations. Bottoms (this volume) discusses an Australian case, *Azzopardi v. R.* [2011] VSCA 372, in which sentences are shortened radically, but in a country in which sentencing jurisprudence celebrates the judge's "intuitive synthesis," no useful generalizations are likely to emerge (Freiberg, 2016). Likewise, in Canada, where the ultimate test is that sentences be "just and appropriate" and in England, where guidelines set starting points and ranges for subcategories of offenses such as robbery, theft, and sexual assault, but treat only sentences outside much broader "offense ranges" as "departures" requiring special justification (Roberts and Ashworth, 2016; Manson, this volume). Case law standards in all these countries resemble Justice Potter Stewart's pornography test in *Jacobellis v. Ohio*, 378 US 184 (1964): "I know it when I see it."

Interoffense Comparisons

One indicator that an aggregate sentence is unduly harsh, *R v M* (CA), (1996) 1 SCR 530 notes, is that it "is substantially above the normal level of a sentence for the most serious of the individual offences involved." Ashworth and Wasik (this volume, p. 214) observe that "intuitively interoffence proportionality is the dominant consideration," and accordingly that "several lesser offences should not combine to produce a sentence above that which is appropriate for a significantly more serious offence."

The unanswered question is why interoffense comparisons should trump an approach in which deserved sentences for each offense are simply totaled? The approach is compatible with the crushing offense intuition, and more generalizable, but still needs justification. There is some evidence from opinion research that public opinion generally supports it, but intuition by itself cannot provide a principled justification (Robinson and Darley, 1995, p. 193; Roberts, 2008, pp. 180–182).

One unnerving answer implies a characterological theory of punishment.[9] The proposition, for example, that no number of burglaries, common or auto thefts, or retail drug sales should be punished as severely as a robbery implies essentialist notions about crimes and criminals. The comparison is implicitly between "burglars" and "robbers"; the latter can justifiably be punished more severely. This, however, categorizes people who are also fathers, husbands, conservatives, Catholics, steelworkers, and tennis players on the basis of one small part of a life. Reification is difficult to reconcile with justice. Once sentencing shifts focus from culpable conduct to characterological assessment, the slope becomes slippery. At its bottom are convictions and punishments for antisocial character or noncriminal behavior.

Mercy

The fourth rationale is that a sense of mercy explains why judges mitigate sentences in multiple-offense cases (Bottoms, 1998). Appellate judges sometimes say that is what they are doing (Bottoms, this volume). Nigel Walker (1999), however, long ago showed that in this context mercy is a protean and elusive concept, possibly even a nonsequitur. If an element of a case, for example, Jean Valjean's motive to steal food to feed a starving family, calls for a mitigated sentence, imposing one is an act of justice, not mercy. For cases in which justice and mercy are not inextricably entangled, there is a fundamental question whether state functionaries have moral standing to grant mercy even if a victim or God might (Murphy and Hampton, 1988). Judges have authority to enforce and apply the law; the source of their authority to be merciful is not obvious. Assuming such authority exists, its exercise is inherently subjective and idiosyncratic unless guided by standards. It is hard to see anything law-like or generalizable in a practice of acknowledging that judges possess ad hoc powers of mercy. That would be a form of "judicial lawlessness" of the sort Judge Marvin Frankel (1973) long ago decried.

Some of these difficulties could easily be sidestepped by substituting "compassion" or "empathy" for mercy. I have never understood why judges and lawyers feel more comfortable claiming to be merciful than claiming to be compassionate.

Openly empowering judges to be compassionate would not be much different from creating a presumption that judges be parsimonious. The *Model Penal Code* did this by creating presumptions against imprisonment in every case and for parole release when prisoners first became eligible. The principal likely objection to a parsimony presumption is the nonsequitur that it would somehow be disrespectful to victims. It has become conventional and politically correct to say that vindication of victims and acknowledgment of their suffering are goals of sentencing, but that cannot be right. Only the state and the defendant are parties in a criminal case.

The criminal law in any case often cannot vindicate victims even should functionaries wish to do so. Conviction and therefore sentencing are often not possible for uncontroversial reasons, for example, when the perpetrator is below the age of criminal responsibility, or incompetent to stand trial, or determined not to have been mentally responsible. Harm to victims may result from offenders' morally innocent violent acts committed, for example, under a mistaken but reasonable belief of the need for self-defense. Defendants are acquitted for many reasons, including insufficient or inadmissible evidence, or simply that a judge or jury is not convinced of guilt beyond reasonable doubt. It would be exceedingly odd in any of those circumstances to say that the victim was treated unfairly or disrespectfully. It is similarly odd to say that the victim is treated unfairly or disrespectfully when a compassionate sentence is imposed.

Each of the lawyers' arguments for the bulk discount is ethically attractive. All try to explain a practice that feels intuitively right. The crushing sentence argument comes closest to escaping the traditional retributive framework, but its proponents need in a generalizable way to explain why a sentence is crushing, and when.

Philosophers' Efforts

Judges and lawyers have been obliged to address multiple-offense sentencing because such cases arise and courts must explain their decisions. Philosophers have not had to consider the problem, and only recently have begun to do so.

The default position for retributivists is that the bulk discount is not justifiable. So Ryberg (this volume) qualifiedly concludes, attributing the underlying supporting intuition in part to scope-insensitivity, a psychological characteristic that makes human beings more sympathetic to concrete problems than to abstract ones, and to small numbers of troubling phenomena than to large ones. A drowned refugee child pulled from the water attracts massive media attention and sympathy; thousands of refugee child less so.

So far little has been written by philosophers about the bulk discount. Two attempts deserve "A"s for effort but something less for persuasiveness. To make their cases, each abandons the mainstream retributive view that punishment is a blaming institution that should censure people in reasonable proportion to the seriousness of their crimes or the extent of their moral culpability.

Making Amends

Bennett (this volume) argues that sentencing is inevitably and rightly discretionary. What counts is "making amends," a phenomenon not closely coupled to the seriousness or number of offenses. Bennett bases his argument on a vignette about one of two business partners who repeatedly embezzles funds from the business. Bennett considers what the victim would regard as adequate amends and concludes that the measure would seldom be the total amount of money involved, restitution in like kind, but something considerably less that expresses suitable remorse. Defendants being punished for multiple offenses, he argues by analogy, may receive discounted sentences if they can reasonably be regarded as making amends.

There are substantial problems. First, people in close private relationships provide an inapt analogy for exercise of state power against—for this purpose—anonymous citizens. Second, making amends inexorably raises the question of who decides. In the vignette, the victim is authoritative, but that cannot be right for the criminal courts. Otherwise sentencing decisions would depend on the luck of the draw in victim identity. If the judge decides, the problems of subjectivity, idiosyncrasy, and inconsistency posed by crushing sentences and mercy arise, but more acutely. Third, making amends effectively abandons concern for proportionality and rule-of-law values including consistency, predictability, and transparency.

Character

Lee (this volume) argues that multiple-offense sentencing should be based primarily on what the offenses reveal about the defendant's character. Thus, a person convicted of five burglaries, thefts, or street-level drug sales should be seen as a burglar, thief, or drug dealer, and an appropriate sentence determined by comparison with sentences received by rapists, robbers, or others convicted of more serious crimes. This resembles the interoffense comparison approach but with a big difference. That approach begins with the offenses and then asks whether any number of them can be regarded as being as serious and deserving of punishment as a more serious crime. It is not whether robbers are worse people than thieves, but whether robberies are more serious crimes than thefts.

Lee essentializes offenders and asks, what do thieves or rapists deserve? There is no way, he writes, "for the criminal justice system to avoid commenting on the actor's bad character traits," and accordingly that the "criminal law punishes persons *for their actions only when* . . . the actions display their character defects." By labeling a person a "rapist," the state is "commenting on a set of traits that the person has that has generated the wrongful act of rape" (this volume, pp. 122–123) This tidily addresses lots of multiple-offense scenarios. Six thefts are no problem because the core message is "He is a thief." A rape and a burglary are no problem since rapists' character traits are even less attractive than burglars'. Nothing worse is shown by the burglary. Punishment for the rape is enough.

There are fundamental problems and practical ones. The first is that criminal law jurisprudence in every democratic country focuses on offenses. Values of consistency, equality, human dignity, and procedural fairness require this. The defendant's identity should not matter. Otherwise the criminal law risks becoming an instrument for the exercise of political, class, racial, economic, or religious power.

It is sometimes said that judges are powerfully influenced by their assessments of defendants' character, and that it is hypocritical and perverse from a crime prevention perspective to pretend otherwise (e.g., Moore et al., 1986). Yes, but. Human beings inevitably sometimes fail to do what they are supposed to do, and some judges no doubt take characterological assessments into account. It is a giant step, however, from the observation that judges sometimes disregard applicable legal and moral norms to the normative claim that it is right that they do so. That needs justification.

The second problem is the elusiveness and artificiality of the concept character "trait" or "defect." In a drunken assault, is the defect lack of self-control, inability to control alcohol intake, poor anger management, or willingness to strike another person? For a trait to be a relevant determining consideration, presumably it has to be a static characteristic like low intelligence, gender, aggressiveness, or callousness. Large fractions, probably large majorities, of sexual and physical assaults, however, are committed while under the influence of alcohol or drugs. Causal explanations have to take account of interactions between static characteristics and substance effects. The dispositive character trait is then presumably something like willingness to use drugs or alcohol under circumstances in which there is a nontrivial chance of an assault occurring. It is not obvious how that can sensibly be related to interoffense comparisons. In any case, much crime is situational, and occurs as much because of background conditions as of static or other traits of individuals. The only conception of character trait that appears workable, and the one Lee seems to have in mind, is a generic characterization of people convicted of robbery as "robbers." This, however, quickly collapses into a simple interoffense comparison. If that is true, the argument provides no distinctive justification for the bulk discount.

A third problem is that drawing inferences of character from multiple offenses of conviction is as a practical matter incomplete unless the logic, like Bennett's making amends theory, abandons any connection to retributive proportionality. Social science research demonstrates impressive congruence among citizens of Western countries in their assessments of the relative seriousness of different kinds of crimes (e.g., Robinson and Darley, 1995). So do the efforts of developers of sentencing guidelines systems.

Beyond that, though, empirical research provides little guidance. For Lee's model, a number of questions need answers. For one, once a person who commits multiple offenses becomes "a burglar" or "a rapist," is the number of offenses germane? On Lee's account, it might be unwarranted to impose harsher sentences for a second or fifth rape; the extras presumably provide no additional information about the offender's "character make-up." For another, should the interoffense comparison for, say, a multiple burglar be made with the normal sentence for a single rape or for multiple rapes? Unless a single rape provides a license for committing others without additional penalty, the number of rapes must matter. If that is true, there is no single benchmark with which multiple burglaries can be prepared.

There is also a fourth, fundamental problem. Four decades of longitudinal, developmental, and criminal careers research show that most offenders are generalists, not specialists (Piquero, Farrington, and Blumstein, 2003; 2007). The essentialization of burglars, robbers, rapists, and drug dealers is an empirical mistake. One can say that a particular defendant was convicted of five burglaries, but seldom accurately that "burglar" is his essential character, even as an offender.

The easy next step to Lee's argument about characterological assessments is to argue that character should be the critical consideration at sentencing and all relevant evidence including unproven allegations, arrests, prosecutions, and convictions are germane (e.g., Moore et al., 1986). Thence came the US Sentencing Commission's relevant conduct rule which required federal judges to take account of all criminality which they believed occurred including offenses for which charges were not filed or were dismissed or of which the defendant was acquitted (Tonry, 2016b, ch. 3).

If positive retributivist theories are correct, every offender convicted of multiple offenses should receive the punishment he or she deserves, no more, no less: if one burglary deserves a one-year prison sentence, 10 burglaries warrant 10 years. Negative retributivist and mixed theories do no better. Their upper limits in principle could bound the workings of both the bulk discount and the recidivist premium, but specifying how those limits should be set in multiple-conviction cases requires justification that retributivist theories cannot provide.

Acknowledging Competing First Principles

Questions of justice in punishment cannot be answered by invocation only of moral theories of punishment. They are "monist," which, asserted Isaiah Berlin, implies the false view that all ethical questions have a single correct answer and that all these answers dovetail within a single, coherent moral system. To the contrary, "the world that we encounter in ordinary experience is one in which we are faced with choices between ends equally ultimate, and claims equally absolute, the realization of some of which must inevitably involve the sacrifice of others" (2002, pp. 213–214). Berlin characterized Kantian retributivist and Benthamite utilitarian theories as monist.

Punishment theories by themselves cannot provide plausible justifications of multiple-offense sentencing. Other fundamental values are at stake. Extreme cases show this. Lee (this volume), for example, describes a series of cases in which people convicted of downloading child pornography received longer-than-lifetime sentences including 10 consecutive 20-year sentences for possession of child pornography. A recent series of US Supreme Court decisions upheld the constitutionality of a life sentence for a $120.75 theft, 50-years-to-life for theft of nine videotapes worth $150, and two consecutive 20-year prison terms for possession of nine total ounces of marijuana.[10] These cases illustrate sentences that reflect the view that the interests of affected offenders, like those of the frogs killed by Bion's boys, do not matter.

Anomalies and injustices such as life sentences for possessing pornography or committing recidivist thefts or drug sales are immoral because they are grossly disproportionate to the seriousness of the crimes for which they are imposed, but also because more is at stake than principles of punishment. That is true whenever a punishment is imposed. Humanity dignity and individualized moral responsibility are at least equally relevant.

Human Dignity

Respect for the human dignity principle is the reason why the bulk discount exists in all Western legal systems: mechanical application of a positive retributivist approach in cases involving multiple offenses would produce punishments that most people would believe to be grossly unjust if imposed on themselves or their children. We live short lives. We all make serious ethical and moral mistakes. Depriving people of the opportunity to live a meaningful portion of their remaining years at liberty because even of grievous mistakes is the moral equivalent of capital punishment.

Part of the explanation the German Constitutional Court gave for declaring full life sentences unconstitutional was that hope for the possibility of a better life in the future is a basic human right (*lebenslange Freiheitsstrafe*, 21 June 1977, 45 BverfGE 187). Similar ideas underlie the much shorter maximum sentences authorized in continental European than in Anglo-Saxon legal systems. Table 14.3, for illustration, shows maximum authorized prison sentences in Scandinavian countries.

Most prison sentences imposed in those countries and elsewhere in Europe are immediately suspended and when executed are usually shortened by one-third remission. In any case, as Table 14.4 shows, sentences longer than two years are exceptionally rare. James Whitman (2016) argues that post-Enlightenment ideas of respect for human dignity and a derivative that he calls a "presumption of mercy" explain why European punishments are so much less severe than those in Anglo-Saxon countries. Only 3.1% of Finnish sentences are to confinement and 2.1% of those (or 0.006% of all sentences) are more than five years. In

Table 14.3 **Maximum Sentences, Four Scandinavian Countries**

Offense	*Finland*	*Sweden*	*Norway*	*Denmark*
Assault	2 years	2 years	1 year	3 years
Aggravated Assault	10 years	6 years	1.5 years*	6 years*
Robbery	6 years	6 years	6 years	6 years
Aggravated Robbery	10 years	10 years	15 years*	10 years
Rape	6 years	6 years	10 years	8 years
Aggravated Rape	10 years	10 years	21 years	12 years
Theft	1.5 years	2 years	2 years	1.5 years
Aggravated Theft	4 years	6 years	6 years	n.a.
Drug Offenses	2 years	3 years	2 years	2 years*
Aggravated Drug Offenses	10 years	10 years	10 years*	16 years

* With some exceptions for highly unusual cases.
Source: Lappi-Seppälä 2016, Table 3.

Germany, only 0.02% of executed sentences are for five years or longer. The principle of respect for human dignity should everywhere be recognized to set powerful restraints on the severity of punishment of individual offenders whether for one, concurrent, or sequential offenses.

Individualized Moral Responsibility

Thinking about appropriate punishments should also take into account the equally important principle of individualized moral reponsibility. By this I refer to the combination of Rawlsian fairness and Dworkinian treatment as an equal. Both require that individualized consideraton be fairly given to the circumstances of offenses and the characteristics and situaltions of offenders. A fundamental failure of the "do the crime, do the time" mindset is that "the crime" consists only of the legal label given to behavior for which an individual was convicted.[11]

The calculus for criminal liability is highly stylized and ignores interpersonal differences that a more humanly sensitive approach would necessarily encompass. Doctrines of mens rea, actus reus, and affirmative defenses may be necessary for purposes of operating high-volume legal processes, but they ignore things that should not be ignored. All robberies or rapes or assaults or thefts are not the same.

Table 14.4 **Prison Sentences in Months before Remission, Selected Countries, 2010**

Country	*Percent sentenced to Prison*	*Of these, percent under 6 months*	*Of these, percent 6–11 months*	*Of these, percent 12–23 months*	*Of these, percent 24–59 months*	*Of these, percent 60–119 months*	*Of these, percent over 120 months*
Austria	n.a.	56.1	16.7	11.9	2.0	1.2	. . .
Finland	3.1	61.2	15.5	11.4	9.3	1.8	0.3
France	17.8	57.2	20.3	17.3	2.8	1.4	1.0
Germany	5.4	24.1	28.6	18.8	24.4	3.5	0.3
Netherlands	23	74.1	10.8	6.3	4.9	1.2	0.4
Sweden	9.6	60.6	14.2	14.3	5.4	3.1	. . .
England	7.5	52.7	17.4	12.6	11.4	3.8	0.7

Sources: Aebi et al. 2014, Tables 3.2.3.1 and 3.2.7.1.

Most writers on the criminal law acknowledge that imperfect assertions of affirmative defenses should often be taken into account at sentencing even if they do not bar a conviction. In Anglo-Saxon countries, successful self-defense claims must usually be based on a reasonable belief of imminent danger, and actions taken must be reasonably proportionate to the perceived danger. Honest but unreasonable beliefs about the existence, imminence, or seriousness of the danger are not adequate bases for a successful defense. In such cases, when the defendant's honesty is accepted, and the defendant in his or her own mind acted in good faith, it should be no surprise that judges often mitigate the punishment they might otherwise impose. Similar analyses apply to defenses of necessity, duress, and defense of others.

The mitigating defenses of diminished capacity and provocation are a step further removed. If accepted, they reduce the seriousness of the offense of conviction. But even if not accepted, they raise ambiguities in imputations of blameworthiness.

Another step away are conditions and circumstances that are not bases for a formal defense or mitigation but are fundamental to individualized assessments of blameworthiness. Recent US Supreme Court decisions in *Graham v. Florida*, 560 US 48 (2010), and *Miller v. Alabama*, 132 S. Ct. 2455 (2012), for example, banned mandatory full-life sentences for juvenile offenders on the basis of neuroscientific and developmental research showing that young offenders' cognitive processes and behavioral controls are fundamentally different from those of adults. Similar differences exist between adults. Ethically sensitive sentencing processes would take them into account.

That is not the end of the individualization road. Some crimes are committed under the influence of drug and alcohol use, addiction, depression, extreme emotion, or exceptional need. Many crimes result from cupidity, stupidity, or 30 seconds' bad judgment. Many drug sales, routine property crimes, and gang activities are committed by people whose lives are fundamentally shaped by extreme economic and social disadvantage, low intelligence, inadequate educations, dysfunctional family lives, few legitimate opportunities, or antisocial peer relationships and role models. None of these things constitute legal defenses but all are germane to individualized assessments of moral blameworthiness.

The principle of individualized moral responsibility explains why sentencing laws in most Western legal systems, except in the United States, set maximum sentences but almost never minimums. Scandinavian sentencing codes, for example, set out exclusive lists of aggravating circumstances that might justify a severer-than-normal punishment, but provide illustrative sets of mitigating circumstances including "and any others" the court believes appropriate (Lappi-Seppälä, 2016).

Pulling Things Together

The shift from monist punishment theories to comprehensive conceptions of just punishment requires substantial modification of most retributive and mixed theories of punishment.[12] This may not be unlikely as may appear. It will require a paradigm shift, which Thomas Kuhn (1962) demonstrated seldom happens in the physical sciences until prevailing ways of thinking shift sufficiently to absorb unfamiliar and previously heretical ideas. However, such things may happen more frequently in other contexts as, for example, when retributive punishment theories quickly displaced consequentialist ones in the 1960s and 1970s. Robert Nozick (1981) explained how that happens in philosophy:

> When a philosopher sees that premisses he accepts logically imply a conclusion he has rejected until now, he faces a choice: he may accept this conclusion or reject one of the previously accepted premisses . . . . His choice will depend on which is greater, the degree of his commitment to the various premisses or the degree of his commitment to denying the conclusion. It is implausible that these are independent of how strongly he wants certain things to be true. The various means of control over conclusions explain why so few philosophers publish ones that (continue to) upset them. (p. 2–3)

This essay was written for a symposium and offers commentary on many of the resulting papers. Taken as a whole, they serve as evidence that a paradigm shift may be underway, at least within the theory class in English-speaking countries. For the past 40 years retributive ideas have in many peoples' minds seemed self-evidently right. Partly that is because they displaced consequentialist ideas embodied in indeterminate sentencing that produced practices and problems that seemed self-evidently wrong. For theorists, retributive proportionality offered promise as a guiding value for fairness, consistency, and equality and as a guard against idiosyncrasy, capriciousness, and racial and other forms of bias.

In practice, as is increasingly recognized, and not only among academics, things did not work out that way. Part of the problem is that politicians, especially in the United States, readily endorsed blameworthiness and deserved punishment, but paid little attention to the entailed ideas about interoffense proportionality. All of the English-speaking countries enacted mandatory minimum sentence and other mechanical and disproportionately severe sentencing laws. In the worlds of policy and politics those laws and their wisdom are being questioned.

The theoretical primacy of retributive ideas is also being questioned (Matravers, 2011). All of the papers I discuss in the second section try to explain or justify departures from punishment patterns that retributivism appears to require. Ryberg (this volume) tentatively concludes that the bulk discount is irreconcilable with retributivism. Hoskins (this volume) argues that retributivist ideas must at least be restrained within mixed theories if they are to address real-world problems. Papers by Frase (this volume), Manson (this volume), Roberts and de Keijser (this volume), and Ashworth and Wasik (this volume) each in its own way offers arguments and concrete proposals that are at best only partly compatible with retributive ideas.

Lippke (this volume) attempts to show that parsimony, the idea of imposing the least severe or intrusive appropriate punishment, adds little or nothing to punishment theorizing. The parsimony idea is not necessary, he says, to explain to retributivists why disproportionately severe punishments are unjust, or to explain to consequentialists why punishments more severe than they need to be for preventive purposes are unjust.

What the concept of parsimony provides, however, is a bridge that connects retributive with consequentialist and other values. Retributivism can provide proportionate upper limits on punishment and consequentialism can guide the imposition of less severe punishments. Parsimony, even if conceptually redundant, provides a rhetorical device that directs decision-makers' attention to the desirability of imposing the least severe appropriate sentence that can be justified on consequentialist grounds.

However, parsimony can do much heavier lifting than that. Negative or limiting retributivism and mixed theories of punishment are not new, but are generally discussed only in relation to punishment and prevention. Extended to encompass other values, including human dignity and individualized moral responsibility, they can coherently and justly resolve the multiple-offense paradox. The parsimony question would then become whether any punishment more severe than is minimally appropriate is justifiable in preventive terms and is reconcilable with human dignity and individualized moral responsibility.

There is nothing new in this. Bentham (1970), despite the view attributed to him that notions of human rights are "nonsense on stilts" (Harrison, 1995), was unambiguously clear that imposition of pain on human beings is an "evil" than can be justified only by a greater than offsetting good. He was emphatic that people who lack individualized moral responsibility because they are insane, mistaken, intoxicated, or unaware that an act was criminal should not be convicted or punished. Parsimony and moral responsibility served in effect as trumps, which is how broader conceptions of human rights and individualized moral responsibility should be treated.

The details of sentencing systems constrained by both negative retributivist and parsimony ideas no doubt would differ from country to country. The issues to be worked through include all of those that lawyers discuss in explanation of the bulk discount: Is a prison sentence longer than X years, or a sentence for a particular offense longer than Y years, ever compatible with human dignity? May a sentence for any number of offenses of one kind ever be punished more severely than is normally appropriate for a clearly more serious offense?

The harder problem is to respect individualized moral responsibility by showing equal concern and respect for every convicted person. Part of the answer is that the broadened parsimony principle calls for the least severe punishment consistent with preventive effects, blameworthiness, and human dignity. Judges should have authority to impose even less severe than otherwise appropriate sentences in cases of people for whom there are extenuating causal circumstances. Another part of the answer is that judges should take important causal and circumstantial factors into account in choosing types of sanctions and requiring that opportunities be provided for participation in relevant social and treatment programs.

The elements of a sentencing system that incorporates interacting principles of penal desert, human dignity, and individualized moral responsibility are straightforward. Among other policies they would require bulk discounts and sharply limit or proscribe recidivist premiums. Structural arrangements should encourage judges to justice.

Sentence maximums should seldom exceed a few years, and never be more than 10 or 12 years whether for single or multiple offenses except possibly for murder. There is nothing original about this. Both the original *Model Penal Code* and the report of the Advisory Council on the Penal System (1978) in England and Wales long ago so proposed.

Offenses should be divided into a sizable number of classes each bearing proportionate maximums. If class maximums were one, two, three, four, five, seven, and nine years, the conviction offense would cap judges' discretion to do worse and the system would give teeth to interoffense comparisons.

Aggregate punishments for any number of offenses of one kind should never exceed the most severe punishment that could be imposed for a single offense of that kind. This is not original but restates in a constrained form the totality policies now in operation in many countries.

Statutes should specify narrow circumstances in which recidivist premiums are allowable and, only in those circumstances, authorize modest increments capped by the authorized maximum for the most serious current offense. No one not a consequentialist has adequately explained in principle why increments of additional punishment for past crimes may justly be imposed.

The bottom line is that no one should be punished more severely than an individualized assessment of his or her moral responsibility would justify. Any adequate theory or system of punishment must reconcile the competing claims of penal desert, human dignity, and individualized moral responsibility and in doing so will necessarily solve the multiple-offense paradox. Sentencing decisions concern the lives of individuals and necessarily require consideration of the circumstances of individual lives. No decision should destroy or debase a human life.

Notes

1. Matt Matravers similarly observed that "the issue is not one of reconciling those practices to desert . . . but rather it is one of thinking about the requirements of liberal justice as a whole" (2011, p. 37).
2. If moral blameworthiness were taken seriously, punishments would be individualized much as the Recording Angel would do at Heaven's Gate (Walker, 1991; Kolber, 2009).
3. The text understates the prevalence of defendants convicted of multiple offenses. The data in Table 1 include only people charged with felonies and by definition omit the much larger number of misdemeanor defendants. In addition, because most felony defendants are prosecuted for felonies on multiple occasions, one-year counts underrepresent the number of separate times they are prosecuted. A first offender is one case. Some multiple offenders have been prosecuted many times and thus represent many cases.
4. Large or general deterrent and incapacitative effects cannot be convincingly demonstrated, but a recent National Academy of Sciences panel concluded that both exist albeit not for all offenses, all offenders, or most of the time (Travis, Western, and Redburn, 2014, ch. 5).
5. See n. 9 for a more detailed explanation.
6. Ashworth and Wasik (this volume) passingly mention a fifth: all else being equal, time in prison makes people more not less likely to reoffend. It is unclear to me why that is germane to sentencing multiple current offenses, but it does offer an ethical argument against the recidivist premium.
7. Essentially, American time off for good behavior.
8. Sentence lengths for multiple current convictions are tightly limited (American Law Institute, 1962, sects. 6.06, 6.07, and 7.06). All prison sentences are indeterminate with minimum and maximum terms; the parole board sets release dates under a presumption that all prisoners should be released when first they become eligible. When consecutive sentences are imposed, the *Code* specifies that minimums and maximums for the most serious offense govern. The longest possible minimum is 10 years for the most serious felonies including murder and aggravated rape (one year is the norm). The longest minimums for other felonies are usually two or three years (one year is the norm). The longest possible maximum for a single offense other than murder is 20 years (for most, five or 10). All minimums and maximums are subject to 12 days per month reduction for good behavior. Good conduct thus can reduce a 20-year maximum to 12, 10 years to six, and five to three. The longest possible net minimum is about six years.
9. Ryberg (this volume) offers the additional objection that offense severity is a continuum, not a stepladder, and that without clear breaks interoffense comparisons are not workable. That is reductionist. Step effects inevitably occur in categorizing phenomena in a natural distribution (for example, how does a teacher draw a line between a b+ and an A-?), and there are practical solutions. Sentencing guidelines grids provide examples.
10. Fuller detail and case citations are provided in Tonry, 2016a.
11. In the United States prosecutors have much greater influence over sentencing than judges. Plea negotiation vagaries (whether concerning charges, counts, sentences, or "facts" that trigger mandatory sentences) often make the offense of conviction an arbitrary and unreliable indicator of offense severity (Lynch, 2003; Stuntz, 2011).

12. Restorative theories are an exception since they accept retributive limits on punishment severity but otherwise prescribe individualized responses to crime (e.g., Braithwaite and Pettit, 2001).

References

Advisory Council on the Penal System. 1978. *Sentences of Imprisonment: A Review of Maximum Penalties*. London: Home Office.

Aebi, M. F., B.A. de Vacarlay, G. Barclay, B. Gurszczyńska, S. Harrendorf, M. Heiskanen, V. Hysi, V. Jaquier, J-M. Jehle, M. Killias, O. Shostko, P. Smit, and R. Borisdottir. 2010. *European Sourcebook of Crime and Criminal Justice Statistics*. 4th ed. The Hague: Research and Documentation Centre, Netherlands Ministry of Justice.

Albrecht, H-J. 1994. *Strafzumessung bei schwerer Kriminalitat: Eine vergleichende theoretische und empirische Studie zur Herstellung und Darstellung des Strafmaßes*. Berlin: Duncker & Humblot.

American Law Institute. 1962. *Model Penal Code*. Proposed Official Draft. Philadelphia: American Law Institute.

Ashworth, A. 2015. *Sentencing and Criminal Justice*. 5th ed. Cambridge: Cambridge University Press.

Asp, P. 2010. "Previous Convictions and Proportionate Punishment under Swedish Law." In J. V. Roberts and A. von Hirsch (eds.), *Previous Convictions at Sentencing: Theoretical and Applied Perspectives*, pp. 207–226. Oxford: Hart Publishing.

Bennett, C. 2010. "'More to Apologise For': Can We Find a Basis for the Recidivist Premium in a Communicative Theory of Punishment?" In J. V. Roberts and A. von Hirsch (eds.), *Previous Convictions at Sentencing: Theoretical and Applied Perspectives*, 73–90. Oxford: Hart Publishing.

Bentham, J. 1970. "The Utilitarian Theory of Punishment." In *An Introduction to the Principles of Morals and Legislation*. In J. H. Burns and H. L. A. Hart (eds.), *The Collected Works of Jeremy Bentham*. London: The Athlone Press reprinted in Why Punish? How Much?, edited by Michael Tonry. New York: Oxford University Press. (pp. 21–40).

Berlin, I. H. Hardy (ed.). 2002. *Liberty*. Oxford: Oxford University Press.

Bottoms, A. E. 1998. "Five Puzzles in von Hirsch's Theory of Punishment." In A. Ashworth and M. Wasik (eds.), *Fundamentals of Sentencing Theory: Essays in Honour of Andrew von Hirsch*, pp. 53–101. Oxford: Clarendon.

Braithwaite, J. 2002. "In Search of Restorative Jurisprudence." In L. Walgrave (ed.), *Restorative Justice and the Law*, pp. 150–167. Cullompton, Devon: Willan.

Braithwaite, J., and P. Pettit. 2001. "Republicanism and Restorative Justice: An Explanatory and Normative Connection." In J. Braithwaite and H. Strang (eds.), *Restorative Justice: Philosophy to Practice*, pp. 145–63. Burlington, VT: Ashgate.

Dworkin, R. 1978. *Taking Rights Seriously*. Cambridge, MA: Harvard University Press.

Ferri, E. 1921. *Relazione sul Progetto Preliminare di Codice Penale Italiano*. Milan Roma: "L'Universelle" Imprimerie Polyglotte.

Frankel, M. 1973. *Criminal Sentences: Law without Order*. New York: Hill & Wang.

Frase, R. S., J. V. Roberts, R. Hester, and K. L. Mitchell. 2015. *Criminal History Enhancement Sourcebook*. Minneapolis: Robina Institute of Criminal Law and Criminal Justice.

Freiberg, A. 2014. *Fox and Freiberg's Sentencing: State and Federal Law in Victoria*. 3rd ed. Melbourne: Thomson Reuters.

Freiberg, A. 2016. "The Road Well Traveled in Australia: Ignoring the Past, Condemning the Future." In M Tonry (ed.), *Crime and Justice: A Review of Research* 45(1): 419–457. Chicago: University of Chicago Press.

Glueck, S. 1928. "Principles of a Rational Penal Code." *Harvard Law Review*. 41(4): 453–482.

Hart, H. L. A. 1968. *Punishment and Responsibility: Essays in the Philosophy of Law*. Oxford: Oxford University Press.

Harrison, R. 1995. "Jeremy Bentham." In T. Honderich (ed.), *The Oxford Companion to Philosophy*, pp. 85–88. Oxford: Oxford University Press.

Hinkkanen, V., and T. Lappi-Seppälä. 2011. "Sentencing Theory, Policy, and Research in the Nordic Countries." In M. Tonry and T. T. Lappi-Seppälä (eds.), *Crime and Justice in Scandinavia*, pp. 349–404. In M. Tonry (ed.), *Crime and Justice: A Review of Research*. 40(1). Chicago: University of Chicago Press.

James, W. 1903. *The Varieties of Religious Experience*. New York: Longmans, Green.

Jareborg, N. 1998. "Why Bulk Discounts in Multiple Offence Sentencing?" In A. Ashworth and M. Wasik (eds.), *Fundamentals of Sentencing Theory: Essays in Honour of Andrew von Hirsch*, pp. 129–140. Oxford: Oxford University Press.

Jolliffe, D., D. P. Farrington, and A. R. Piquero. 2015. *Life-Course Persistent Offenders: A Literature Review and Secondary Data Analysis*. London: Ministry of Justice.

Kant, I. 1965 [1787]. "The Penal Law and the Law of Pardon." In *The Metaphysical Elements of Justice*, pp. 137–44. trans. J. Ladd. Indianapolis: Bobbs-Merrill.

Kolber, A. 2009. "The Subjective Experience of Punishment." *Columbia Law Review* 109(1): 182–236.

Kuhn, T. 1962. *The Structure of Scientific Revolutions*. Chicago: University of Chicago Press.

Lappi-Seppälä, T. 2016. "Nordic Sentencing." In M. Tonry (ed.), *Sentencing Policies and Practices in Western Countries: Comparative and Cross-National Perspectives*, pp. 17–82. In M. Tonry (ed.), *Crime and Justice: A Review of Research* 45(1). Chicago: University of Chicago Press.

Lee, Y. 2010. "Repeat Offenders and the Question of Desert." In J. V. Roberts and A. von Hirsch (eds.), *Previous Convictions at Sentencing: Theoretical and Applied Perspectives*, pp. 49–72. Oxford: Hart Publishing.

Lovegrove, A. 1997. *The Framework of Judicial Sentencing: A Study in Legal Decision Making*. Cambridge: Cambridge University Press.

Luban, D. 2007. *Legal Ethics and Human Dignity*. Cambridge: Cambridge University Press.

Lynch, G. E. 2003. "Screening versus Plea Bargaining: Exactly What Are We Trading Off?" *Stanford Law Review* 55(4): 1399–1408.

Manson, A., P. Healy, G. Trotter, J. V. Roberts, and D. Ives (eds.). 2008. *The Law of Sentencing and Penal Policy in Canada*. 2nd ed. Toronto: Emond Montgomery.

Matravers, M. 2011. "Is Twenty-First Century Punishment Post-Desert?" In M. Tonry (ed.), *Retributivism Has a Past: Has it a Future?*, pp. 30–45. New York: Oxford University Press.

Moore, M. H., S. R. Estrich, D. McGillis, and W. Spelman. 1986. *Dangerous Offenders: The Elusive Target of Justice*. Cambridge, MA: Harvard University Press.

Moore, M. S. 1993. "Justifying Retributivism." *Israeli Law Review* 27(1/2): 15–49.

Morris, N. 1974. *The Future of Imprisonment*. Chicago: University of Chicago Press.

Murphy, J., and J. Hampton. 1988. *Justice and Mercy*. New York: Cambridge University Press.

Nozick, R. 1981. *Philosophical Explanations*. Cambridge, MA: Harvard University Press.

Piquero, A. R., D. P. Farrington, and A. Blumstein. 2003. "The Criminal Career Paradigm." In M. Tonry (ed.), *Crime and Justice: A Review of Research* 30: 359–506. Chicago: University of Chicago Press.

Piquero, A. R., D. P. Farrington, and A. Blumstein, 2007. *Key Issues in Criminal Career Research: New Analyses of the Cambridge Study in Delinquent Development*. New York: Cambridge University Press.

Plutarch, M. 1957. "Whether Land or Sea Animals Are Cleverer." In *Moralia* Vol. 12, trans. H. Cherniss. Cambridge, MA: Harvard University Press.

Rawls, J. 1958. "Justice as Fairness." *The Philosophical Review* 67(2): 164–194.

Reaves, B. A. 2013. *Felony Defendants in Large Urban Counties, 2009—Statistical Tables*. Washington, DC: US Department of Justice, Bureau of Justice Statistics.

Reitz, K. 2010. "The Illusion of Proportionality: Desert and Repeat Offenders." In J. V. Roberts and A. von Hirsch (eds.), *Previous Convictions at Sentencing: Theoretical and Applied Perspectives*, pp. 137–160. Oxford: Hart Publishing.

Roberts, J. V. (ed.) 2008. *Punishing Persistent Offenders: Exploring Community and Offender Perspectives*. Oxford: Oxford University Press.

Roberts, J. V. 2011. "The Future of State Punishment. The Role of Public Opinion in Sentencing." In M. Tonry (ed.), *Retributivism Has a Past. Has It a Future?*, pp. 101–129. Oxford: Oxford University Press.

Roberts, J. V., and A. Ashworth. 2016. "The Evolution of Sentencing Policy and Practice in England and Wales, 2003–2015." In M. Tonry (ed.), *Sentencing Policies and Practices in Western Countries: Comparative and Cross-National Perspectives*, pp. 307–358. In M Tonry (ed.), *Crime and Justice: A Review of Research*. 45(1). Chicago: University of Chicago Press.

Roberts, J. V., and J. Pina-Sanchez. 2014. "Previous Convictions at Sentencing: Exploring Empirical Trends in the Crown Court." *Criminal Law Review* 8: 575–588.

Robinson, P. H., and J. M. Darley. 1995. *Justice, Liability, and Blame*. Boulder, CO: Westview.

Rocque, M. 2015. "A Comparative, Cross-cultural Criminal Career Analysis." *European Journal of Criminology* 12(4): 400–19.

Snacken, S. 2015. "Punishment, Legitimate Policies, and Values: Penal Moderation, Dignity, and Human Rights." *Punishment & Society* 17(3): 397–423.

Stuntz, W. J. 2011. *The Collapse of American Criminal Justice*. Cambridge, MA: Harvard University Press.

Thomas, D. A. 1979. *Principles of Sentencing: The Sentencing Policy of the Court of Appeal Criminal Division*. 2nd ed. London: Heinemann.

Tonry, M. 1994. "Proportionality, Parsimony, and Interchangeability of Punishments." In R. A. Duff, S. E. Marshall, R. E. Dobash, and R. P. Dobash (eds.), *Penal Theory and Penal Practice*, pp. 59–84. Manchester: Manchester University Press.

Tonry, M. 2010. "The Questionable Relevance of Previous Convictions to Punishments for Later Crimes." In J. V. Roberts and A. von Hirsch, *Previous Convictions at Sentencing: Theoretical and Applied Perspectives*, pp. 91–116. Oxford: Hart Publishing.

Tonry, M. 2016a. "Equality and Human Dignity: The Missing Ingredients in American Sentencing." In M. Tonry (ed.), *Sentencing Policies and Practices in Western Countries: Comparative and Cross-national Perspectives*, pp. 459–496. In M Tonry (ed.) *Crime and Justice: A Review of Research* 45(1). Chicago: University of Chicago Press.

Tonry, M. 2016b. *Sentencing Fragments: Penal Reform in America, 1975–2025*. New York: Oxford University Press.

Travis, J., B. Western, and S. Redburn (eds.) 2014. *The Growth of Incarceration in the United States: Exploring Causes and Consequences*. Washington, DC: National Academies Press.

Vibla, N. 2015. "More Than One Crime: Sentencing the Multiple Conviction Offender." In J. V. Roberts (ed.), *Exploring Sentencing Practice in England and Wales*, pp. 221–234. London: Palgrave Macmillan.

Von Hirsch, Andrew. 1976. *Doing Justice: The Choice of Punishments*. New York: Hill & Wang.

Walker, N. 1991. *Why Punish?* Oxford: Oxford University Press.

Walker, N. 1999. *Aggravation, Mitigation, and Mercy in English Criminal Justice*. London: Blackstone's.

Whitman, J. 2004. "The Two Western Cultures of Privacy: Dignity versus Liberty." *Yale Law Journal* 113(6): 1151–1221.

Whitman, J. 2016. "Presumption of Innocence or Presumption of Mercy? Weighing Two Western Modes of Justice." *Texas Law Review* 94(5): 933–993.

INDEX

Note: Page references followed by "*t*" indicate table; "*f*" indicate figure.

9 780190 607